AACD
ETHICAL STANDARDS
CASEBOOK

Fourth Edition

Barbara Herlihy, PhD
University of Houston—Clear Lake

Larry Golden, PhD
University of Texas at San Antonio

American Association for Counseling and Development
5999 Stevenson Avenue
Alexandria, VA 22304

American Association for Counseling and Development
5999 Stevenson Avenue
Alexandria, VA 22304

Cover design by Sarah Jane Valdez

Library of Congress Cataloging-in-Publication Data

American Association for Counseling and Development.
    AACD ethical standards casebook / Barbara Herlihy. Larry Golden.—
    4th ed.
      p.   cm.
    ISBN 1-55620-069-2
    1. American Association for Counseling and Development.
  2. Counseling—United States—Moral and ethical aspects.
  3. Counselors—Professional ethics—United States.   4. Counseling—
  United States—Moral and ethical aspects—Case studies.
  5. Counselors—Professional ethics—United States—Case studies.
  I. Herlihy, Barbara.   II. Golden, Larry.   III. Title.
  BF637.C6A37   1989
  174'.915—dc20   89-27226
                                                                        CIP

Printed in the United States of America

CONTENTS

FOREWORD

This casebook will prove useful for a class in ethics in counseling or for other settings where ethical issues are considered. The variety of the casebook keeps the interest of the reader, and it offers plenty of material for exchange of ideas and opinions.

The short **Incidents** that illustrate the AACD *Ethical Standards* are good examples and serve to clarify the intent of the various standards. I hope readers will use these incidents as examples to reflect on and to examine their own views and practices. The incidents leave room for plenty of discussion. The reasons why certain practices were rated as ethical or unethical can be a fruitful focus of discussion. Readers may find that they disagree with some of the ratings, which could be helpful in promoting critical thinking about ethical decision making.

The **Case Studies** section is excellent. Again, I like the variety of issues presented and the descriptive vignettes. As these cases demonstrate, ethical dilemmas are rarely simple. The ethical concerns that confront us often are subtle and complex, and these cases provide readers with an opportunity to explore the kinds of cases that are brought before an ethics committee.

The **Essays on Ethics in Professional Practice** section is a real plus in the casebook. Readers have a chance to review issues pertaining to topics such as confidentiality, advertising, multicultural counseling, dual relationships, child abuse, counseling records, and counselor impairment. Each essay is well thought out, and the issues selected for discussion are all important. This is a good teaching tool to promote small group discussion and interaction in class.

The casebook provides readers with help they will need to formulate guidelines in working with the variety of ethical and professional concerns they will inevitably encounter in their practice. My hope is that the AACD *Ethical Standards* and this casebook serve the purpose of challenging students and practitioners to review their own views and practices. Learning to make sound ethical decisions is an ongoing process as opposed to a one-time event. We all could benefit from taking the time to examine honestly what we are doing and saying to determine if we are working toward the enhancement of our clients.

Professional codes of ethics are not chiseled into concrete. They are a set of guidelines designed by a group of interested practitioners who organize themselves into a committee. Therefore, it is a mistake to think of ethical codes as legal documents. If these codes truly serve the profession and the consumer, they inform counselors about parameters of acceptable practice. These ethical codes do not make decisions *for* practitioners, rather they present and clarify the thinking of a professional group. Those who study the AACD *Ethical Standards* and use this casebook will be better equipped to think through the issues surrounding ethical dilemmas. The casebook offers a range of cases to sharpen critical thinking and give practice in applying general standards to specific situations.

The class discussion based on the reading of the material in this casebook can certainly demonstrate that ethics does not have to be a dry subject. Ethics education can be exciting, challenging, controversial, and even fun. Ideally, readers will be encouraged to reflect on their own philosophy and practice so that they can refine their positions on issues. My hope is that readers be willing to discuss their cases and their ethical struggles with their fellow students and colleagues.

—*Gerald Corey, EdD*
Professor and Coordinator of Human Services Program
California State University, Fullerton

THE AUTHORS

Barbara Herlihy, PhD, was Chair of the AACD Ethics Committee 1987–89 and member 1986–87. She served as Co-Chair of the ACES Ethics and Professional Practices Interest Network 1986–89. She has co-authored numerous articles on ethical and legal issues in counseling that have appeared in such journals as *Journal of Counseling and Development, Counselor Education and Supervision*, and *The School Counselor*. Currently, Dr. Herlihy is Associate Professor of Counselor Education at the University of Houston—Clear Lake. She is a National Board Certified Counselor and Texas Licensed Professional Counselor.

Larry Golden, PhD, was a member of the AACD Ethics Committee 1987–90. He served as Chair of the Texas Association for Marriage and Family Therapy Ethics Committee during 1980–83. He has co-authored articles on ethical issues in *Counseling and Values* and the *Oregon Personnel and Guidance Journal*. Previous books are *Preventing Adolescent Suicide* (1988), *Helping Families Help Children: Family Interventions With School-Related Problems* (1986), and *Psychotherapeutic Techniques in School Psychology* (1984). Currently, Dr. Golden is Associate Professor of Counseling and Guidance at the University of Texas at San Antonio. He is a Licensed Psychologist in Texas.

ACKNOWLEDGMENTS

Many people have contributed to this edition of the casebook, some known to us and some not. First and perhaps foremost are those who contributed to the previous editions. We are especially indebted to the authors of the third edition—Robert Callis, Sharon K. Pope, and Mary E. DePauw—who gave us the foundation on which to build.

The AACD Ethics Committee's deliberations are reflected throughout the casebook. Besides ourselves, Ethics Committee members in 1989 are Bonnie Baker, Beverly O'Bryant, Louis Paradise, and Karen Prichard. We are also indebted to Virginia B. Allen, former chair of the Ethics Committee, whose work in revising the ethical standards preceded our work on the casebook.

Natalie S. Eldridge, Madelyn Healy, and Pat Nellor Wickwire provided descriptions of incidents that illustrate the standards as well as helpful suggestions regarding content and format.

Members of the AACD Media Committee served as our editorial review board. Nancy J. Garfield and Kathy Hotelling thoroughly read the draft document. We are grateful for their extremely helpful comments and suggestions.

The AACD headquarters staff have assisted in numerous ways throughout the process. Special thanks go to W. Mark Hamilton, Director of Professional Publications, Elaine Pirrone, Acquisitions and Development Editor, and their staff. It has been a joy to work with such a capable and conscientious publications crew. Executive Director Patrick J. McDonough has been facilitative as always, maintaining the communications link between headquarters and the field. Nancy Pinson-Millburn, Assistant Executive Director for Association and Professional Relations, has been a marvel of swift response to all requests for information and assistance.

Patricia Parma, Sandra Seckel, and Mari Sica spent many long hours deciphering our scrawls and inputting material into the word processor. They performed their tedious task with skill, accuracy, and good cheer.

Many other people gave us suggestions in informal conversation. Graduate students, participants in workshops and conferences, and various colleagues and other individuals served as sounding boards when we shared material from the casebook in its early drafts. Although we cannot thank them all by name, we are grateful for their contributions.

INTRODUCTION TO THE FOURTH EDITION

A primary responsibility of the AACD Ethics Committee is to inform the membership and others of the AACD *Ethical Standards* and their implications for practice. Early in its history, the Committee determined that a casebook would be one means to fulfill this responsibility. Periodically since 1961, the ethical standards have been updated and revised, and revised editions of the casebook have followed. Thus, the casebook has evolved along with the ethical standards.

OBJECTIVES OF THE CASEBOOK

1. To inform current, new, and prospective members of AACD of the ethical responsibilities assumed with membership.
2. To inform nonmembers—including consumers of counseling services and professional associates of members—of the ethical standards to which members are expected to adhere in their professional work.
3. To stimulate consideration, discussion, and questions regarding ethical issues and the AACD *Ethical Standards*.
4. To provide specific examples that illustrate and clarify the meaning and intent of each of the standards that comprise the association's code of ethics.
5. To provide a source of information about ethical standards and ethical issues that will be useful in the preservice and inservice education of counselors.
6. To provide material that will assist the Ethics Committee in executing its responsibilities, especially in adjudicating complaints of alleged violations of the ethical standards.

ORGANIZATION OF THE CASEBOOK

Section 1 of the casebook presents the revised AACD *Ethical Standards* adopted by the Governing Council in March 1988.

In **section 2**, each individual ethical standard is followed by several incidents intended to illustrate and clarify the meaning of the standard. Because standards vary in their complexity, the number of examples given also varies. When a standard contains more than one concept, an attempt has been made to present at least one positive and one negative incident associated with each concept. Incidents that illustrate compliance are presented first and are marked plus (+). They are followed by incidents that illustrate violation, marked minus (−). The incidents vary in their seriousness, ranging from gross unethical conduct to behavior reflecting poor practice or questionable judgment.

Section 3 presents a series of case studies that are more detailed and complex than the incidents in the previous section and are more typical of the situations a member may encounter. Each case study involves a number of considerations and needs to be studied in light of more than one standard to conduct an ethical analysis. The case studies reflect the types of complaints that the Ethics Committee receives as well as the current and emerging concerns of the membership.

Section 4 presents a series of essays intended to provide further information and provoke thought about ethical issues of particular concern to counselors. The essays have been contributed by members with particular expertise in these issues.

Certain **terms** have consistent meaning throughout the casebook. *Member* always refers to a member of AACD. In each incident when not explicitly stated, it is to be assumed that at least one party involved in the incident is an AACD member. This holds true regardless of the person's professional title—counselor, therapist, student affairs administrator, dean, director, professor, counselor educator, to mention a few. *Standard* is a numbered statement in one of the sections of the AACD *Ethical Standards*. For instance, standard F.8 states that "It is unethical to use one's institutional affiliation to recruit clients for one's private practice."

The **appendices** contain information to which the member may need to refer from time to time. Appendix A contains the divisional codes of ethics for ACPA, AMHCA, ARCA, ASCA, ASGW, and NCDA. Members of a division are responsible for observing the divisional code of ethics as well as the AACD code. Appendix B presents the ethical standards of the National Board for Certified Counselors. Appendix C, the AACD Policies and Procedures for Processing Complaints of Ethical Violations, describes the steps to be followed in reporting and processing allegations of unethical behavior by a current or former member. Appendix D describes the purpose and procedures of the AACD Legal Action Program that is designed to give eligible members financial assistance in resolving legal disputes regarding their professional practices.

EVOLUTION OF THE CASEBOOK

In 1961 the Board of Directors adopted a code of ethics for APGA. In 1963 the Ethics Committee began to solicit and compile incidents having ethical implications, both positive and negative, that would illustrate the standards. Because that first casebook was "started from scratch," it was a lengthy process to collect material, write, review, and rewrite to prepare the final draft. The **first edition** of the *Ethical Standards Casebook* was published by the association in 1965, 4 years after the ethical standards were officially adopted.

About 1972 it was recognized that the ethical standards needed to be revised, which would require a revision of the casebook. To reduce the time lag between adoption of the standards and publication of the casebook, two committees were appointed to work simultaneously—one to revise the standards and the other to revise the casebook. The first committee completed its work when the Board of Directors adopted the revised APGA *Ethical Standards* in 1974. The second committee collected a wide variety of incidents that would illustrate by concrete examples how each ethical standard should be implemented in practice. The APGA president then asked a single individual to collate these incidents and edit the **second edition** of the casebook, which was published 2 years after the standards were revised.

In a further effort to control the time lag between revision of the standards and revision of the casebook, the APGA president appointed the editor of the second casebook to be an ex officio member of the Ethics Committee for the purpose of accumulating material that might be relevant to the next edition. The APGA *Ethical Standards* were revised and adopted by the Board of Directors in 1981. The editor of the second edition, with the assistance of two co-editors, prepared the **third edition** of the casebook, which was published in 1982.

The association (now AACD) adopted a revised code of ethics in 1988. Two of the lessons learned from previous experience were that a casebook should be published as soon as possible after the ethical standards are revised, and that the casebook authors must be aware of the thought processes that cause the standards to be revised. Therefore, soon after the adoption of the revised code of ethics, the Chair and a member of the Ethics Committee were asked to undertake the current revision. Once again, input was solicited from a wide variety of sources to determine what changes were needed in the casebook to maximize its usefulness. That input is reflected throughout the current **fourth edition**.

The counseling and human development profession is constantly growing, developing, and changing. Ethical standards, as a guide to proper professional practice, will also continue to develop and undergo further revision. Ethical standards and the casebook should grow out of and reflect the experiences of the profession. No ethics committee or group of authors can do this task alone. Members can help make these documents authentic. Members are requested and urged to report incidents involving ethical issues to AACD headquarters, where they will be accumulated and studied for inclusion in future revisions. Reports of such incidents should be factually accurate and complete but disguised to prevent identification of individuals and institutions. They should be marked for the attention of the Ethics Committee and noted "For Information Only: This is not a formal complaint." To file a formal complaint, follow the procedures outlined in Appendix C.

ETHICAL STANDARDS
of the American Association for Counseling and Development
(As Revised by AACD Governing Council, March 1988)

PREAMBLE

The Association is an educational, scientific, and professional organization whose members are dedicated to the enhancement of the worth, dignity, potential, and uniqueness of each individual and thus to the service of society.

The Association recognizes that the role definitions and work settings of its members include a wide variety of academic disciplines, levels of academic preparation, and agency services. This diversity reflects the breadth of the Association's interest and influence. It also poses challenging complexities in efforts to set standards for the performance of members, desired requisite preparation or practice, and supporting social, legal, and ethical controls.

The specification of ethical standards enables the Association to clarify to present and future members and to those served by members the nature of ethical responsibilities held in common by its members.

The existence of such standards serves to stimulate greater concern by members for their own professional functioning and for the conduct of fellow professionals such as counselors, guidance and student personnel workers, and others in the helping professions. As the ethical code of the Association, this document establishes principles that define the ethical behavior of Association members. Additional ethical guidelines developed by the Association's Divisions for their specialty areas may further define a member's ethical behavior.

Section A: General

1. The member influences the development of the profession by continuous efforts to improve professional practices, teaching, services, and research. Professional growth is continuous throughout the member's career and is exemplified by the development of a philosophy that explains why and how a member functions in the helping relationship. Members must gather data on their effectiveness and be guided by the findings. Members recognize the need for continuing education to ensure competent service.

2. The member has a responsibility both to the individual who is served and to the institution within which the service is performed to maintain high standards of professional conduct. The member strives to maintain the highest levels of professional services offered to the individuals to be served. The member also strives to assist the agency, organization, or institution in providing the highest caliber of professional services. The acceptance of employment in an institution implies that the member is in agreement with the general policies and principles of the institution. Therefore the professional activities of the member are also in accord with the objectives of the institution. If, despite concerted efforts, the member cannot reach agreement with the employer as to acceptable standards of conduct that allow for changes in institutional policy conducive to the positive growth and development of clients, then terminating the affiliation should be seriously considered.

3. Ethical behavior among professional associates, both members and nonmembers, must be expected at all times. When information is possessed that raises doubt as to the ethical behavior of professional colleagues, whether Association members or not, the member must take action to attempt to rectify such a condition. Such action shall use the institution's channels first and then use procedures established by the Association.

4. The member neither claims nor implies professional qualifications exceeding those possessed and is responsible for correcting any misrepresentations of these qualifications by others.

5. In establishing fees for professional counseling services, members must consider the financial status of clients and locality. In the event that the established fee structure is inappropriate for a client, assistance must be provided in finding comparable services of acceptable cost.

6. When members provide information to the public or to subordinates, peers, or supervisors, they have a responsibility to ensure that the content is general, unidentified client information that is accurate, unbiased, and consists of objective, factual data.

7. Members recognize their boundaries of competence and provide only those services and use only those techniques for which they are qualified by training or experience. Members should only accept those positions for which they are professionally qualified.

8. In the counseling relationship, the counselor is aware of the intimacy of the relationship and maintains respect for the client and avoids engaging in activities that seek to meet the counselor's personal needs at the expense of that client.

9. Members do not condone or engage in sexual harassment which is defined as deliberate or repeated comments, gestures, or physical contacts of a sexual nature.

10. The member avoids bringing personal issues into the counseling relationship, especially if the potential for harm is present. Through awareness of the negative impact of both racial and sexual stereotyping and discrimination, the counselor guards the individual rights and personal dignity of the client in the counseling relationship.

11. Products or services provided by the member by means of classroom instruction, public lectures, demonstrations, written articles, radio or television programs, or other types of media must meet the criteria cited in these standards.

Section B:
Counseling Relationship

This section refers to practices and procedures of individual and/or group counseling relationships.

The member must recognize the need for client freedom of choice. Under those circumstances where this is not possible, the member must apprise clients of restrictions that may limit their freedom of choice.

1. The member's primary obligation is to respect the integrity and promote the welfare of the client(s), whether the client(s) is (are) assisted individually or in a group relationship. In a group setting, the member is also responsible for taking reasonable precautions to protect individuals from physical and/or psychological trauma resulting from interaction within the group.

2. Members make provisions for maintaining confidentiality in the storage and disposal of records and follow an established record retention and disposition policy. The counseling relationship and information resulting therefrom must be kept confidential, consistent with the obligations of the member as a professional person. In a group counseling setting, the counselor must set a norm of confidentiality regarding all group participants' disclosures.

3. If an individual is already in a counseling relationship with another professional person, the member does not enter into a counseling relationship without first contacting and receiving the approval of that other professional. If the member discovers that the client is in another counseling relationship after the counseling relationship begins, the member must gain the consent of the other professional or terminate the relationship, unless the client elects to terminate the other relationship.

4. When the client's condition indicates that there is clear and imminent danger to the client or others, the member must take reasonable personal action or inform responsible authorities. Consultation with other professionals must be used where possible. The assumption of responsibility for the client's(s') behavior must be taken only after careful deliberation. The client must be involved in the resumption of responsibility as quickly as possible.

5. Records of the counseling relationship, including interview notes, test data, correspondence, tape recordings, electronic data storage, and other documents are to be considered professional information for use in counseling, and they should not be considered a part of the records of the institution or agency in which the counselor is employed unless specified by state statute or regulation. Revelation to others of counseling material must occur only upon the expressed consent of the client.

6. In view of the extensive data storage and processing capacities of the computer, the member must ensure that data maintained on a computer is: (a) limited to information that is appropriate and necessary for the services being provided; (b) destroyed after it is determined that the information is no longer of any value in providing services; and (c) restricted in terms of access to appropriate staff members involved in the provision of services by using the best computer security methods available.

7. Use of data derived from a counseling relationship for purposes of counselor training or research shall be confined to content that can be disguised to ensure full protection of the identity of the subject client.

8. The member must inform the client of the purposes, goals, techniques, rules of procedure, and limitations that may affect the relationship at or before the time that the counseling relationship is entered. When working with minors or persons who are unable to give consent, the member protects these clients' best interests.

9. In view of common misconceptions related to the perceived inherent validity of computer-generated data and narrative reports, the member must ensure that the client is provided with information as part of the counseling relationship that adequately explains the limitations of computer technology.

10. The member must screen prospective group participants, especially when the emphasis is on self-understanding and growth through self-disclosure. The member must maintain an awareness of the group participants' compatibility throughout the life of the group.

11. The member may choose to consult with any other professionally competent person about a client. In choosing a consultant, the member must avoid placing the consultant in a conflict of interest situation that would preclude the consultant's being a proper party to the member's efforts to help the client.

2

12. If the member determines an inability to be of professional assistance to the client, the member must either avoid initiating the counseling relationship or immediately terminate that relationship. In either event, the member must suggest appropriate alternatives. (The member must be knowledgeable about referral resources so that a satisfactory referral can be initiated.) In the event the client declines the suggested referral, the member is not obligated to continue the relationship.

13. When the member has other relationships, particularly of an administrative, supervisory, and/or evaluative nature with an individual seeking counseling services, the member must not serve as the counselor but should refer the individual to another professional. Only in instances where such an alternative is unavailable and where the individual's situation warrants counseling intervention should the member enter into and/or maintain a counseling relationship. Dual relationships with clients that might impair the member's objectivity and professional judgement (e.g., as with close friends or relatives) must be avoided and/or the counseling relationship terminated through referral to another competent professional.

14. The member will avoid any type of sexual intimacies with clients. Sexual relationships with clients are unethical.

15. All experimental methods of treatment must be clearly indicated to prospective recipients, and safety precautions are to be adhered to by the member.

16. When computer applications are used as a component of counseling services, the member must ensure that: (a) the client is intellectually, emotionally, and physically capable of using the computer application; (b) the computer application is appropriate for the needs of the client; (c) the client understands the purpose and operation of the computer application; and (d) a follow-up of client use of a computer application is provided to both correct possible problems (misconceptions or inappropriate use) and assess subsequent needs.

17. When the member is engaged in short-term group treatment/training programs (e.g., marathons and other encounter-type or growth groups), the member ensures that there is professional assistance available during and following the group experience.

18. Should the member be engaged in a work setting that calls for any variation from the above statements, the member is obligated to consult with other professionals whenever possible to consider justifiable alternatives.

19. The member must ensure that members of various ethnic, racial, religious, disability, and socioeconomic groups have equal access to computer applications used to support counseling services and that the content of available computer applications does not discriminate against the groups described above.

20. When computer applications are developed by the member for use by the general public as self-help/stand-alone computer software, the member must ensure that: (a) self-help computer applications are designed from the beginning to function in a stand-alone manner, as opposed to modifying software that was originally designed to require support from a counselor; (b) self-help computer applications will include within the program statements regarding intended user outcomes, suggestions for using the software, a description of the conditions under which self-help computer applications might not be appropriate, and a description of when and how counseling services might be beneficial; and (c) the manual for such applications will include the qualifications of the developer, the development process, validation data, and operating procedures.

Section C:
Measurement & Evaluation

The primary purpose of educational and psychological testing is to provide descriptive measures that are objective and interpretable in either comparative or absolute terms. The member must recognize the need to interpret the statements that follow as applying to the whole range of appraisal techniques including test and nontest data. Test results constitute only one of a variety of pertinent sources of information for personnel, guidance, and counseling decisions.

1. The member must provide specific orientation or information to the examinee(s) prior to and following the test administration so that the results of testing may be placed in proper perspective with other relevant factors. In so doing, the member must recognize the effects of socioeconomic, ethnic, and cultural factors on test scores. It is the member's professional responsibility to use additional unvalidated information carefully in modifying interpretation of the test results.

2. In selecting tests for use in a given situation or with a particular client, the member must consider carefully the specific validity, reliability, and appropriateness of the test(s). General validity, reliability, and related issues may be questioned legally as well as ethically when tests are used for vocational and educational selection, placement, or counseling.

3. When making any statements to the public about tests and testing, the member must give accurate information and avoid false claims or misconceptions. Special efforts are often re-

quired to avoid unwarranted connotations of such terms as IQ and grade equivalent scores.

4. Different tests demand different levels of competence for administration, scoring, and interpretation. Members must recognize the limits of their competence and perform only those functions for which they are prepared. In particular, members using computer-based test interpretations must be trained in the construct being measured and the specific instrument being used prior to using this type of computer application.

5. In situations where a computer is used for test administration and scoring, the member is responsible for ensuring that administration and scoring programs function properly to provide clients with accurate test results.

6. Tests must be administered under the same conditions that were established in their standardization. When tests are not administered under standard conditions or when unusual behavior or irregularities occur during the testing session, those conditions must be noted and the results designated as invalid or of questionable validity. Unsupervised or inadequately supervised test-taking, such as the use of tests through the mails, is considered unethical. On the other hand, the use of instruments that are so designed or standardized to be self-administered and self-scored, such as interest inventories, is to be encouraged.

7. The meaningfulness of test results used in personnel, guidance, and counseling functions generally depends on the examinee's unfamiliarity with the specific items on the test. Any prior coaching or dissemination of the test materials can invalidate test results. Therefore, test security is one of the professional obligations of the member. Conditions that produce most favorable test results must be made known to the examinee.

8. The purpose of testing and the explicit use of the results must be made known to the examinee prior to testing. The counselor must ensure that instrument limitations are not exceeded and that periodic review and/or retesting are made to prevent client stereotyping.

9. The examinee's welfare and explicit prior understanding must be the criteria for determining the recipients of the test results. The member must see that specific interpretation accompanies any release of individual or group test data. The interpretation of test data must be related to the examinee's particular concerns.

10. Members responsible for making decisions based on test results have an understanding of educational and psychological measurement, validation criteria, and test research.

11. The member must be cautious when interpreting the results of research instruments possessing insufficient technical data. The specific purposes for the use of such instruments must be stated explicitly to examinees.

12. The member must proceed with caution when attempting to evaluate and interpret the performance of minority group members or other persons who are not represented in the norm group on which the instrument was standardized.

13. When computer-based test interpretations are developed by the member to support the assessment process, the member must ensure that the validity of such interpretations is established prior to the commercial distribution of such a computer application.

14. The member recognizes that test results may become obsolete. The member will avoid and prevent the misuse of obsolete test results.

15. The member must guard against the appropriation, reproduction, or modification of published tests or parts thereof without acknowledgement and permission from the previous publisher.

16. Regarding the preparation, publication, and distribution of tests, reference should be made to:

a. "Standards for Educational and Psychological Testing," revised edition, 1985, published by the American Psychological Association on behalf of itself, the American Educational Research Association and the National Council of Measurement in Education.

b. "The Responsible Use of Tests: A Position Paper of AMEG, APGA, and NCME," *Measurement and Evaluation in Guidance*, 1972, 5, 385-388.

c. "Responsibilities of Users of Standardized Tests," APGA, *Guidepost*, October 5, 1978, pp. 5-8.

Section D:
Research and Publication

1. Guidelines on research with human subjects shall be adhered to, such as:

a. *Ethical Principles in the Conduct of Research with Human Participants*, Washington, D.C.: American Psychological Association, Inc., 1982.

b. Code of Federal Regulation, Title 45, Subtitle A, Part 46, as currently issued.

c. *Ethical Principles of Psychologists*, American Psychological Association, Principle #9: Research with Human Participants.

d. Family Educational Rights and Privacy Act (the Buckley Amendment).

e. Current federal regulations and various state rights privacy acts.

4

2. In planning any research activity dealing with human subjects, the member must be aware of and responsive to all pertinent ethical principles and ensure that the research problem, design, and execution are in full compliance with them.

3. Responsibility for ethical research practice lies with the principal researcher, while others involved in the research activities share ethical obligation and full responsibility for their own actions.

4. In research with human subjects, researchers are responsible for the subjects' welfare throughout the experiment, and they must take all reasonable precautions to avoid causing injurious psychological, physical, or social effects on their subjects.

5. All research subjects must be informed of the purpose of the study except when withholding information or providing misinformation to them is essential to the investigation. In such research the member must be responsible for corrective action as soon as possible following completion of the research.

6. Participation in research must be voluntary. Involuntary participation is appropriate only when it can be demonstrated that participation will have no harmful effects on subjects and is essential to the investigation.

7. When reporting research results, explicit mention must be made of all variables and conditions known to the investigator that might affect the outcome of the investigation or the interpretation of the data.

8. The member must be responsible for conducting and reporting investigations in a manner that minimizes the possibility that results will be misleading.

9. The member has an obligation to make available sufficient original research data to qualified others who may wish to replicate the study.

10. When supplying data, aiding in the research of another person, reporting research results, or making original data available, due care must be taken to disguise the identity of the subjects in the absence of specific authorization from such subjects to do otherwise.

11. When conducting and reporting research, the member must be familiar with and give recognition to previous work on the topic, as well as to observe all copyright laws and follow the principles of giving full credit to all to whom credit is due.

12. The member must give due credit through joint authorship, acknowledgement, footnote statements, or other appropriate means to those who have contributed significantly to the research and/or publication, in accordance with such contributions.

13. The member must communicate to other members the results of any research judged to be of professional or scientific value. Results reflecting unfavorably on institutions, programs, services, or vested interests must not be withheld for such reasons.

14. If members agree to cooperate with another individual in research and/or publication, they incur an obligation to cooperate as promised in terms of punctuality of performance and will full regard to the completeness and accuracy of the information required.

15. Ethical practice requires that authors not submit the same manuscript or one essentially similar in content for simultaneous publication consideration by two or more journals. In addition, manuscripts published in whole or in substantial part in another journal or published work should not be submitted for publication without acknowledgement and permission from the previous publication.

Section E: Consulting

Consultation refers to a voluntary relationship between a professional helper and help-needing individual, group, or social unit in which the consultant is providing help to the client(s) in defining and solving a work-related problem or potential problem with a client or client system.

1. The member acting as consultant must have a high degree of self-awareness of his/her own values, knowledge, skills, limitations, and needs in entering a helping relationship that involves human and/or organizational change and that the focus of the relationship be on the issues to be resolved and not on the person(s) presenting the problem.

2. There must be understanding and agreement between member and client for the problem definition, change of goals, and prediction of consequences of interventions selected.

3. The member must be reasonably certain that she/he or the organization represented has the necessary competencies and resources for giving the kind of help that is needed now or may be needed later and that appropriate referral resources are available to the consultant.

4. The consulting relationship must be one in which client adaptability and growth toward self-direction are encouraged and cultivated. The member must maintain this role consistently and not become a decision maker for the client or create a future dependency on the consultant.

5. When announcing consultant availability for services, the member conscientiously adheres to the Association's Ethical Standards.

6. The member must refuse a private fee or other remuneration for consultation with per-

sons who are entitled to these services through the member's employing institution or agency. The policies of a particular agency may make explicit provisions for private practice with agency clients by members of its staff. In such instances, the clients must be apprised of other options open to them should they seek private counseling services.

Section F:
Private Practice

1. The member should assist the profession by facilitating the availability of counseling services in private as well as public settings.

2. In advertising services as a private practitioner, the member must advertise the services in a manner that accurately informs the public of professional services, expertise, and techniques of counseling available. A member who assumes an executive leadership role in the organization shall not permit his/her name to be used in professional notices during periods when he/she is not actively engaged in the private practice of counseling.

3. The member may list the following: highest relevant degree, type and level of certification and/or license, address, telephone number, office hours, type and/or description of services, and other relevant information. Such information must not contain false, inaccurate, misleading, partial, out-of-context, or deceptive material or statements.

4. Members do not present their affiliation with any organization in such a way that would imply inaccurate sponsorship or certification by that organization.

5. Members may join in partnership/corporation with other members and/or other professionals provided that each member of the partnership or corporation makes clear the separate specialties by name in compliance with the regulations of the locality.

6. A member has an obligation to withdraw from a counseling relationship if it is believed that employment will result in violation of the Ethical Standards. If the mental or physical condition of the member renders it difficult to carry out an effective professional relationship or if the member is discharged by the client because the counseling relationship is no longer productive for the client, then the member is obligated to terminate the counseling relationship.

7. A member must adhere to the regulations for private practice of the locality where the services are offered.

8. It is unethical to use one's institutional affiliation to recruit clients for one's private practice.

Section G:
Personnel Administration

It is recognized that most members are employed in public or quasi-public institutions. The functioning of a member within an institution must contribute to the goals of the institution and vice versa if either is to accomplish their respective goals or objectives. It is therefore essential that the member and the institution function in ways to: (a) make the institutional goals specific; and public; (b) make the member's contribution to institutional goals specific; and (c) foster mutual accountability for goal achievement.

To accomplish these objectives, it is recognized that the member and the employer must share responsibilities in the formulation and implementation of personnel policies.

1. Members must define and describe the parameters and levels of their professional competency.

2. Members must establish interpersonal relations and working agreements with supervisors and subordinates regarding counseling or clinical relationships, confidentiality, distinction between public and private material, maintenance and dissemination of recorded information, work load, and accountability. Working agreements in each instance must be specified and made known to those concerned.

3. Members must alert their employers to conditions that may be potentially disruptive or damaging.

4. Members must inform employers of conditions that may limit their effectiveness.

5. Members must submit regularly to professional review and evaluation.

6. Members must be responsible for in-service development of self and/or staff.

7. Members must inform their staff of goals and programs.

8. Members must provide personnel practices that guarantee and enhance the rights and welfare of each recipient of their service.

9. Members must select competent persons and assign responsibilities compatible with their skills and experiences.

10. The member, at the onset of a counseling relationship, will inform the client of the member's intended use of supervisors regarding the disclosure of information concerning this case. The member will clearly inform the client of the limits of confidentiality in the relationship.

11. Members, as either employers or employees, do not engage in or condone practices that are inhumane, illegal, or unjustifiable (such as considerations based on sex, handicap, age, race) in hiring, promotion, or training.

6

Section H:
Preparation Standards

Members who are responsible for training others must be guided by the preparation standards of the Association and relevant Division(s). The member who functions in the capacity of trainer assumes unique ethical responsibilities that frequently go beyond that of the member who does not function in a training capacity. These ethical responsibilities are outlined as follows:

1. Members must orient students to program expectations, basic skills development, and employment prospects prior to admission to the program.

2. Members in charge of learning experiences must establish programs that integrate academic study and supervised practice.

3. Members must establish a program directed toward developing students' skills, knowledge, and self-understanding, stated whenever possible in competency or performance terms.

4. Members must identify the levels of competencies of their students in compliance with relevant Division standards. These competencies must accommodate the paraprofessional as well as the professional.

5. Members, through continual student evaluation and appraisal, must be aware of the personal limitations of the learner that might impede future performance. The instructor must not only assist the learner in securing remedial assistance but also screen from the program those individuals who are unable to provide competent services.

6. Members must provide a program that includes training in research commensurate with levels of role functioning. Paraprofessional and technician-level personnel must be trained as consumers of research. In addition, personnel must learn how to evaluate their own and their program's effectiveness. Graduate training, especially at the doctoral level, would include preparation for original research by the member.

7. Members must make students aware of the ethical responsibilities and standards of the profession.

8. Preparatory programs must encourage students to value the ideals of service to individuals and to society. In this regard, direct financial remuneration or lack thereof must not be allowed to overshadow professional and humanitarian needs.

9. Members responsible for educational programs must be skilled as teachers and practitioners.

10. Members must present thoroughly varied theoretical positions so that students may make comparisons and have the opportunity to select a position.

11. Members must develop clear policies within their educational institutions regarding field placement and the roles of the student and the instructor in such placement.

12. Members must ensure that forms of learning focusing on self-understanding or growth are voluntary, or if required as part of the educational program, are made known to prospective students prior to entering the program. When the educational program offers a growth experience with an emphasis on self-disclosure or other relatively intimate or personal involvement, the member must have no administrative, supervisory, or evaluating authority regarding the participant.

13. The member will at all times provide students with clear and equally acceptable alternatives for self-understanding or growth experiences. The member will assure students that they have a right to accept these alternatives without prejudice or penalty.

14. Members must conduct an educational program in keeping with the current relevant guidelines of the Association.

7

INCIDENTS THAT ILLUSTRATE THE ETHICAL STANDARDS

SECTION A: GENERAL

A.1. **The member influences the development of the profession by continuous efforts to improve professional practices, teaching, services, and research. Professional growth is continuous throughout the member's career and is exemplified by the development of a philosophy that explains why and how a member functions in the helping relationship. Members must gather data on their effectiveness and be guided by the findings. Members recognize the need for continuing education to ensure competent service.**

+ *A.1.(a)* A member is appointed chair of the state branch's task force on human rights of people with AIDS. She corresponds with colleagues in several surrounding states who hold similar positions. As a result of sharing mutual concerns, she organizes a regional conference on counseling people with AIDS and their families.

+ *A.1.(b)* A school counselor in a rural area works to have university extension classes and a series of inservice education workshops brought to his isolated community. He establishes a newsletter to inform counselors in his own and neighboring school districts about these offerings.

− *A.1.(c)* A community college counselor earns her certification from the National Board for Certified Counselors. Over the next 5 years, she finds that she is too busy to attend workshops and conferences to earn continuing education clock hours. She lets her certification expire.

− *A.1.(d)* A counselor employed by the state juvenile probation and parole system uses principles of reality therapy in dealing with clients. When his supervisor asks him to show evidence of its effectiveness, he replies that practitioners do not have time to do research. Instead, he refers the supervisor to a journal article that supports the effectiveness of reality therapy.

A.2. **The member has a responsibility both to the individual who is served and to the institution within which the service is performed to maintain high standards of professional conduct. The member strives to maintain the highest** levels of professional services offered to the individuals to be served. The member also strives to assist the agency, organization, or institution in providing the highest caliber of professional services. The acceptance of employment in an institution implies that the member is in agreement with the general policies and principles of the institution. Therefore the professional activities of the member are also in accord with the objectives of the institution. If, despite concerted efforts, the member cannot reach agreement with the employer as to acceptable standards of conduct that allow for changes in institutional policy conducive to the positive growth and development of clients, then terminating the affiliation should be seriously considered.

+ A.2.(a)   A newly employed director of a community mental health care center is concerned that there is an unusually long waiting list for clients to see a counselor. She meets with the faculty of the counselor education department at a nearby university and arranges for the mental health center to serve as a practicum station for the department's graduate students. Supervision of the graduate students' work is jointly conducted by the mental health center staff and university faculty, involving all parties in continuing professional growth and reducing client waiting time.

+ A.2.(b)   A member is employed as a counselor in a residential facility for juvenile offenders. The director of the facility institutes a policy that involves administering harsh punishments to residents who break the rules. The member consults with the director about his ethical opposition to such methods. The director insists that he participate. When the differences are determined to be irreconcilable, the member seeks employment elsewhere.

− A.2.(c)   A counselor intern is uncertain what to do after a client admits to having committed a crime. The intern, afraid that admitting his ignorance will affect his grade, fails to consult with his supervisor or take any other action.

− A.2.(d)   A residence hall director repeatedly refuses to report a drug abuse violation by a student, even though she has accepted her position in full knowledge that the institution's policies require her to report such violations. Also, she states her opposition to these policies to the students for whom she is responsible.

A.3.   Ethical behavior among professional associates, both members and nonmembers, must be expected at all times. When information is possessed that raises doubt as to the ethical behavior of professional colleagues, whether Association members or not, the member must take action to rectify such a condition. Such action shall use the institution's channels first and then use procedures established by the Association.

+ A.3.(a)   An employment service supervisor is concerned that a new counselor, who has stated that he "likes a challenge," is spending more and more time with a few difficult-to-place clients to the exclusion of others seeking counseling. The supervisor confers twice with the counselor, who begins seeing "less challenging" clients but dealing with them on a perfunctory basis. The supervisor files an inquiry with the AACD Ethics Committee to determine what to do next.

+ A.3.(b) A principal makes public only those standardized test results that tend to show the school in a favorable light. Information that might discredit the school's efforts is withheld. The director of guidance brings to the attention of the principal the ethical questions involved. The principal defends the practice. The director then asks that they both confer with the superintendent.

− A.3.(c) A rehabilitation counselor learns from his client that a volunteer worker in the hospital has revealed confidential information about the client to neighbors in social conversation. Because the client does not seem particularly upset by the disclosure, the counselor decides not to pursue the issue.

− A.3.(d) A career counselor is aware that one of her colleagues, who failed to attend inservice training on a new career interest inventory, has been misinterpreting the results of that inventory to clients. The counselor is a close friend of the colleague and realizes that the colleague is under considerable stress at home. Therefore, the counselor does nothing to correct the situation.

A.4. The member neither claims nor implies professional qualifications exceeding those possessed and is responsible for correcting any misrepresentations of those qualifications by others.

+ A.4.(a) A student with a wide variety of work experience drafts her resume when she completes her MA degree in student personnel administration. She asks her faculty advisor to review the draft to ensure its accuracy and appropriateness before making it available to prospective employers.

+ A.4.(b) A licensed professional counselor in private practice is sometimes mistakenly labeled as a psychologist by prospective clients and members of the community. Whenever this occurs, the counselor carefully explains his credentials to clarify the distinction.

− A.4.(c) A member has taken a course that included didactic study of individual psychological tests but has had no supervised practice in administering or interpreting such tests. In an employment interview, he is told that his prospective job will include administering and interpreting the MMPI. When asked if he "knows how to give" this test, he answers in the affirmative.

− A.4.(d) A counselor is approached by a local church to give a weekend marriage enrichment seminar. The counselor has had no training in this area, but because she is a member of the church and is familiar with its views on marriage, she agrees to conduct the seminar.

A.5. **In establishing fees for professional counseling services, members must consider the financial status of clients and locality. In the event that the established fee structure is inappropriate for a client, assistance must be provided in finding comparable services of acceptable cost.**

+ *A.5.(a)*   A member who has been in private practice in New York City moves to a small midwestern town. The member goes to the department chair of counseling psychology at the local university, introduces himself, and indicates he is interested in opening his own practice. He asks the department chair to recommend four professionals who are established in private practice in town. After speaking with these four people, the member decides to lower his fee from $80 an hour, which he had previously been receiving, to $50 an hour in keeping with local practice.

+ *A.5.(b)*   The guidance director of a school district asks a private practitioner to provide a workshop series on preventing youth suicide. The guidance director explains that, athough their need for the workshop series is great, their budget is limited. The member, realizing that the district cannot pay her fee and that her schedule is already full during the time in question, recalls an excellent workshop she had attended on the topic, which was presented by qualified professionals of high repute in the community. She contacts the presenters and learns that they are available at a nominal fee. She then gives the guidance director these presenters' names, phone numbers, and background.

− *A.5.(c)*   A member has a private practice located in a wealthy suburban area. The member feels that a sliding fee is unnecessary for this locality and refuses to do any "charity" work. When a prospective client from the few residents in the area who are not very well off financially makes an appointment to see her and indicates that he cannot afford the fee, she simply says she will not see him. She does not refer him to any other agency that he might be better able to afford.

− *A.5.(d)*   A couple have been in marriage counseling for 4 months. They have consistently paid promptly for services. The husband falls ill and misses 2 weeks of work, causing him to lose income for this period. When the couple is able to resume counseling, the wife calls to explain their tight financial situation. She asks if they might work out a payment plan for the next month. She proposes that they pay half the fee during the next 4 weeks with the understanding that the entire bill will be paid in full at the end of the month. The counselor responds that this would not be possible and that they should delay resumption of counseling until they can afford it.

A.6.   **When members provide information to the public or to subordinates, peers, or supervisors, they have a responsibility to ensure that the content is general, unidentified client information that is accurate, unbiased, and consists of objective, factual data.**

11

+ A.6.(a) The four counselors in a high school have been asked by the PTA to present a panel discussion at the June meeting on the problems of the students they have counseled during the academic year. The counselors meet several times to plan their presentation. They determine that they will organize their data by presenting problems, year in school, and gender of student. They are careful to present these data in general, concise, accurate form so that no individual student can be identified by the audience.

+ A.6.(b) A counselor educator maintains a limited private practice on Saturdays. His graduate students at the university ask him to share his experiences as a private practitioner. He responds by informing them in general terms about presenting problems he typically encounters, ratio of male to female clients, average duration of counseling, and strategies he has found effective in dealing with various types of concerns. He takes care to withhold any information that might reveal the identity of an individual client.

− A.6.(c) A college wants to attract minority students to its campus. A member who is in charge of recruiting efforts conducts a special one-day campus visit for minority high school seniors. When the minority students come to campus, they begin their day with a tour in small groups. Then they are all brought together for an informal reception to which college freshmen have also been invited. At the reception a Black high school senior, mistaking seniors from other high schools for freshmen at the college, remarks to the counselor, "I had no idea there were so many minority students on this campus." The member does nothing to correct this false impression.

− A.6.(d) The department chair of a counseling psychology program is asked to write a letter of reference for an assistant professor in her department. The assistant professor, whose job performance has been marginal at best, is applying for similar positions elsewhere. The department chair wants to avoid having to make a negative tenure recommendation about the professor. She writes a glowing and misleading letter in the hope that the professor will be hired elsewhere.

A.7. Members recognize their boundaries of competence and provide only those services and use only those techniques for which they are qualified by training or experience. Members should only accept those positions for which they are professionally qualified.

+ A.7.(a) A member is asked to give a seminar on trends in humanistic psychology in the classroom. Because the member is a behaviorist by orientation, training, and experience, he declines the invitation. He provides the names and telephone numbers of several well-known humanistic educators as alternative presenters.

+ A.7.(b) A member whose primary interest is personal counseling accepts a position in an employment service whose major concern is job placement. The member limits his activities to those that would assist clients to obtain gainful employment. To satisfy his interest in personal counseling, he joins the staff of a private counseling agency where he sees clients on Saturday mornings.

− A.7.(c) A member is counseling with a client who had been sexually abused as a child. The client expresses frustration that she cannot remember the earliest incidents of abuse and insists that hypnosis would help her break through this barrier. Although the counselor has no specific training in hypnosis, she agrees to purchase a hypnosis audiotape and attempt the procedure with the client.

− A.7.(d) A member applies for a university counseling center position that has been advertised as entailing vocational counseling and developing a career information center. When she is interviewed, she learns that recent staff reassignments have caused the job description to be changed. It now involves primarily clinical assessment and personal-emotional counseling duties for which the member feels only partially qualified. The university makes her an attractive offer, which she accepts.

A.8. In the counseling relationship, the counselor is aware of the intimacy of the relationship and maintains respect for the client and avoids engaging in activities that seek to meet the counselor's personal needs at the expense of that client.

+ A.8.(a) A school counselor has strong beliefs against abortion. A 15-year-old girl comes to the counselor because she is pregnant and wants information about the physical and emotional effects of an abortion. The counselor responds with factual information about the emotional effects and suggests she consult a physician about the physical effects. The counselor asks whether the girl has discussed this decision with her parents, and the girl asks if she could bring her parents in to talk the situation over in the counselor's presence. The counselor agrees. Throughout the entire discussion the counselor is objective and does not try to push her antiabortion beliefs onto the client or her parents.

+ A.8.(b) A pastoral counselor is experiencing personal difficulties in her marital relationship. During a counseling session with a married couple, she becomes aware that this couple are dealing with many of the same issues that are unresolved in the counselor's own marriage. The counselor questions whether she can work effectively with the couple at this time. After consulting with colleagues, she offers to refer the couple to a counselor who would be better able to work with their situation.

− A.8.(c) The nephew of a school superintendent comes to his elementary school counselor because he is failing in math. The counselor, who is new to the school district, wants to make a positive impression on the administration. She counsels with the nephew three times a week and provides extra services including tutoring him in math. Other students with similar concerns are seen weekly at most.

13

– A.8.(d) A young woman makes an appointment with a counselor in private practice because she has been feeling depressed. This depression seems to be a reaction to the death of the client's mother several months ago. The young woman can afford to continue in counseling only if her health insurance company will reimburse. Her policy strictly limits the number of visits allowed for certain diagnoses including adjustment disorders. The counselor diagnoses "major depression" although this diagnosis is not justified on the basis of his assessment.

A.9. Members do not condone or engage in sexual harassment which is defined as deliberate or repeated comments, gestures, or physical contacts of a sexual nature.

+ A.9.(a) A member is cofacilitating a weekend personal growth group for young adults. As the group progresses through its Saturday session, the member notices that his female cofacilitator is flirting with a male group member and hugs him inappropriately during breaks. At the first opportunity, the member confronts the cofacilitator and explains his ethical objections to her behavior. The cofacilitator ceases her sexual harassment of the group member.

+ A.9.(b) At lunchtime, a school counselor is dining in the faculty lounge with a group of teachers. A student office worker, a teenage girl who is physically well developed, enters the lounge to deliver a message to a teacher. As she is leaving, one of the teachers makes an inappropriate and suggestive remark. It is possible that the girl may have overheard the remark. The counselor takes the teacher aside and explains his ethical objections to the teacher's behavior.

– A.9.(c) A graduate student tells her faculty advisor that she has received several "indecent proposals" from one of her professors. The student fears that her grade will be adversely affected if the professor should learn that she has told someone about his behavior. She proposes that she drop the course, even though this action would delay completion of her degree and cause her financial hardship. The faculty advisor approves her withdrawal from the course and takes no further action.

– A.9.(d) A counselor in a community mental health clinic is counseling a recent divorcee regarding her mild depression and sexual dysfunction that are related to some incidents with her father during her adolescence. After a few sessions, the counselor begins using psychodrama techniques with the client in which he plays the role of her father. The counselor begins to flirt and try to persuade her to have an affair with him, saying that in doing so he can desensitize her to some of her sexual "hangups."

A.10. The member avoids bringing personal issues into the counseling relationship, especially if the potential for harm is present. Through awareness of the negative impact of both racial and sexual stereotyping and discrimi-

nation, the counselor guards the individual rights and personal dignity of the client in the counseling relationship.

+ *A.10.(a)*   A Black high school senior has been accepted at a state university. The student's counselor attended the same university many years ago. The student tells the counselor that she plans to go through sorority rush. She asks the counselor to write a letter of recommendation for her to the sorority of which the counselor was a member. The counselor agrees, and also points out that the sorority system has changed during the years since the counselor attended the university. Years ago, the counselor's sorority was the only Black sorority on campus, but today Black women belong to many sororities. The student agrees to go through rush with her mind open to all possibilities.

+ *A.10.(b)*   A community college freshman has been coming to the counseling center for career counseling. The results of the career interest inventory he has completed show a strong similarity between the student's interests and those of nurses. The college counselor interprets the results to the student, who indicates enthusiasm for a nursing career but expresses his concern that this is a "female" occupation. The counselor, in exploring the student's concerns with him, gives factual information about the growing numbers of men in nursing and is careful to remain objective and avoid sexual stereotyping.

+ *A.10.(c)*   A counselor works in a junior high school that has an ethnically and racially diverse student population. The counselor reviews a set of English teacher recommendations for students to be placed in the gifted and talented program, and notices that almost all the students who have been recommended are White and middle class. The counselor also notes that several minority students would qualify for the gifted program on criteria other than teacher recommendation. The counselor decides to speak with the teachers about this discrepancy.

− *A.10.(d)*   A counselor in a university counseling center is assigned a male client. During the first session, the client reports that he feels depressed and alienated. He discloses that these feelings are linked to a break-up with his male lover. One of his goals in counseling is to learn how to meet other gay male students with the hope of developing new friendships and, perhaps, romantic relationships. The counselor becomes aware of his negative feelings toward the student when the student discloses his gay orientation. Nevertheless, the counselor does not share his values with the client nor does he offer to refer him to a counselor who might be better able to work with him.

− *A.10.(e)*   A male counselor has been working with a high school student regarding her career development concerns. She has a C average at the end of her first semester senior year and attained a below-average score on the natural sciences subtest of the ACT. Her career goal is to become a surgeon. The counselor does not discuss with her the possibility that this goal might not be consistent with her academic achievement and talents demonstrated to date. The counselor fears that he'll be accused of sex-role stereotyping and thus keeps quiet.

− *A.10.(f)* A counselor in private practice conducts prescreening interviews for a codependency group she is forming. Although 12 individuals have expressed interest in the group, the counselor wants to limit group size to 8 members. After screening, she eliminates the 4 prospective members who are minority group members, and justifies her decision on the basis that minority group members are more likely to drop out of counseling.

A.11. Products or services provided by the member by means of classroom instruction, public lectures, demonstrations, written articles, radio or television programs, or other types of media must meet the criteria cited in these standards.

+ *A.11.(a)* A counselor is asked to record a public service announcement that will be broadcast by a local radio station to promote National Mental Health Week. Before agreeing to participate, the counselor prepares his announcement and carefully reviews the AACD *Ethical Standards* to ensure that his message is fully in compliance.

− *A.11.(b)* A member is asked to give a demonstration of a new group counseling technique with real clients in front of an audience. Although the member is concerned that adequate precautions have not been taken either to safeguard confidentiality or to provide follow-up services to the clients, he agrees to give the demonstration.

SECTION B:
COUNSELING RELATIONSHIP

This section refers to practices and procedures of individual and/or group counseling relationships.

The member must recognize the need for client freedom of choice. Under those circumstances where this is not possible, the member must apprise clients of restrictions that may limit their freedom of choice.

B.1. The member's primary obligation is to respect the integrity and promote the welfare of the client(s), whether the client(s) is (are) assisted individually or in a group relationship. In a group setting, the member is also responsible for taking reasonable precautions to protect individuals from physical and/or psychological trauma resulting from interaction within the group.

+ B.1.(a) A high school senior athlete contacts an admissions counselor at a private liberal arts college that many of her friends plan to attend. She expresses her intention to pursue a career in physical education. The admissions counselor informs the student that the college offers only a minimum curriculum in this field, and raises the question of whether the required liberal arts curriculum is consistent with the student's interests and career goals.

+ B.1.(b) A counselor is facilitating a growth group session. At one point, a group member expresses some personal concerns that indicate he may have serious emotional problems. The counselor detects this and guides the group focus away from that member. After the group session, the counselor privately encourages the person to seek individual counseling.

+ B.1.(c) A high school student, new to a major metropolitan area, comes with his parents to register for school. On the basis of records brought by the parents, and after talking with the student, the counselor considers the specialized curriculum at one of the district's magnet schools to be more suitable. After explaining her rationale to the student and parents and obtaining their consent, she arranges an appointment for them at the magnet school so that they can further explore this alternative.

− B.1.(d) A teacher recommends an unusually shy student for an ongoing social skills group. There are two children in the group who are engaged in an angry conflict. The counselor fails to consider that this conflict may upset the shy child. During his first session, the shy child is so disturbed by the angry outbursts that he refuses to talk, and then refuses to come to any more group meetings.

− *B.1.(e)* A 70-year-old client is seeing a counselor in private practice. The client, who has suffered a series of minor strokes, speaks haltingly and experiences difficulty in expressing herself. Although the counselor becomes bored and finds his attention wandering during the sessions, he continues to see the client on a weekly basis.

− *B.1.(f)* A junior high school boy tells his counselor that one of his teachers is picking on him. The counselor believes the situation can be straightened out and asks the student's permission to discuss the problem with the teacher. The student refuses, fearing that the teacher will retaliate against him. Convinced that the student has underestimated this teacher, the counselor tells the teacher what the student has said.

B.2. Members make provisions for maintaining confidentiality in the storage and disposal of records and follow an established record retention and disposition policy. The counseling relationship and information resulting therefrom must be kept confidential, consistent with the obligations of the member as a professional person. In a group counseling setting, the counselor must set a norm of confidentiality regarding all group participants' disclosures.

+ *B.2.(a)* A high school student comes to the counselor because he is having difficulty interacting with one of his teachers. After discussing the problem the counselor suggests that a meeting between the student and teacher, with the counselor serving as facilitator, might be one effective approach. The student agrees. Over the course of two such meetings, the student and teacher come to understand the nature of the problem and identify ways to resolve it. The counselor does not reveal the content of the initial session to the teacher.

+ *B.2.(b)* A community college counselor is leading a counseling group. She explains to the members of the group during the first session that everything said within the group is to be confidential. The group agrees to this. One day, while at the student union, she hears one of the group members discussing things that had happened in the last meeting with some of his friends. The counselor speaks with the group member individually, and at the next group meeting discusses this incident and again stresses the importance of confidentiality in the group. The group reiterates its agreement with the norm.

+ *B.2.(c)* New clerical staff members are hired to work in a counseling agency. As part of the training program, a session is devoted to discussing the importance of the confidential nature of counseling. Appropriate management of case files to protect the clients is emphasized. The staff is instructed not to reveal information regarding persons receiving services or the nature of services in response to inquiries made by phone, letter, or in person. Staff members are instructed to channel such inquiries to the director of the agency.

+ *B.2.(d)* A counselor in a family counseling agency receives a phone call from the husband of one of his clients. The husband requests information about his wife's progress in counseling. The counselor clarifies the confidential nature of the relationship. At the next session with the wife, the counselor informs her of the phone conversation and they discuss options. Following the client's decision not to invite her husband to a conjoint session at this time, the counselor assists the client to identify ways to respond to the husband's inquiries and express her feelings about this.

− *B.2.(e)* A graduate of a counselor education program has completed 3 years of post-master's supervised counseling experience, and wishes to apply for her state professional counselor licensure. To complete her application, she must document details of her master's level practicum experience. She contacts the university professor who supervised her practicum. The professor informs the student that he has not kept detailed records and that only the student's transcript is available to her.

− *B.2.(f)* Joe, an 18-year-old high school senior, was convicted of illegal possession of controlled substances and is now on a 2-year probation. He is seeing the counselor about his post-high school plans. Joe's probation officer contacts the counselor and requests a report on the counselor's contacts with Joe. Although Joe has not signed a release of information, the counselor complies, fearing that not to do so might cause the probation officer to file an adverse report on Joe to the court.

− *B.2.(g)* A five-session assertiveness training workshop is offered through a college counseling service. The workshop uses role play incidents brought to the workshop by participants. Other feedback exercises also involve self-disclosure by participants. No mention is made by the leaders at any of the sessions regarding the importance of respecting the confidentiality of the disclosures made by participants during the workshop.

− *B.2.(h)* A counselor in a family counseling service discovers that a bowling teammate is the estranged husband of one of her clients. As their contact increases the counselor finds herself drawn into discussions of the husband's feelings about his wife. Because the counselor knows that the wife wants a reconciliation, she continues the discussions in the hope that this will help effect the reconciliation.

B.3. If an individual is already in a counseling relationship with another professional person, the member does not enter into a counseling relationship without first contacting and receiving the approval of that other professional. If the member discovers that the client is in another counseling relationship after the counseling relationship begins, the member must gain the consent of the other professional or terminate the relationship, unless the client elects to terminate the other relationship.

+ *B.3.(a)* Susan, a college sophomore, goes to the college counseling center because she is unable to make a vocational choice. During the first interview, the counselor learns that Susan is currently in counseling with a psychologist at a local mental health center. He explains that he cannot counsel with her unless he obtains the permission of the psychologist. Susan agrees, and after conferring with the psychologist, the college counselor continues to work with Susan on her vocational decisions. Several sessions later, Susan asks to discuss some of her personal problems. She says she is more comfortable with the college counselor and would rather see him for all of her counseling. The counselor suggests that she discuss this with the psychologist. The psychologist has no objections, and Susan terminates at the mental health center. She continues in counseling with the college counselor.

+ *B.3.(b)* A counselor offers a group counseling experience through a community mental health agency. A woman applies for admission to the group and says during the screening interview that she is currently in counseling at another agency. The group counselor requests permission to contact the other counselor. The woman agrees. The group counselor and the individual counselor agree that concurrent group and individual counseling experiences would be advisable.

− *B.3.(c)* A counselor is approached by a student who is having difficulty with his parents. After several sessions, a good working relationship is established and the counselor is satisfied with the progress the student is making. The counselor then learns that the student has been seeing a private psychologist for some time. The counselor says that she must contact the psychologist. The student refuses to give his permission, stating that he doesn't accomplish anything with the psychologist and goes only because his parents make him. The counselor does not want to terminate the student while he is making such progress, so she drops the subject.

− *B.3.(d)* Robert requests counseling from a counselor in private practice. He indicates that he and his wife are involved in marriage counseling as a couple through an agency in town. Robert says that he is undecided about continuing the marriage and would like to sort out his feelings and reach a decision. He intends to continue couple counseling in the meantime. The counselor agrees to provide counseling for Robert without requesting permission to contact the other counselor.

B.4. When the client's condition indicates that there is clear and imminent danger to the client or others, the member must take reasonable personal action or inform responsible authorities. Consultation with other professionals must be used where possible. The assumption of responsibility for the client's(s') behavior must be taken only after careful deliberation. The client must be involved in the resumption of responsibility as quickly as possible.

+ *B.4.(a)* A student contacts a college counselor and indicates that he has been feeling despondent over breaking up with his girlfriend. He reveals that

20

the previous evening he attempted to slash his wrists but stopped when he began to draw blood. After exploring his current emotional state, the counselor suggests that he consider admission to the student health service. The student agrees. He cannot state that he will not attempt his self-destructive behavior again. The counselor contacts the student health center psychiatrist to arrange for admission and evaluation. The counselor also suggests that the student contact his family to share his concerns and request their support. After the student is released from the health center, counseling is resumed and a contract is made in which the student agrees to contact the counselor if self-destructive impulses should recur and before acting on them in any way.

+ *B.4.(b)* A woman enters into a counseling relationship with a counselor at a mental health center soon after she completes an inpatient treatment program for addiction to alcohol. The woman has a history of violent behavior when intoxicated. She maintains her sobriety for several months and makes satisfactory progress in counseling. Then one evening, obviously intoxicated, she calls the counselor. She threatens to kill her mother. Although she is incoherent, the counselor discerns that she has a gun. The counselor attempts to explain that his obligation to warn and protect supersedes confidentiality in this situation, but the woman is not receptive. The counselor calls the mother but is unable to reach her. He calls the police, telling them only the specific nature of the threat and the names and addresses of the client and her mother.

+ *B.4.(c)* A teacher refers a fifth-grade girl to the school counselor. The teacher informs the counselor that the girl has written some poetry that graphically describes violence and that the girl also wears long-sleeved clothing on very hot days. The counselor interviews the student, who reveals that her stepfather physically abuses her and her mother. The counselor explains that she is required to report the abuse to child welfare authorities. The girl tearfully requests that this not be done because she fears the stepfather's retaliation. The counselor asks for permission to discuss this with the mother. The girl agrees and the counselor confers jointly with the girl and her mother. Because the mother shares the girl's fears, the counselor refers them to the local shelter for battered women where they can stay while the report is made and an investigation takes place.

− *B.4.(d)* A young woman makes an appointment to see her clergyman, who conducts pastoral counseling services. She requests help in managing her eating behaviors. During the initial interview it becomes apparent that she is bulimic as evidenced by marked weight loss, maintenance of a compulsive exercise program, and repetitive binge eating and vomiting. The counselor does not want to frighten the client by emphasizing the dangers to her health of these behaviors. However, he does suggest that the client consult a physician. The client dismisses the suggestion, insisting that she is in perfect health. The counselor continues to work with the client, although attempts to modify eating behaviors meet with little success.

21

- *B.4.(e)* A counselor at a community mental health center is seeing a client who believes that he is being threatened by members of a certain religious denomination. The client makes repeated threats to set fire to the local church of this denomination. Although the client has a history of attempted arson, the counselor does not believe that the client will act on the threat. The counselor pursues his own convictions against the advice of colleagues who have discussed the case in a staff conference. Subsequently, the client is arrested for arson in connection with a fire in this church.

- *B.4.(f)* A high school counselor is contacted by a teacher who reports that one of his students has threatened to kill herself. The teacher states that the student has a habit of making overly dramatic statements and he questions whether the remark was made with serious intent. The counselor, alarmed by statistics he has seen regarding the high rate of adolescent suicide, informs the principal and arranges for a conference with the student's parents. The counselor does not confer with the student before taking these actions.

B.5. Records of the counseling relationship, including interview notes, test data, correspondence, tape recordings, electronic data storage, and other documents are to be considered professional information for use in counseling, and they should not be considered a part of the records of the institution or agency in which the counselor is employed unless specified by state statute or regulation. Revelation to others of counseling material must occur only upon the expressed consent of the client.

+ *B.5.(a)* So that a school counselor may have control over his counseling interview notes, a separate locking file is provided for the counselor's office. This permits the counseling notes to be kept confidential and separate from students' educational records that are accessible to parents under provisions of the Family Educational Rights to Privacy Act (FERPA).

+ *B.5.(b)* A college counselor decides that her client's problem is beyond her level of education and experience. The counselor suggests to the client the possibility of referral to a private practicing psychiatrist. The client agrees, is interviewed by the psychiatrist, and decides to begin intensive psychotherapy with her. The psychiatrist calls the college counselor and requests confidential information that might be helpful in understanding the new client. The college counselor explains that this information cannot be provided until a written release is obtained from the client. When written permission is received, the information is sent to the psychiatrist.

+ *B.5.(c)* A client of a rehabilitation counselor is informed that an interview is to be recorded and will be held confidential, to be used only by the counselor in completing an interview record form and then erased. After completing the interview, the counselor privately listens to the recording while entering information directly onto an interview record form stored on her computer.

When the counselor completes the form, she prints it, deletes the data from the computer, and erases the tape.

− B.5.(d) A lawyer contacts a marriage counselor who has worked with a couple to resolve their marital discord. The lawyer asks for information about the marriage and says that he is representing the wife, who has filed suit for divorce. He indicates that he will subpoena the counseling records if the counselor does not cooperate via telephone. Deciding that the information will eventually be available to the lawyer anyway, the counselor provides all information requested.

− B.5.(e) Upon completing a session with a client, the counselor makes a few personal notes that he leaves on his desk in an open notebook. He then leaves his office for a moment. The next client enters while the counselor is out and casually reads the remarks from the open record on the counselor's desk.

− B.5.(f) A counselor in a halfway house for adult offenders is providing services to two residents who are friends. The friends have a disagreement. One client reports the disagreement to the counselor, and they work on strategies for resolution and expression of the client's feelings. The second client raises the disagreement in an interview later the same week. In an effort to open communication between the friends, the counselor shares the perspective of the first client with the second. This angers the second client, who now suspects that the counselor is revealing information about him to his friend. This client refuses to return for further counseling because he believes the counselor can't be trusted.

B.6. In view of the extensive data storage and processing capacities of the computer, the member must ensure that data maintained on a computer is: (a) limited to information that is appropriate and necessary for the services being provided; (b) destroyed after it is determined that the information is no longer of any value in providing services; and (c) restricted in terms of access to appropriate staff members involved in the provision of services by using the best computer security methods available.

+ B.6.(a) A rehabilitation counselor is conducting a research study. Because raw data include confidential information about individual subjects, the counselor deletes all identifying data before giving material to the secretary for entering into the computer.

+ B.6.(b) A faculty advisor is asked to write a letter of recommendation for one of her advisees. The advisor goes to the student records office and obtains a computer printout of the student's grades to gain information about the student's academic performance. Upon completing the recommendation, the advisor destroys the computer printout.

− B.6.(c) A counselor intern is leading a personal growth group at a university counseling center. The intern wants to make a record after each group meeting of the members' participation and issues discussed. To save time, he decides to type the information on a computer located in the reception area. While he is entering the data, he is called away from the computer to answer a question. He leaves his work in progress on the screen where it is scanned by a student who walks in.

− B.6.(d) A school counselor stores her private counseling interview notes on a computer in her office. She refers one of her student clients for intensive psychotherapy with a psychiatrist in private practice. The psychiatrist sends her a request, accompanied by a signed release, for a summary of her counseling sessions with the student. Because the counselor's computer is not functioning properly, she hands the diskette containing the interview notes to a clerk in the attendance office and asks the clerk to print the information for her. The clerk has not been trained regarding confidentiality of counseling information.

B.7. Use of data derived from a counseling relationship for purposes of counselor training or research shall be confined to content that can be disguised to ensure full protection of the identity of the subject client.

+ B.7.(a) A professor of counselor education selects tapes of counseling sessions to illustrate the process of psychotherapy. In one of the tapes the client reveals student and professor names involved in the client's problem. The professor edits out the names mentioned in order to protect the identity of the client and others involved.

+ B.7.(b) Client files are to be reviewed as part of a research project on counseling effectiveness. Counselors are instructed to use pseudonyms or false initials for clients when writing the counseling records. Before the case record review, the researcher examines all materials and marks out any information included accidentally or peripherally that might allow for identification of any client.

− B.7.(c) A counselor travels to another state to attend a conference on interpreting psychological tests. During the conference, she presents the case of one of her former clients. For discussion purposes she provides copies of the client's actual test results. Because the client lives in a different state, she does not take the precaution of removing the client's name from copies of the test results.

− B.7.(d) In an article in a state rehabilitation counseling journal, a counselor discusses several case studies to illustrate a new intervention technique. One of the cases involves a disabled teenage boy who is the son of a leading political figure in the community. Readers who are familiar with the counselor's residence can easily identify this client as the mayor's son.

B.8. The member must inform the client of the purposes, goals, techniques, rules of procedure, and limitations that may affect the relationship at or before the time that the counseling relationship is entered. When working

with minors or persons who are unable to give consent, the member protects these clients' best interests.

+ *B.8.(a)* A counselor intern explains to each of her clients at the first session that she is a trainee and will be available to provide services under supervision for the duration of the semester. She also explains that her supervisor may be observing the sessions from behind the one-way mirror and will consult with her about her work. She invites clients to ask any questions or express any concerns related to her status as a trainee and how this might affect the counseling process.

+ *B.8.(b)* A middle-aged woman seeks counseling about her recurring depression. The counselor discerns that her depression is related to difficulties in her marriage to an abusive husband. He explains to her that she may experience changes in her marital relationship as a result of counseling. He warns that it is even possible that she may eventually wish not to continue the marriage if the husband continues to be abusive.

+ *B.8.(c)* An army private comes to see a counselor on the military base where he is stationed. The private states that he has learned that a friend is in serious trouble, but that he cannot tell what the trouble is unless the counselor promises to keep it in the strictest confidence and not tell anyone. The counselor assures the client that he will treat any information as confidential and will do everything possible to make sure that no innocent parties are involved or hurt. However, he cannot agree to terms such as those proposed by the client. He asks the client to elaborate on his concern for secrecy so that they can determine the best course of action for the client to take.

− *B.8.(d)* A college counseling center arranges for all initial interviews to be conducted by intake counselors. A student arrives at the counseling center in tears. Because the student is in such distress the intake counselor decides not to explain center procedures at the beginning of the interview but to help the client express his concerns immediately. Toward the end of the interview the counselor explains that the client will be receiving services from a counselor other than the intaker. The client says that he cannot bear to "go through the whole thing again" and refuses to return for counseling.

− *B.8.(e)* A young man is seeing a counselor in private practice to overcome his intense anxiety about meeting women in social situations. Several strategies to decrease the client's anxiety and increase his interpersonal effectiveness have met with little success. The counselor gives the client a "relaxation tape" to listen to at home, but neglects to tell the client that the tape contains a subliminal message.

− *B.8.(f)* A counselor is a staff member of a women's center on a university campus. The university policy for the women's center limits to three the number of counseling sessions that can be held with any individual client. This limitation is meant to identify the women's center as a place for support, not an adjunct mental health center. The counselor does not inform clients of these limitations at the outset. When counseling for more than three sessions is needed, she informs clients of the rule but says that she will meet with them one or two more times.

B.9. **In view of common misconceptions related to the perceived inherent validity of computer-generated data and narrative reports, the member must ensure that the client is provided with information as part of the counseling relationship that adequately explains the limitations of computer technology.**

+ *B.9.(a)* A counselor is preparing to interpret a career interest inventory to a client. When the client sees the computer-generated scores and narrative report she remarks, "This is impressive. Now I can find out what career I should choose." The counselor carefully explains that the inventory cannot tell the client what she "should" do, and that the results are only one tool for helping her to make her own decisions.

+ *B.9.(b)* A high school student is disappointed with his very low score on the social sciences subtest of a scholastic aptitude test. The student places great faith in the computer-generated results and says that he will give up his plans to become a history teacher. The counselor explains the limitations of test results and helps the student explore a wide range of factors that could have a bearing on his career plans.

− *B.9.(c)* All high school juniors are given a general aptitude test battery. The tests are sent to the testing company for scoring and are returned with a score profile and narrative explanation. Because the results seem self-explanatory, the junior counselor distributes the results without discussing them with students.

− *B.9.(d)* A counselor employed in an employee assistance program receives the computer-generated results of a test that purports to indicate management potential. Susan, who is employed as a management trainee with the company, does not score well on the test although her supervisor's ratings of her work have been extremely positive. Susan tells the counselor that the test results have caused her to cancel her plans to return to school for her MBA. The counselor does not discuss the test's limitations with Susan nor does he explore with her other data that indicate that she may have good management potential.

B.10. **The member must screen prospective group participants, especially when the emphasis is on self-understanding and growth through self-disclosure. The member must maintain an awareness of the group participants' compatibility throughout the life of the group.**

+ *B.10.(a)* An elementary school counselor wants to conduct a group for children whose parents are divorced. After soliciting teacher recommendations and student self-referrals, she interviews prospective group members and obtains their parents' support for their participation. She begins the group with 10 members. After four sessions the group is floundering. Using a sociometric device, the counselor identifies two subgroups and suggests that they might function better if they split into two groups and meet at separate times. All group members are agreeable and many state that they would feel more comfortable in a smaller group.

+ B.10.(b) Several women apply to join a group being formed for women over 30 who are searching for educational, occupational, or personal alternatives to their present situations. The counselor interviews and gives a personality inventory to each applicant for the group. Severe personality problems are revealed in the case of one applicant. The counselor suggests to her that her needs might be better filled by other services that are offered at the counseling center. She is then referred to another counselor in the center to further explore her needs and the services available.

+ B.10.(c) A couples enrichment group is offered through a local church. During the third session it becomes obvious that one couple is using the group not for enrichment, as agreed in the screening interview, but to decide about the viability of their marriage. Following this session the group counselor speaks with the couple about arranging for marriage counseling at a local agency. It is agreed that the couple may continue for the final two sessions of the group with the stipulation that they not focus on their problems in a manner that is disruptive to the group.

− B.10.(d) An elementary school counselor wants to begin working with first- and second-grade students who are exhibiting disruptive behavior. The counselor has decided to use a group approach. Because time does not allow for interviewing prospective group members, the counselor asks each teacher to identify two students for inclusion in the group. Groups are formed based on teacher selection.

− B.10.(e) Two members of a therapy group frequently engage in conflict during group meetings. Even though this has occurred for several weeks, they have obeyed the rule established by the group about no physical violence in the group. Consequently, the facilitator chooses not to intervene even though they continually threaten one another. He believes that, given enough time, the group will deal with the situation. After one very intense session, the two group members exit together and engage in a scuffle in the parking lot. The police have to be called to break up the two men. When the issue is brought up at the next meeting, another group member points out that the two really did not violate group rules because they were in the parking lot when the incident occurred. Therefore, it is suggested the group move on and let the two men handle their own problems. No one objects, so the facilitator says nothing, believing that the group has chosen to deal with the situation as it wishes.

− B.10.(f) A trainee in a college counseling center is forming personal growth groups to serve as the subjects for her dissertation research. Following the initial screening interviews, it becomes clear that she will be five members short of the number needed to complete the research study. Rather than delay the start of the project, she reviews those persons whom she had originally excluded by the established criteria and chooses several members to fill the groups.

B.11. The member may choose to consult with any other professionally competent person about a client. In choosing a consultant, the member must avoid placing the consultant in a conflict of interest situation that would preclude the consultant's being a proper party to the member's efforts to help the client.

+ *B.11.(a)* Lisa, a fourth grader, describes to the counselor her conflicts at home with her stepmother. She says that they always seem to be fighting. Little progress seems to occur during five counseling sessions. The counselor asks for a case consultation at the next meeting with other elementary school counselors in the district. The consultation produces several new perspectives and a variety of suggestions, and alternative counseling strategies are generated.

+ *B.11.(b)* A student is referred by a faculty member to the college counseling center because she is in serious academic difficulty and unable to function in the field placement necessary to complete her degree. The counselor works regularly with the student. Also, with the client's consent, the counselor consults periodically with the faculty member to monitor the student's progress. With counseling and faculty support, the student is able to meet the demands of her coursework and field placement.

+ *B.11.(c)* A community mental health agency counselor is providing services for Alan, who is concerned about his lack of interest in sexual intercourse with his wife. Alan relates his concerns to his strict religious upbringing. In order to better assist Alan, the counselor contacts a minister of Alan's faith, inquires about that church's views on sexuality, and requests any information that might assist in situations such as the current one.

− *B.11.(d)* An elementary school counselor is working with a child who is distraught over the recent death of a pet. The counselor wonders about the intensity of the child's reaction. The counselor has never worked with a case of this type before but does not seek consultation with another professional who has had such experience nor does he look for publications that might assist him.

− *B.11.(e)* During sessions with a male client, a counselor at a mental health agency finds that she experiences strong feelings of attraction toward the client. She realizes that her feelings interfere with her ability to assist the client. Rather than discuss this situation during weekly meetings of the professional staff, the counselor decides that she will find a way to handle it herself.

− *B.11.(f)* A counselor at a small college is perplexed about a hostile male client. She seeks consultation with the Dean of Students, who is also the chief discipline officer of the college. In the process of consultation, the counselor reveals information that allows the dean to discern that this client is one of the students who broke into a professor's office and stole some examinations.

B.12. If the member determines an inability to be of professional assistance to the client, the member must either avoid initiating the counseling relationship or immediately terminate that relationship. In either event, the member must suggest appropriate alternatives. (The member must be knowledgeable about referral resources so that a satisfactory referral can be initiated.) In the event the client declines the suggested referral, the member is not obligated to continue the relationship.

+ *B.12.(a)* A counselor for the juvenile court is assigned to work with a young man who has serious problems relating to authority figures. The young man constantly ridicules and insults police, administrators, and other authority figures with whom he interacts. The counselor is unable to develop rapport with the client and finds it difficult to work with or around this attitude. He refers the client to another counselor who has a record of success in working with rebellious young people.

+ *B.12.(b)* After two interviews a counselor realizes that a client's extreme hostility, resentment, and tendency to act out are beyond her expertise to manage. The counselor suggests a referral. When the client agrees, the counselor refers the client to a psychiatric clinic and makes the needed transfer arrangements.

+ *B.12.(c)* A college freshman goes to the counseling center to get help in improving his study skills. The student feels inadequate to handle college work and mentions that it was once suggested that he might be dyslexic. Although he was able to get through high school, he believes his dyslexia is interfering with his college work. The counselor refers the student to the diagnostic evaluation clinic on campus as a step toward understanding the problem.

− *B.12.(d)* A school counselor is working with a student who is distressed about her family situation, which involves abuse of "crack" cocaine. The counselor has no training in cocaine addiction counseling but feels confident about working with the student. The counselor continues to counsel with the student, unaware that a local family service center has an excellent program for teenagers from substance abusive homes that is available at no charge.

− *B.12.(e)* After a period of 4 months, a counselor in a college counseling center reviews her work with a certain client and decides that no progress has been made. The counselor feels increasingly frustrated with the client. Because the relationship will be terminated in 3 weeks at the end of the semester, the counselor continues to meet with the client and "just talk" rather than confronting the issue of no progress toward goals. At the end of counseling, the client is dissatisfied with counseling and says that he will not consider returning next year or recommending the center.

− B.12.(f) A counselor in private practice has had three interviews with a client. It has become apparent that the client's needs could best be met through career counseling. Because the counselor has neither the training nor the resources needed for career counseling, he offers to refer the client to a qualified career counselor. The client refuses to accept the suggested referral. The counselor then continues to work with the client and attempts to address her career concerns.

B.13. When the member has other relationships, particularly of an administrative, supervisory, and/or evaluative nature with an individual seeking counseling services, the member must not serve as the counselor but should refer the individual to another professional. Only in instances where such an alternative is unavailable and where the individual's situation warrants counseling intervention should the member enter into and/or maintain a counseling relationship. Dual relationships with clients that might impair the member's objectivity and professional judgement (e.g., as with close friends or relatives) must be avoided and/or the counseling relationship must be terminated through referral to another competent professional.

+ B.13.(a) A college student approaches his psychology teacher after class and says he has been very depressed lately and even has thought about suicide. He asks the teacher for help because she is also on staff at the college counseling center. The teacher expresses her concern but explains that it would be inadvisable to work with him as a client because they already have a teacher-student relationship. She recommends another counselor and walks with him to the center to help him arrange for an appointment.

+ B.13.(b) A counselor receives a frantic phone call from a personal friend whose wife has been working with another counselor for 8 months. The wife's counselor has been out of town on vacation for 2 weeks. During that time the client has become increasingly troubled and has stated that she wants to end her life. The friend is frightened and asks the counselor to talk with her just this once. Her counselor will be back in 2 days but the friend is afraid to wait that long. The counselor agrees to see her to assess whether any immediate intervention such as hospitalization is warranted.

+ B.13.(c) A counselor in a mental health agency is concerned about his increasing feelings of isolation. He shares his concerns with a fellow staff counselor. After saying how helpful it is to air his feelings, he suggests that they meet weekly for lunch to work on his concerns. The counselor replies that she is willing to be a good friend and listen, but believes it important that he explore these concerns in a formal counseling relationship. She explains her concern that their friendship and collegial relationship will interfere with her ability to be objective and give candid feedback. He agrees and they discuss counselors whom he might contact for assistance.

– *B.13.(d)* Jan has been working as a secretary at a family counseling center for the past year. She has been having marital difficulties and her husband has agreed to try counseling to work out solutions. Jan asks one of the counselors at the agency to provide marriage counseling for her and her husband. The counselor declines because he is her work supervisor and suggests two other marriage counselors in the area. Jan pleads with him to change his mind because Jan's husband already knows the counselor and likes him. The counselor reluctantly agrees to see them.

– *B.13.(e)* A counselor educator also has a part-time private practice. One of her graduate students makes an appointment to see her. The student says that the course has brought up some personal issues for him. He asks to be a client in her private practice. She agrees to work with him.

– *B.13.(f)* A residence hall director who is responsible for hall discipline has training in counseling. He is approached by students living in his hall who say they would like to address some personal concerns and want him to be their counselor. Although the college has services available through the counseling center, the residence hall director arranges weekly sessions for counseling.

B.14. The member will avoid any type of sexual intimacies with clients. Sexual relationships with clients are unethical.

+ *B.14.(a)* A client suggests to her counselor that they see each other socially, on a dating basis, because they have such a good relationship. She also indicates that she finds him sexually attractive. The counselor explains that, due to the nature of the counseling relationship, this would not be appropriate or possible.

+ *B.14.(b)* A student is seeing a counselor at a university counseling center. During the first two interviews, the client has made several sexually suggestive comments. In the third session, he asks the counselor if she is married. The counselor discerns that the client is interested in pursuing the possibility of a social and sexual relationship. When confronted, the client admits this is the case. The counselor explains that such a relationship would be unethical and cannot be considered.

– *B.14.(c)* A counselor in private practice has been counseling with a woman who feels devastated by the breakup of her marriage. During one session she begins to sob and asks to be held. The counselor complies with her request, and the situation leads to mutual caresses of a sexual nature. The counselor continues, rationalizing that the client could not handle another rejection.

– *B.14.(d)* An employment counselor enters into a sexual relationship with one of her clients. When a colleague questions her behavior, she says that her personal relationship with the client is irrelevant to the employment counseling she is conducting with him.

31

B.15. All experimental methods of treatment must be clearly indicated to prospective recipients, and safety precautions are to be adhered to by the member.

+ *B.15.(a)* College counseling center counselors offer a group counseling experience for students experiencing eating disorders. Prospective participants are informed that the group will be conducted by professional staff members and may offer assistance with their concerns. Counselors explain clearly to the students seeking this experience that there are no definitive research findings regarding the efficacy of this approach. Students are also told that alternative assistance will be available if needed and that this group is an attempt to find a more effective treatment approach for eating disorders.

+ *B.15.(b)* A therapist in a community mental health agency is contacted by a client seeking hypnosis for control of pain associated with a degenerative disease. The client says no other agencies in the community offer this service and he cannot afford to seek the assistance available in a large metropolitan area several hours away. The therapist explains that she has studied hypnosis techniques, has used them with clients for anxiety management, and is willing to see if they will assist the client in pain control. The therapist also asks to consult with the client's physician and with other practitioners of hypnosis about the client's case.

− *B.15.(c)* A mental health counselor offers a group experience in attitudinal healing for cancer patients. After the fourth group session one of the participants approaches the counselor and says that attitudinal healing is so powerful that she intends to cancel plans to return to the hospital for her prescribed chemotherapy. The counselor does not warn her of the dangers of this decision.

− *B.15.(d)* A client consults a therapist because she experiences high levels of anxiety in social situations where others are consuming alcohol. The problem relates to adolescent experiences with an alcoholic parent. The counselor has read about systematic desensitization and believes it may be an effective approach with this client. The counselor does not explain that he has not actually used this procedure in working with previous clients. The client agrees to proceed with desensitization techniques.

B.16. When computer applications are used as a component of counseling services, the member must ensure that: (a) the client is intellectually, emotionally, and physically capable of using the computer application; (b) the computer application is appropriate for the needs of the client; (c) the client understands the purpose and operation of the computer application; and (d) a follow-up of client use of a computer application is provided to both correct possible problems (misconceptions or inappropriate use) and assess subsequent needs.

+ B.16.(a) A high school counselor encourages students to use a computerized guidance information system to investigate various colleges. He meets with students individually to assess their capability to use computer applications and shows them how to operate the system. When the students complete their work on the computer, he meets with them again to discuss their findings and help them determine what steps to take next.

+ B.16.(b) An employment counselor is working with a man who is unemployed. When counseling has progressed to the point where the client has identified specific types of jobs he wants to seek, the counselor shows him how to access employment listings on a computer. When he completes his search, they meet to plan the next phase of his job search.

− B.16.(c) A newly employed counselor in a community college is assigned to do career and personal counseling. She prefers the personal counseling aspect of her work. To allow more time for personal counseling, she administers the same computer-generated and -scored career interest inventory to every student who requests career counseling.

− B.16.(d) A counselor and his client agree that the client will conduct a self-directed search on a computer as part of the career counseling process. The counselor gives the materials to the client and helps him get started at a computer terminal located in a workroom. A few minutes later, the client has difficulty following the instructions that appear on the computer screen. He goes to the counselor's office to ask for assistance, but the counselor is not in. The client leaves in frustration and does not return for counseling.

B.17. When the member is engaged in short-term group treatment/training programs (e.g., marathons and other encounter-type or growth groups), the member ensures that there is professional assistance available during and following the group experience.

+ B.17.(a) A widow seeks an encounter-type group experience after the death of her husband. Because she feels lonely and confused, she believes being with others would help. The group experience, however, is very painful for her and she breaks into uncontrollable tears on several occasions. When the group facilitator speaks with her, she says that she just doesn't seem able to "deal with people yet." The facilitator suggests that she work with another counselor who is available for individual assistance and postpone her decision about participating in group experiences.

+ B.17.(b) Several members of a 6-week assertiveness training group wish to continue developing their assertiveness skills. The group facilitator suggests several alternatives. The members decide to select works from the reading list that the facilitator had given them. The facilitator reminds them that additional contact or referral information can be arranged at any time in the future.

– *B.17.(c)* An interview preparation workshop is being conducted at a community career development agency. As part of the workshop, practice interviews are videotaped. As the facilitator prepares to replay the interviews, one man becomes visibly anxious and agitated. The facilitator decides to proceed with the replay and suggests to the man that he "get a cup of coffee from the receptionist and try to calm down." The man leaves the workshop and does not return. No further contact is initiated by the facilitator.

– *B.17.(d)* A rape education program is offered through a local rape emergency assistance center. This 2-hour workshop includes a film that depicts the brutality of rape and the vulnerability of women to this experience. Following the film, the presenter leads a brief discussion of reactions that participants might experience as a result of the workshop. However, she does not identify ways for participants to arrange for professional assistance or debriefing after this presentation.

B.18. Should the member be engaged in a work setting that calls for any variation from the above statements, the member is obligated to consult with other professionals whenever possible to consider justifiable alternatives.

+ *B.18.(a)* An applicant is interviewed for a counseling position in a religious center. The applicant is told that the center has strict beliefs against abortion and expects that counselors will not advise any client to have an abortion. The applicant accepts the position after deciding that he can work compatibly with the center's philosophy. To safeguard client integrity and to avoid initiating a relationship in which he may be unable to be of professional assistance, the counselor informs all clients concerned with unwanted pregnancies about the center's position. Clients are given the opportunity to choose whether they want to continue counseling at the center or seek help elsewhere.

+ *B.18.(b)* A newly appointed superintendent of schools institutes a policy that counseling files must be kept open to teachers. A counselor expresses her ethical objections. She is told that the policy will be reconsidered at a later date but must be adhered to in the interim. She consults with her fellow counselors, who agree that they will make only the most general written records while they are preparing their proposal to change the policy.

– *B.18.(c)* After being hired for an industrial counseling position, a counselor discovers that notes of all counseling interviews are expected to be maintained in the employee's permanent record. The counselor objects because this violates confidentiality. He is told that compliance is expected with this standard company policy. The counselor acquiesces to the employer's demands.

– *B.18.(d)* A high school counselor is required to have an open file of students' standardized test scores available to all teachers. No control is placed upon the use of tests or test scores within the school. Neither are teachers provided any training regarding the tests used by the school. The counselor opposes this practice but says nothing because it is her first year of employment.

B.19. The member must ensure that members of various ethnic, racial, religious, disability, and socioeconomic groups have equal access to computer applications used to support counseling services and that the content of available computer applications does not discriminate against the groups described above.

+ *B.19.(a)* A school counselor discovers that a computerized test used for placement purposes has been found to have low validity for Hispanic students. He arranges for an alternative test to be acquired by the school district.

+ *B.19.(b)* A college hires a counselor to create a personal and career counseling program for visually handicapped students. The counselor orders equipment needed to visually enhance material that appears on computer screens in the counseling center and arranges for a reader to be available to assist students who cannot read the enhanced screens.

− *B.19.(c)* A community college center purchases for student use a variety of self-help, stand-alone computer applications. Students who have home computers make use of the new applications. Students who are inexperienced with computer use do not avail themselves of the resources, and the counseling center staff does not arrange to assist these students.

− *B.19.(d)* A high school counseling staff holds a career day during which a number of computerized career guidance information systems are made available to students. The career day is held on a date when many Jewish students are absent due to a religious holiday.

B.20. When computer applications are developed by the member for use by the general public as self-help/stand-alone computer software, the member must ensure that: (a) self-help computer applications are designed from the beginning to function in a stand-alone manner, as opposed to modifying software that was originally designed to require support from a counselor; (b) self-help computer applications will include within the program statements regarding intended user outcomes, suggestions for using the software, a description of the conditions under which self-help computer applications might not be appropriate, and a description of when and how counseling services might be beneficial; and (c) the manual for such applications will include the qualifications of the developer, the development process, validation data, and operating procedures.

+ *B.20.(a)* A counselor educator develops a self-help, stand-alone computer application intended to help individuals identify their life stressors. In the accompanying manual, she carefully describes results and other factors that would alert the individual to seek counseling for stress management.

35

+ *B.20.(b)* Three college counselors work to develop a computer program to assist entering students to choose the most appropriate freshman English course. They want to design the software so that students can complete the program without assistance. Over a period of 2 years, the program is pilot tested and validation studies are conducted. When the program is completed, the development and validation procedures are fully described in the manual.

− *B.20.(c)* A school system purchases a computerized software package for 4-year course planning that is designed for students to complete with counselor assistance. To save time, the counselor writes an instruction manual to accompany the software and instructs students to complete the process independently in the school's computer lab.

− *B.20.(d)* A career counselor develops a computerized initial decision-making program that is designed for clients to take home and complete at their leisure. Although it is the counselor's intention that clients will bring the results of this initial exploration to the next counseling session for further discussion, he fails to include this information in the software. Several clients complete the program at home but fail to return for further counseling.

SECTION C:
MEASUREMENT AND
EVALUATION

The primary purpose of educational and psychological testing is to provide descriptive measures that are objective and interpretable in either comparative or absolute terms. The member must recognize the need to interpret the statements that follow as applying to the whole range of appraisal techniques including test and nontest data. Test results constitute only one of a variety of pertinent sources of information for personnel, guidance, and counseling decisions.

C.1. The counselor must provide specific orientation or information to the examinee(s) prior to and following the test administration so that the results of testing may be placed in proper perspective with other relevant factors. In so doing, the member must recognize the effects of socioeconomic, ethnic, and cultural factors on test scores. It is the member's professional responsibility to use additional unvalidated information carefully in modifying interpretation of the test results.

+ *C.1.(a)* One week prior to the administration of achievement tests to the sophomore class, the counselor visits classrooms in order to explain the purpose of this test series. After the results become available, the counselor again meets with the sophomore classes and provides information about how test scores should be interpreted. Further, the counselor invites students who have questions about their own scores to make an appointment to speak with him individually.

+ *C.1.(b)* A male client wants to become a nurse. He has some doubt, however, about whether this is really the right field. The counselor suggests a vocational interest test. The test results do not support his interest in the nursing field. The counselor explains that although the test shouldn't be the only factor in his decision, the results do mean that the student's interests are different from those of a recent sample of men who are in the nursing profession.

− *C.1.(c)* A week prior to the test administration date, the counselor makes this announcement over the school's intercom: "Attention, students in the junior class! On Monday, October 12th, at 9:00 in the morning, please assemble in the cafeteria to take the Test of Academic Skills and Knowledge."

The students are not told the purpose of the test or how the results will be used.

− C.1.(d) A client wants to enter an apprenticeship in a local shipyard to become a draftsman. The client has scored below the minimal standard on the admissions test. The counselor lies and reports passing scores, believing that this "adjustment" balances out the educational disadvantages the client suffered by attending poor schools in the barrio.

C.2. In selecting tests for use in a given situation or with a particular client, the member must consider carefully the specific validity, reliability, and appropriateness of the test(s). General validity, reliability, and related issues may be questioned legally as well as ethically when tests are used for vocational and educational selection, placement, or counseling.

+ C.2.(a) The manager of an employment agency asks her counseling staff for advice on the purchase of an attractive new test of manual dexterity. The counselors evaluate the test manual. They advise against using the test because there is no evidence that the test is valid.

+ C.2.(b) In counseling with a university sophomore, a counselor has the Strong Vocational Interest Blank also scored for the Psychology Specialty keys. The student has expressed interest in a career in psychology. In discussing the sophomore's interest similarities, the counselor is careful to distinguish the meaning of the scores on the general occupations from those on the specialty keys and explains the differences between the reference groups.

− C.2.(c) A 12th-grade client has lived only a few years in this country, and although fluent in oral communication, has a considerable handicap in interpreting written English. The counselor administers a standard academic ability test and interprets it against 12th-grade norms as indicating that the student has poor potential for college work.

C.3. When making any statements to the public about tests and testing, the member must give accurate information and avoid false claims or misconceptions. Special efforts are often required to avoid unwarranted connotations of such terms as I.Q. and grade equivalent scores.

+ C.3.(a) After achievement test results for the sixth-grade class have been received, the school counselor goes further than merely sending the scores to the parents. She writes a cover letter that explains the meaning of test scores in lay rather than psychometric terminology. She also invites parents to come to the school and discuss the results.

− C.3.(b) In revising a standardized achievement test battery, the test publisher decides to change the nature of the norm group. The change results in more "difficult" norms and is carefully described in the test manual. The test representative considers this information too technical for school personnel to understand or appreciate and fails to call this to the attention of potential customers. One school system switches from the old to the new edition, only to find that students score considerably lower on the new edition. The superintendent concludes that the teachers (recently unionized) are simply not working as hard as before. The test representative makes no effort to correct this possible misinterpretation.

C.4. Different tests demand different levels of competence for administration, scoring, and interpretation. Members must recognize the limits of their competence and perform only those functions for which they are prepared. In particular, members using computer-based test interpretations must be trained in the construct being measured and the specific instrument being used prior to using this type of computer application.

+ C.4.(a) The director of a mental health agency asks a counselor to administer a projective personality test to a client. The counselor is not trained in the administration of this test. She tells her director and they agree that another staff counselor will administer the test.

− C.4.(b) A counselor who works with prisoners in the county jail is asked for a personality assessment of a newly incarcerated inmate. As this counselor has little knowledge of personality tests, she administers a test that can be computer-scored and interpreted. She goes ahead with her personality assessment based on the computer printout.

C.5. In situations where a computer is used for test administration and scoring, the member is responsible for ensuring that administration and scoring programs function properly to provide clients with accurate test results.

+ C.5.(a) Prior to using a computer administered and scored test with clients, the counselor goes through the entire test-taking and scoring process herself to make sure that the computer program works properly.

− C.5.(b) Over the course of a year, 50 students take a computerized assessment of vocational interest. The counselor routinely makes a small error in operating the program with the result that students are given inaccurate information. The counselor had neglected to master the operation of the program or test the accuracy of the results.

− C.5.(c) All first graders are administered a test of basic skills that requires the children to "bubble in" their answers on a computer-scanned form. The school counselor is assigned to make sure that each form is properly bubbled in. However, the counselor finds the task tedious and decides to check every fifth test rather than every test.

C.6. Tests must be administered under the same conditions that were established in their standardization. When tests are not administered under standard conditions or when unusual behavior or irregularities occur during the testing session those conditions must be noted and the results designated as invalid or of questionable validity. Unsupervised or inadequately supervised

39

test-taking, such as the use of tests through the mails, is considered unethical. On the other hand, the use of instruments that are so designed or standardized to be self-administered and self-scored, such as interest inventories, is to be encouraged.

+ C.6.(a) During the administration of a standardized test, a breakdown in the clocks causes the time to be 7 minutes short for a subtest. The error is discovered a week later when the clocks are used again. The principal is reluctant to report the matter to the national testing service, but the counselor insists that it be reported, pointing out how this could adversely affect the total test results.

+ C.6.(b) A counselor gives a client a self-administering interest inventory and tells the client that he can complete the inventory at home and mail it back.

− C.6.(c) The director of testing at a university is scheduled to administer the LSAT. Enroute to administer the test, the counselor has a flat tire. By the time she gets the tire changed she is quite late. The students, who were already anxious, are angry by the time the counselor arrives. To offset the students' distress, she decides to give the students 30 minutes extra time beyond that allotted in the directions to complete the testing. She does not report these events to the testing service.

− C.6.(d) Three students are competing for a scholarship offered by a local service club. One of the requirements is that they must take a standardized aptitude test at the school. The counselor starts the students on the test, sets the interval timer, and leaves. He returns to the room 2 hours later to collect the tests.

C.7. The meaningfulness of test results used in personnel, guidance, and counseling functions generally depends on the examinees's unfamiliarity with the specific items of the test. Any prior coaching or dissemination of the test materials can invalidate test results. Therefore, test security is one of the professional obligations of the member. Conditions that produce most favorable test results must be made known to the examinee.

+ C.7.(a) A counselor's friend has a son who is applying for admission to law school. The friend knows that the counselor works in the testing center at a neighboring university and asks the counselor for some questions from the law admissions test in addition to the samples already provided. The counselor refuses on ethical grounds but does suggest a textbook that might be helpful in preparing for the exam.

+ C.7.(b) A provision for security is that no test booklets are to be taken out of the testing rooms by anyone. One of the proctors starts to leave the room with a test booklet. The counselor reminds him of the rule and has him leave the test copy in the room.

+ C.7.(c) A student is scheduled to take a college entrance examination. The counselor becomes aware that the student is upset over the recent death of his mother. The counselor suggests that the student postpone the examination, explaining that the results could be negatively influenced by the student's emotional state.

– C.7.(d) A department chair telephones a university testing officer to request a copy of the Graduate Record Examination given in his subject area. Although the regulations governing the security of this test are fully explained, and he is given the sample questions provided by ETS, he is not satisfied. The testing officer decides to "go along" and sends a copy of the test.

– C.7.(e) A counselor is administering an achievement test to a group of ninth-grade students. Toward the end of the test, the counselor notices one student who has put her head down on the desk. When questioned, the student replies that she has a terrible headache and feels nauseated. The counselor doesn't tell the student that she could retake a different form of the test at a later date.

C.8. The purpose of testing and the explicit use of the results must be made known to the examinee prior to testing. The counselor must ensure that instrument limitations are not exceeded and that periodic review and/or retesting are made to prevent client stereotyping.

+ C.8.(a) A private practitioner regularly administers a personality test to his clients. He carefully explains the purpose of the test and how the results will be used in the therapeutic process.

+ C.8.(b) A school counselor encourages strict adherence to the ruling that special education students must be reevaluated every 3 years.

– C.8.(c) A business administrator asks the personnel counselor to administer a battery of tests to five employees who are being considered for promotion. The personnel counselor assumes that the employees have been informed of how the company will use the results. A follow-up reveals that two employees were fired shortly after the testing and that they had not been told about the purpose of the tests. Shortly thereafter another group of employees are sent for testing. The personnel counselor tests this group also.

– C.8.(d) A physically disabled person is applying for vocational rehabilitation assistance to pursue job retraining. The rehabilitation counselor gets achievement test scores from the client's high school records. Although these scores are 5 years old, the counselor uses them to advise the client regarding his abilities for various training programs.

C.9. The examinee's welfare and explicit prior understanding must be the criteria for determining the recipients of the test results. The member must see that specific interpretation accompanies any release of individual or group test data. The interpretation of test data must be related to the examinee's particular concerns.

+ *C.9.(a)* A counselor who is the personnel officer for a large department store has been asked by her superiors to "do something" in order to determine which job applicants are prone to tardiness and absenteeism due to hypochondriacal tendencies (calling in sick). The counselor proposes a correlational study comparing results from instruments that measure hypochondriacal tendencies with actual employee promptness and attendance over a 10-month period. The counselor explains that until and unless sufficient correlation can be found between actual employee performance and test data, no individual employee's test result can be considered relevant to the problem of absenteeism.

+ *C.9.(b)* A high school student asks a counselor to evaluate his vocational interests. The counselor administers an interest inventory. The student's folder also contains an old report from a personality test that is concerned with identifying psychopathology. Although the results of the personality test are interesting, the counselor thinks that they don't have anything to do with the student's request. Consequently, the counselor interprets the results of the interest inventory and doesn't mention the results of the personality test.

− *C.9.(c)* A faculty adviser in a graduate program is required by departmental policy to interpret advisory test battery results to his students in counseling. Because the students have taken or will take courses in testing, the adviser simply gives the students the raw test data and recommends a book that will help them make their own interpretations.

− *C.9.(d)* The director of a community vocational center wants his counseling staff to be more proficient in test interpretation. He instructs staff members to administer a personality instrument, a vocational interest inventory, and an intelligence test to all clients regardless of their presenting problem in order to practice interpreting all kinds of tests.

C.10. Members responsible for making decisions based on test results have an understanding of educational and psychological measurement, validation criteria, and test research.

+ *C.10.(a)* A school counselor frequently serves on admission, review, and dismissal (ARD) committees. An ARD committee evaluates a wide range of information, including test data, and then decides if a child qualifies for special education services. Finally, the ARD committee recommends an individualized educational plan. The counselor has a thorough understanding of testing and measurement. She is able to help other committee members see the test results in proper perspective and use them in making wise decisions.

− *C.10.(b)* Rather than admit to an embarrassing lack of knowledge or go to the trouble of learning more about testing, a counselor simply avoids those aspects of his responsibilities that require an understanding of testing.

− *C.10.(c)* A school counselor tells parents of a third grader that their child's high achievement in the classroom coupled with superior scores on the Wechsler Intelligence Scale for Children-Revised (WISC-R) would predict success should the child be advanced a grade above his age level. However, the counselor really does not understand how WISC-R scores are derived or what abilities they represent.

C.11. The member must be cautious when interpreting the results of research instruments possessing insufficient technical data. The specific purposes for the use of such instruments must be stated explicitly to examinees.

+ *C.11.(a)* A counselor administers a newly developed ability test to a prospective college student. The test's predictive validity has not been established. In interpreting the scores, the counselor advises the client that he can only compare his scores with other students' and that he can draw only limited inferences about his chances for success in college.

+ *C.11.(b)* The director of testing at a community college has been contacted by a testing company that wants to use the college students as part of the item analysis group. The director agrees to help and explains to student volunteers that they are participating in the development of this test and that they won't be able to get any meaningful information from it.

− *C.11.(c)* A counselor is mailed a sample copy of a new vocational interest test that is in the process of being standardized. The counselor surveys the contents of the test, is impressed, and decides to use it in vocational counseling with his current clients. The counselor fails to tell his clients that the test results may be unreliable.

C.12. The member must proceed with caution when attempting to evaluate and interpret the performance of minority group members or other persons who are not represented in the norm group on which the instrument was standardized.

+ *C.12.(a)* A Mexican-American transfer student is recommended for a class for slow learners based on poor performance on a mental ability test. The school counselor learns that Mexican-Americans are not represented in the norm group for the test in question and that the student has always performed well academically. The counselor puts together a variety of more appropriate measures to use as a basis for placement.

+ *C.12.(b)* A counselor learns from a well-researched journal article that there are several race-related or race-sensitive items on the Minnesota Multiphasic Personality Inventory (MMPI), enough so that standard scoring and norms of the MMPI might not be fully appropriate for use with Black clients. The data in the article enable him to adjust the scoring of the MMPI for Black clients so that the standard norms and profile can be used.

– *C.12.(c)*   A Black student is denied admission to a university because of poor performance on the entrance examination. Even after it is pointed out that a local study has shown that the test has zero predictive validity for Black students, the director of admissions refuses to reconsider the student's application.

– *C.12.(d)*   A visually handicapped student applies for admission to a graduate program in counseling psychology. One of the requirements for admission to this program is a Miller Analogies Test (MAT) raw score of 50 or higher. The applicant took the MAT under standard conditions (including time limit). The student scored 32 on the MAT. He appended a note to his application saying that he had difficulty reading the questions because of his poor vision. The departmental admissions committee denies him admission to the program solely on the basis of the MAT score.

C.13.   When computer-based test interpretations are developed by the member to support the assessment process, the member must ensure that the validity of such interpretations is established prior to the commercial distribution of such a computer application.

+ *C.13.(a)*   A counselor develops a computer program that generates an interpretation of the Wechsler Intelligence Scale for Children-Revised (WISC-R). In collaboration with the Psychological Corporation, the WISC-R's publisher, a thorough study of validity and reliability is undertaken prior to marketing the program.

– *C.13.(b)*   A counselor develops a computer program that generates a profile of suicide risk. There seems to be a "common sense" justification for the program's interpretation of test data. For example, the program describes self-reported feelings of depression as elevating suicide potential. The counselor rents an exhibit booth and sells the program at a national conference.

C.14.   The member recognizes that test results may become obsolete. The member will avoid and prevent the misuse of obsolete test results.

+ *C.14.(a)*   A counselor in a university admissions office argues that Graduate Record Exam (GRE) results that are more than 10 years old should not be used as a criterion for admission to graduate school. The argument is persuasive and the admissions policy is changed.

– *C.14.(b)*   A counselor discourages a reentry college student from enrolling in an electrical engineering degree program because of a low algebra score on an achievement test taken 8 years ago.

C.15.   The member must guard against the appropriation, reproduction, or modification of published tests or parts thereof without acknowledgement and permission from the previous publisher.

+ *C.15.(a)* By empirical study, a psychologist determines that a test of academic motivation can be constructed by drawing selected items from each of several published personality and interest inventories. She then obtains permission from the several publishers to use these items in her new inventory.

+ *C.15.(b)* A counseling psychologist who has authored an inventory of study skills learns that a competitor has mimeographed his inventory under a new title, "College Educational Skills Inventory." The author tells the competitor that unauthorized use of his inventory will be referred to the AACD Ethics Committee and/or a lawyer unless immediate changes are made. The retitled instrument is withdrawn.

− *C.15.(c)* An elementary school counselor, finding that his budget for test materials will not permit purchase of the publisher's answer sheets for next fall's testing program, duplicates the answer sheet.

− *C.15.(d)* A counselor item-analyzes a standard commercial achievement test and replaces the original test with his adapted version that takes less testing time. He doesn't contact the test publisher regarding authorization for such use.

C.16. Regarding the preparation, publication, and distribution of tests, reference should be made to:

a. *Standards for Educational and Psychological Testing*, **revised edition, 1985, published by the American Psychological Association on behalf of itself, the American Educational Research Association, and the National Council on Measurement in Education.**

b. The Responsible Use of Tests: A Position Paper of AMEG, APGA, and NCME. *Measurement and Evaluation in Guidance*, **1972, *5*, 385–388.**

c. "Responsibilities of Users of Standardized Tests," APGA, *Guidepost*, **October 5, 1978, pp. 5–8.**

SECTION D: RESEARCH AND PUBLICATION

D.1. Guidelines on research with human subjects shall be adhered to, such as:

a. *Ethical Principles in the Conduct of Research with Human Participants*, Washington, DC: American Psychological Association, Inc., 1982.

b. Code of Federal Regulations, Title 45, Subtitle A, Part 46, as currently issued.

c. *Ethical Principles of Psychologists*, American Psychological Association, Principle #9: Research With Human Participants.

d. Family Educational Rights and Privacy Act (the Buckley Amendment).

e. Current federal regulations and various state rights privacy acts.

D.2. In planning any research activity dealing with human subjects, the member must be aware of and responsive to all pertinent ethical principles and ensure that the research problem, design, and execution are in full compliance with them.

+ *D.2.(a)* The university's Research With Human Subjects Committee is evaluating a proposal to compare the side effects caused by a promising new asthma medicine with those caused by a placebo. Student volunteers will be paid to participate in the experiment. The committee consults an outside medical expert to find out whether the potential side effects can be harmful.

− *D.2.(b)* The university's Research With Human Subjects Committee meets with a researcher who is proposing a study on the effects of sleep deprivation on short-term memory. Student volunteers will be paid to participate in the experiment. The researcher has impressive credentials and, because the members of the committee aren't experts, they accept the researcher's assurance that the experiment is harmless.

D.3. Responsibility for ethical research practice lies with the principal researcher, while others involved in the research activities share ethical obligation and full responsibility for their own actions.

46

+ *D.3.(a)* The administrators of a school district grant permission to a researcher to study the impact of parental divorce on achievement test scores of elementary school pupils. The study requires the assistance of the school counselor on each campus. Before agreeing to help, the school counselors read the proposal carefully in order to be sure that the study falls within ethical guidelines.

− *D.3.(b)* A counselor in the Air Force allows the videotaping of her interviews with basic trainees as part of a research study. The videotaped interviews will subsequently be analyzed. As the study has been approved by her commanding officer, the counselor does not feel obliged to decide for herself if the research falls within ethical guidelines.

D.4. In research with human subjects, researchers are responsible for the subjects' welfare throughout the experiment, and they must take all reasonable precautions to avoid causing injurious psychological, physical, or social effects on their subjects.

+ *D.4.(a)* An investigator's research protocol requires an extended period of time from each subject. For some subjects the experience may be extremely fatiguing and frustrating. The investigator arranges the procedure so that there is a brief rest period at the end of each hour if the subject desires one. Also, ample time is allowed to confer with all subjects as they finish to offer support, answer questions, and provide information about the study.

+ *D.4.(b)* A counselor working in a college residence hall wants to study social communication among roommates. The most rigorous design for the purpose of this investigation would require splitting certain roommates and reassigning them to other rooms. However, the counselor alters the design to one that will not disrupt students' social relationships because the ratio of expected benefit to risk does not justify the original design.

+ *D.4.(c)* Dr. Zapata is conducting a study to evaluate the impact of systematic relaxation on pain tolerance. The pain tolerance technique used requires submersion of one's arm in ice water for as long as possible. Dr. Zapata uses a stopwatch to measure elapsed time and sets the maximum time period allowed *under* the length at which physiological damage may be expected to ensue.

− *D.4.(d)* The impact of a meditation technique is evaluated in a prison population. The researcher arranges for 20 of the prisoners to be verbally abused by the guards, thereby causing stress symptoms. The experimental group is taught to use the meditation technique; the control group receives no treatment. The study demonstrates the efficacy of the meditation technique.

− *D.4.(e)* An investigator studies the effects of jogging on stress management. A group of dedicated joggers is identified. These joggers are encouraged to run to their limit each day for a period of 1 month. No precautions are taken and no physical examinations are introduced prior to the investigation.

− D.4.(f) An investigator studies the effects of feedback on changes in communication style in a small group. Participants are encouraged to be totally honest and not hold back when reporting their feelings about others. No clear guidelines for feedback are established. The investigator does not monitor for any negative impact on the subjects.

D.5. All research subjects must be informed of the purpose of the study except when withholding information or providing misinformation to them is essential to the investigation. In such research the member must be responsible for corrective action as soon as possible following completion of the research.

+ D.5.(a) A doctoral student proposes to investigate the effect of tape recording of interviews on client-counselor freedom of expression and spontaneity. Information will be withheld from half of the counselors and clients as to whether a particular interview is being recorded. The counselors will be told what has been done at a later date, but not the clients. The student plans to confer with the doctoral adviser and the department's human experimentation committee before proceeding.

NOTE: A study such as the one outlined above is replete with ethical difficulties. The ethical behavior that is highlighted is the process; the student openly proposes what is actually intended, confers with the adviser, and submits the study for review by the human experimentation committee. Although it is likely that the study will not be conducted as submitted, the important behavior is review by and consultation with professionals who will scrutinize the study in light of ethical and legal regulations for human experimentation.

+ D.5.(b) Subjects participate in a simulated counseling interview. Although the purpose of the experiment is to study subjects' reactions to the interviewer, it is desirable that subjects believe that it is the content of the interview that is under investigation. After completing the dependent measures, all subjects are informed of the true purpose of the study and the reason for the deception.

+ D.5.(c) A counselor educator uses two groups of trainees as subjects for an experiment in group morale. Some of the subjects feel anxious about the strong feelings expressed in the groups. The investigator listens to their concerns and tries to help them understand the purpose of the experiment. He reiterates that they are free to drop out of the experiment at any time.

− D.5.(d) An investigator wants to study the impact of nonreinforcement on risk-taking behavior. In several general psychology laboratory sections, the teaching assistants are instructed not to orally reinforce correct responses to questions by certain student subjects. The impact of this oral nonreinforcement is judged in terms of the willingness of these students to volunteer responses to the teaching assistant's questions. No debriefing session or explanation of the teaching assistant's behavior is given upon completion of the study.

- − D.5.(e) A group of educationally retarded children have taken tests as part of a research project. The researcher wants to motivate the children to do their best on the next test. To that end, the researcher lies and tells them that they are performing at a superior level as compared with other students. The lie is not corrected when the experiment is completed.

D.6. Participation in research must be voluntary. Involuntary participation is appropriate only when it can be demonstrated that participation will have no harmful effects on subjects and is essential to the investigation.

- + D.6.(a) A study is designed to compare the effectiveness of different teaching approaches in elementary school mathematics. The student subjects will be studying the topic at the same time that they normally would in the curriculum. Previous research shows that none of the teaching approaches used in the study are ineffective. Thus, the researchers do not ask for voluntary participation on the part of the student subjects.

- + D.6.(b) A study investigates the depth of self-disclosure that takes place in a small group experience. Some of the experiences are emotionally intense and bring out intimate aspects of the participants' lives. It is decided that only volunteer participants will be used. All subjects will be informed of the general nature of the experiment and the potential harm of such group experiences. As an additional precaution, each volunteer is screened for sufficient ego strength.

- + D.6.(c) An investigator wishes to study the impact of a coeducational residential living environment on the academic achievement of college students. A list of grade point averages is obtained for students living in coeducational and same-sex residence halls over a 3-year period. Because information is analyzed after student graduation and without identification of individuals, consent of the subjects is not obtained.

- − D.6.(d) A professor is teaching a course in which the students would be suitable subjects for an experiment. The study requires subjects to complete a personality inventory. The inventory results will be compared with the subjects' behavior in small task-oriented groups held during class. Participation is mandatory even though it is not specifically related to the content of the course.

- − D.6.(e) School district administrators design a study to be conducted in elementary schools for the purpose of comparing various textbooks. Teachers are required to participate in the study. Furthermore, teachers must use unfamiliar texts, make major changes in semester lesson plans, and, in some cases, alter established teaching styles.

– *D.6.(f)* A community mental health agency wants to study the personality traits and presenting symptoms of clients seeking services. All clients are required to complete an extensive test battery including personality instruments and behavioral data as part of the intake procedures. Those clients unwilling to complete the battery are refused services until all data have been obtained.

D.7. When reporting research results, explicit mention must be made of all variables and conditions known to the investigator that might affect the outcome of the investigation or the interpretation of the data.

+ *D.7.(a)* The research director of a school system summarizes the data of the year's dropouts. One counselor knows that some schools routinely include summer dropouts in their reports whereas others do not. The counselor tells the research director about this discrepancy so that the report can be corrected.

+ *D.7.(b)* A state employment service supervisor is preparing a job analysis on a relatively new occupation. A careful training program is held for the 10 counselors who are to conduct interviews throughout the state. Before the interviews begin one counselor moves away, one is promoted, one resigns, and another dies. Four additional counselors are assigned to carry out the project, but only superficial training can be provided due to the impending deadline. When reporting the results, the supervisor makes special mention of the variance in qualifications of the interviewers who collected the data.

– *D.7.(c)* A master's candidate receives permission to gather data for a thesis from a stratified sample of a large school system. The study is supposed to show how well school counselors are informed about vocational rehabilitation services available to handicapped students and to determine what referrals are being made. A preliminary study of the raw data shows that a school in the lower socioeconomic area of the city is referring large numbers of students for rehabilitation services. The counselors in an upper socioeconomic school, on the other hand, refuse to identify any handicapped students. The master's candidate reports the data in such a way as to suggest that the results are representative of the entire school system.

D.8. The member must be responsible for conducting and reporting investigations in a manner that minimizes the possibility that results will be misleading.

+ *D.8.(a)* An investigator wants information about the resolution of adult developmental crises. A questionnaire is mailed to clients who have sought services for such issues through a community counseling agency. In the manuscript, the investigator reports that a 44% return was obtained from the initial survey, and an additional 22% return was obtained by a telephone follow-up. The investigator notes that the results reflect the perspective of only slightly more than two thirds of those initially seeking services for adult developmental crises concerns. Caution in making generalizations is emphasized because the data are incomplete.

+ *D.8.(b)* A researcher, well known for espousing a particular theoretical position, conducts an experiment that only partially supports her point of view. In the discussion section of the report, the researcher interprets the data first in light of their support of her favored theory, then in light of their support of an opposing theory, and concludes the paper with the statement that the choice of interpretation depends upon the reader's own theoretical orientation.

+ *D.8.(c)* *After* completing an experiment, an investigator discovers that an important variable was not controlled. In reporting the results, the implications of this uncontrolled variable and consequent limitations of the study are discussed.

− *D.8.(d)* A researcher discovers that the data do not meet the assumptions for the statistical test of significance that is being used. The results are reported without mention of this discovery.

− *D.8.(e)* A counselor investigates peer-group acceptance of severely handicapped college students, all of whom are confined to wheelchairs. In the manuscript submitted for publication, the discussion implies that these data generalize to *all* forms of disability.

− *D.8.(f)* A researcher studying hospitalized psychiatric patients finds that about one third of the subjects simply refuse to participate in the experiment. In reporting the findings, the researcher states that the data were obtained on a given number of subjects but fails to point out that this number reflects only two thirds of the total defined group.

NOTE: Research findings must be reported honestly. Researchers must resist the temptation to manipulate statistical results or overgeneralize in order to support desired conclusions. Editors who evaluate manuscripts for publication have an opportunity and, therefore, a responsibility to exclude unethical or faulty research.

D.9.   The member has an obligation to make available sufficient original research data to qualified others who may wish to replicate the study.

+ *D.9.(a)* The faculty of a graduate department establishes a policy that all theses and dissertations completed by students in that department include the "raw data" as an appendix so that another investigator would be able to check for computation errors or perform a different analysis. The data must be presented in such a way as to protect the anonymity of individual subjects.

− *D.9.(b)* A well-known authority in the field of counseling publishes an article that shows positive results from the application of his favorite counseling technique. He fails to report the very narrow subject selection criteria that may have "stacked the deck" in favor of positive results. Furthermore, he "loses" the raw data that would enable others to check the methodology of the study.

− D.9.(c) In one of the programs at a professional growth conference, a counselor presents a paper reporting how students in her school rate the guidance program using a new survey form. The students are highly enthusiastic about their guidance experiences. A counselor from a different school has used the same survey form and asks for a detailed report in order to make comparisons. The counselor involved with the first study refuses, maintaining that the data are confidential and cannot be disclosed.

D.10. When supplying data, aiding in the research of another person, reporting research results, or making original data available, due care must be taken to disguise the identity of the subjects in the absence of specific authorization from such subjects to do otherwise.

+ D.10.(a) The superintendent of schools asks an elementary school principal for records of students involved in disciplinary incidents during the past year as part of a district study. As the request comes in the summer, the principal is unable to contact the parents of five of the students involved. The principal submits the records for those students from whose parents written permission has been obtained and explains that five reports are omitted because the parents could not be contacted.

+ D.10.(b) A researcher asks several college counseling centers for reports of cases involving eating disorders. The researcher specifies that the case reports must omit any identifying information. When a report is received that has identifying information, it is returned for revision.

+ D.10.(c) A counselor who has submitted an article for publication uses real names and photographs of persons and events to dramatize their rehabilitation. The counselor obtained the written permission of each of the individuals before submitting the materials to the journal.

− D.10.(d) A researcher is studying depression as evidenced by certain types of profiles on the Minnesota Multiphasic Personality Inventory (MMPI). Counselors from a community mental health agency are asked to submit MMPI data and completed case reports. Because of a time problem, one counselor photocopies the profiles without editing out identifying data. Client permission to use the files had not been obtained.

− D.10.(e) A counselor at a university counseling center is assigned to work with several students who have tested positive for the human immunodeficiency virus (HIV). The counselor describes the experience in a professional paper. Although pseudonyms are used, there is sufficient information for a clever local newspaper reporter to write a story that enables many people to speculate about the identity of the students involved.

− D.10.(f) A professor is contacted by a graduate student who wants to replicate a study. The professor sends the complete data that include a list of student subjects by name and their scores on various tests used in the original study. The students had not signed consent forms giving permission to disclose their identity.

D.11. When conducting and reporting research, the member must be familiar with and give recognition to previous work on the topic, as well as to observe all copyright laws and follow the principles of giving full credit to all to whom credit is due.

+ *D.11.(a)*   A researcher reviews relevant literature before completing the design of a study. This practice strengthens the design and the interpretations, and provides a bibliography for future investigations.

+ *D.11.(b)*   A doctoral student submits a dissertation proposal that has some shortcomings. Previous work published on the topic has not been fully reviewed. Furthermore, the student fails to cite references for all of his sources. With the help of his major adviser, the problems are corrected.

+ *D.11.(c)*   A counselor replicates a study that was terminated by the death of the original researcher. In reporting this investigation, the counselor acknowledges the original researcher as author of the hypothesis and design of the study.

− *D.11.(d)*   In lecturing before local civic clubs, a counselor reports on her successful work with alcohol abusers in the workplace. The counselor presents this work as if it were original and without crediting earlier projects that have been reported in the professional literature.

− *D.11.(e)*   In writing a textbook, the author cites references for the research data. In the presentation of theoretical material, however, it is not clear which theorists are responsible for particular ideas and positions. The author paraphrases and summarizes material without citing references.

D.12. The member must give due credit through joint authorship, acknowledgement, footnote statements, or other appropriate means to those who have contributed significantly to the research and/or publication, in accordance with such contributions.

+ *D.12.(a)*   A graduate student carries out a study. This student is the sole investigator but he gets direction and assistance from his major professor. Later, when the study is developed into a chapter for a new book, the counselor acknowledges the contribution of the professor.

+ *D.12.(b)*   Three counselors write a descriptive study about brief family interventions. In reporting the study, all three counselors are listed as coauthors. The order of presentation of the authors' names is determined in relation to the contribution of each to the project.

− *D.12.(c)*   In a graduate course in counseling techniques students are assigned a paper on the philosophy and approaches of an outstanding authority in the field. The professor writes a book and uses a student's paper with only minor editing. No mention is made of the student's original work.

− *D.12.(d)* Dr. Jones agrees to conduct a study with Dr. Smith on the topic of at-risk adolescents. Dr. Jones loses interest and contributes little. When a manuscript is finally produced, thanks entirely to the persistence of Dr. Smith, Dr. Jones insists that he be credited as an equal coauthor.

D.13. The member must communicate to other members the results of any research judged to be of professional or scientific value. Results reflecting unfavorably on institutions, programs, services, or vested interests must not be withheld for such reasons.

+ *D.13.(a)* A college student personnel counselor conducts a study of student alcohol use. The results show that students exhibit a higher level of use than had been suspected. The results are made available in booklet form to other college counselors and administrators, and plans for an alcohol education program are set in motion.

− *D.13.(b)* A professor has carried out well-designed research that demonstrates the predictive power of a widely used test of college ability. The professor discusses the study in classroom lectures. However, he does not submit the study for consideration as an article in a journal or for a paper to be read at a conference.

− *D.13.(c)* A school counselor surveys substance abuse by students at an affluent high school. The results suggest that substance abuse is widespread. Such information could be upsetting to parents. The counselor takes the principal's "hint" that the results should go unreported.

D.14. If members agree to cooperate with another individual in research and/or publication, they incur an obligation to cooperate as promised in terms of punctuality of performance and with full regard to the completeness and accuracy of the information required.

+ *D.14.(a)* Two professors agree to divide tasks for a book they are coauthoring. One of them chooses to do a critical review of the research literature. Shortly after starting the project, she begins to think that her partner is better prepared to review certain areas. Subsequently, the coauthors renegotiate their respective work loads.

+ *D.14.(b)* Graduate student volunteers are sought from students in a counselor training program to facilitate growth groups for another student's doctoral dissertation. During the training session for these volunteers, the importance of conducting activities according to the time schedule is emphasized. Volunteer facilitators are punctual in arriving for the groups, keep accurate records following each group session, and return research materials within the established time frame.

− *D.14.(c)* A counselor agrees to complete a lengthy questionnaire as part of a national survey on professional ethics. Soon, he receives the survey instrument. A month passes before he looks at the questionnaire only to discover that it had to be completed and returned within 2 weeks. He throws the questionaire away rather than send it in late.

D.15. Ethical practice requires that authors not submit the same manuscript or one essentially similar in content for simultaneous publication consideration by two or more journals. In addition, manuscripts published in whole or in substantial part in another journal or published work should not be submitted for publication without acknowledgement and permission from the previous publication.

+ *D.15.(a)* A counselor completes a study on the impact of a tutoring program on high school student attrition. He rank orders journals in terms of desirability and submits the article to the journal he considers the most authoritative. The counselor decides that if the article is not accepted by the top journal, he will send it to the next one on the list and continue this process until the article is accepted.

+ *D.15.(b)* A counselor expands a published journal article on adolescent development into a chapter for a new book on developmental theories. She negotiates with the journal's publisher for a release of tables from the original article that she wants to reproduce in the book chapter.

− *D.15.(c)* An assistant professor is employed in a "publish or perish" institution. Aware that the acceptance, revision, and publication process can easily take more than a year, he submits the same article to two journals simultaneously.

− *D.15.(d)* A professor replicates a study with additional variables. She submits the new manuscript to a journal without getting permission to include the graphs published in the original article. She believes that acknowledgment through citation is sufficient.

SECTION E: CONSULTING

Consultation refers to a voluntary relationship between a professional helper and help-needing individual, group or social unit in which the consultant is providing help to the client(s) in defining and solving a work-related problem or potential problem with a client or client system.

E.1. The member acting as consultant must have a high degree of self-awareness of his/her own values, knowledge, skills, limitations, and needs in entering a helping relationship that involves human and/or organizational change and that the focus of the relationship be on the issues to be resolved and not on the person(s) presenting the problem.

+ *E.1.(a)* A professor of counseling and guidance who is an expert on women's issues has become acquainted with a representative of the U.S. Department of Labor. The representative knows of the professor's reputation and asks her to consult at the regional conference of union apprenticeship directors. The unions have had problems recruiting women to their apprenticeship programs. Although the professor is knowledgeable about women's issues, she knows very little about unions. She agrees to work with the apprenticeship directors, however, with the understanding that the Department of Labor will send a letter to the apprenticeship directors asking them to respond to questions about their difficulties.

+ *E.1.(b)* The president of a publishing house hires a consultant to investigate the unexpectedly low sales of one of the company's new academic achievement tests. The consultant talks with sales personnel and the director of sales and finds animosity toward the president. The sales people are frustrated because they feel they're expected to sell so many different tests that they can't do justice to any of the instruments, much less this new test with which customers are unfamiliar. The consultant tells the president that one of two decisions should be made: (a) the sales force needs to be increased or (b) the tests available for sale need to be placed in priority order so the sales force will know where to place their maximal efforts. The consultant does not mention the negative attitude of the sales force toward the president on the assumption that these attitudes will improve when the recommended changes are made.

− *E.1.(c)* The board of directors of a community agency hires a consultant to find out why drug users make up such a large proportion of the clientele. In his report, the consultant explains that the director of the agency holds the conviction that treating adolescent drug abusers is a top priority. The consultant does not say, however, that the data show a very high level of drug abuse by adolescents in the local community.

− *E.1.(d)* A consultant is asked by a large corporation to deliver a series of workshops on developing understanding between able-bodied and disabled employees. The consultant agrees even though she personally believes that too much emphasis is placed on promoting disabled individuals at the expense of women. During the workshops she pursues her hidden agenda of making her audience aware of women's struggles in various job settings. At the end of the workshops, the employees feel they have learned nothing about relationships between the able-bodied and the handicapped.

E.2. There must be understanding and agreement between member and client for the problem definition, change of goals, and prediction of consequences of interventions selected.

+ *E.2.(a)* A school district guidance coordinator attempts to mediate a conflict between counseling staff and faculty in a neighboring school district. Representatives of the faculty tell the coordinator that they want the counselors to ". . . get out of their offices and do something other than generate paperwork." Counselors tell the coordinator that the faculty needs to be educated about the counselors' role. The coordinator goes back to the principal to be certain that she has (a) a clear idea of her task and (b) the principal's full support. Receiving affirmation, the coordinator calls a meeting of the principal, the faculty representatives, and counseling staff to outline goals and define the problems they will be working to solve.

+ *E.2.(b)* An employee has had some serious adjustment problems that obviously have reduced his job efficiency. The manager suggests that the company's consulting psychologist "counsel" the employee to resign and find another job. The psychologist sees this as a violation of his role and explains his position to the manager.

− *E.2.(c)* A consultant is asked to recommend improvements in the operation of a psychiatric unit of a hospital. The consultant learns that the unit fails to meet minimal standards of care for such facilities. He recommends strategies that would enable the hospital to come into compliance. The hospital administrator tells the consultant to delete all reference to the deficiencies from his formal report. The consultant complies with the administrator's wishes.

E.3. The member must be reasonably certain that she/he or the organization represented has the necessary competencies and resources for giving the kind of help that is needed now or may be needed later and that appropriate referral resources are available to the consultant.

+ *E.3.(a)* A professor accepts a position as a consultant to a research project. She understands that she is to help with the measurement and evaluation part of the study. After several meetings it becomes clear that she is expected to provide technical help with computer procedures, an area in which she lacks expertise. Therefore, she steps down and suggests the names of several qualified consultants.

− E.3.(b) A psychologist eagerly accepts an opportunity to consult with a psychiatric hospital in establishing an adult substance abuse unit. However, the psychologist knows virtually nothing about treating substance abuse.

E.4. The consulting relationship must be one in which client adaptability and growth toward self-direction are encouraged and cultivated. The member must maintain this role consistently and not become a decision maker for the client or create a future dependency on the consultant.

+ E.4.(a) A consultant to a state psychiatric hospital is charged with helping set up an outpatient clinic. She offers illustrations of approaches taken by other hospitals and encourages the staff to assume responsibility for design and implementation of the new service.

+ E.4.(b) The faculty at a university with a new counselor education program asks two professors from a well-established program to consult with them. The consultants work closely with the developing program's faculty for 2 years, but at the end of the second year believe that they are no longer needed. They state that the new program is well established and there is no reason to continue the consulting on an ongoing basis.

−E.4.(c) A consultant is retained by an employment service to help staff with their professional development, especially interviewing skills. The consultant agrees to the goals and the fee of $400 per day of service. The entire process could easily be completed in five sessions; however, the member purposefully draws the sessions into eight by obfuscating and not moving the group of employees along as quickly as possible.

E.5. When announcing consultant availability for services, the member conscientiously adheres to the Association's Ethical Standards.

NOTE: The reader is referred to Section F, Parts 2, 3, and 4. These standards for advertisement apply equally to private practice and consultation.

E.6. The member must refuse a private fee or other remuneration for consultation with persons who are entitled to these services through the member's employing institution or agency. The policies of a particular agency may make explicit provisions for private practice with agency clients by members of its staff. In such instances, the clients must be apprised of other options open to them should they seek private counseling services.

+ E.6.(a) A campus fraternity is hosting a regional leadership conference for all the chapters in a surrounding seven-state area. The fraternity president asks the director of student development, an exciting public speaker, if she will be the keynote speaker. He offers to pay an honorarium. Because fraternity advisement is one of the responsibilities of the director's office, she declines the fee.

+ *E.6.(b)* A graduate student asks a professor of counseling psychology for private counseling, offering to pay. The policy of the university permits any professor to engage in outside consultation or private practice. However, the professor's policy is not to accept as clients students who are enrolled in the counseling psychology program. He helps the students explore other options for getting help.

− *E.6.(c)* During the summer, a counselor who is under a 12-month contract to his high school advertises in the daily paper that college entrance information is available by telephoning his residence number after 6:00 p.m. He does not identify himself by name or school title. A parent of one of his high school clients calls and finds out that little specific information can be obtained over the phone. At his suggestion, she then signs up for a $100.00 evaluation session.

SECTION F: PRIVATE PRACTICE

F.1. The member should assist the profession by facilitating the availability of counseling services in private as well as public settings.

+ *F.1.(a)* The United Way wants to sponsor a crisis telephone line. A counselor accepts a 3-year term of service on the "hotline" advisory council.

+ *F.1.(b)* A recent graduate of a counseling program wants to establish a private practice. The state licensing law requires 2 years of postgraduate supervised practice as a condition for licensure. He negotiates an arrangement with a licensed counselor who agrees to provide supervision for a relatively low fee, thereby enabling the new professional to start a practice.

+ *F.1.(c)* A private practitioner is contacted by an individual who needs help for a sexual dysfunction. The practitioner does not handle such cases but is aware of a competent specialist as well as a program offered by a community mental health agency. She tells the individual about both alternatives and facilitates a referral.

− *F.1.(d)* A counselor is considering relocating to a community to establish a private practice. She contacts several AACD members to get information about mental health services currently offered in the community. The members, wanting to discourage competition from another practice in their locality, refuse to meet with her.

−*F.1.(e)* A practitioner is often approached by couples seeking marriage counseling, which the practitioner doesn't provide. A nearby church-affiliated family counseling center is providing marriage counseling. The practitioner regularly refers to several agencies but has not sought information about the church-affiliated center because he is adamantly agnostic and believes no worthwhile counseling could be provided by a religiously oriented agency.

F.2. In advertising services as a private practitioner, the member must advertise the services in a manner that accurately informs the public of professional services, expertise, and techniques of counseling available. A member who assumes an executive leadership role in the organization shall not permit his/her name to be used in professional notices during periods when he/she is not actively engaged in the private practice of counseling.

+ *F.2.(a)* A brochure is mailed to community organizations outlining the programs of a pastoral counseling center. Information about counseling services, the fee structure, and a roster of staff identified by name, services, degree, and state certification held is included.

− *F.2.(b)* A successful independent practitioner establishes a family counseling center. Eventually, he comes to devote all of his efforts to administration and consulting. However, clients are attracted to the center by his strong reputation as a counselor. The director continues to be listed as a staff counselor in advertising materials.

F.3. The member may list the following: highest relevant degree, type and level of certification and/or license, address, telephone number, office hours, type and/or description of services, and other relevant information. Such information must not contain false, inaccurate, misleading, partial, out-of-context, or deceptive material or statements.

+ *F.3.(a)* In establishing a private practice, a counselor places advertisements in the yellow pages and the newspaper, and mails announcements to local professionals. The advertisements and announcements read:

SUSAN S. SMITH, MASTER OF ARTS IN EDUCATION
Licensed Professional Counselor
National Certified Counselor
Individual Counseling
Behavior Modification—Stress Management

− *F.3.(b)* The following advertisement is placed in the telephone book:

ALICIA SMITH, MASTER OF COUNSELING
• Relief from Depression and Anxiety
• Improved Marital Relationships
• Greater Satisfaction in Living

NOTE: This individual's degree, which, in fact, is a master of education degree in counseling, is not accurately represented. Also, the advertisement implies that clients will receive benefits that Ms. Smith may not be able to deliver.

− *F.3.(c)* A counselor relocates from another state and joins a private partnership. State regulations for licensure as a clinical mental health counselor require a review of credentials by the state board of examiners and the satisfactory completion of a written licensure examination. This counselor allows her partner to send out announcements implying licensure for both of them prior to the board review or the examination.

F.4. Members do not present their affiliation with any organization in such a way that would imply inaccurate sponsorship or certification by that organization.

+ *F.4.(a)* A counselor explains to her clients the actual meaning of her various credentials. For example, she helps clients understand the distinction between the school counselor certificate she has been granted by the state education agency and a license to practice counseling.

− *F.4.(b)* An AACD member advertises that he is "Recognized by the American Association for Counseling and Development."

NOTE: This statement is misleading in that it implies that the AACD recognizes, and thereby assesses and certifies, competence of its members.

F.5. Members may join in partnership/corporation with other members and/or other professionals provided that each member of the partnership or corporation makes clear the separate specialties by name in compliance with the regulations of the locality.

+ *F.5.(a)* A counselor joins with other professionals to establish a corporation that provides a hospital-based alcohol treatment program. Advertisements accurately portray the roles and services provided by counselors, social workers, psychologists, and psychiatrists.

− *F.5.(b)* Three practitioners incorporate a private family counseling service. Information describing the staff indicates that all are providing *psychological* services. These three practitioners include one counselor, one social worker, and one psychologist. The practice is established in a state that has licensure for psychologists. State statute specifically prohibits professionals except psychologists presenting themselves to the public by any description incorporating the term "psychologist" or "psychological."

F.6. A member has an obligation to withdraw from a counseling relationship if it is believed that employment will result in violation of the Ethical Standards. If the mental or physical condition of the member renders it difficult to carry out an effective professional relationship or if the member is discharged by the client because the counseling relationship is no longer productive for the client, then the member is obligated to terminate the counseling relationship.

+ *F.6.(a)* A counselor believes that a client's desire to terminate may be premature. She discusses her reasoning with the client but conveys respect for whatever decision the client makes.

+ *F.6.(b)* A counselor in private practice experiences intense anxiety when he and his wife divorce. He finds that his ability to be objective and facilitate problem resolution in marriage counseling is hampered by his personalization of client concerns. The counselor arranges to get counseling for himself from another professional, examines the impact of his anxiety on his current cases, and decides to obtain supervision for the marital cases he is currently carrying and not to initiate any new marriage counseling cases until his personal concerns have been resolved.

− *F.6.(c)* A private practitioner suffers a stroke that results in partial aphasia. Upon returning to work, he recognizes that his counseling is seriously impaired. He is unable to find the words to reflect client concerns. Nevertheless, the counselor continues to practice. This leaves the decision to terminate counseling to clients. Several clients experience distress about deciding to terminate the nonproductive counseling relationship because they sympathize with the counselor's debility.

− *F.6.(d)* A counselor, Mr. Jones, has worked with a client for several months. The client complains that counseling hasn't helped and contacts another counselor, Mr. Green. Mr. Green gets permission from the client to request information from Mr. Jones. When Mr. Green calls, Mr. Jones becomes angry and says that Mr. Green is colluding in the client's denial of the problem. Subsequently, Mr. Jones calls the client and insists on a termination interview. After the interview, the client concludes that it was a waste of time and money and only met Mr. Jones's needs.

F.7. A member must adhere to the regulations for private practice of the locality where the services are offered.

+ *F.7.(a)* State regulations for private practice require a minimum number of continuing education credits over a 3-year period. A counselor conscientiously arranges for experiences that will fulfill these requirements.

− *F.7.(b)* A counselor practicing under supervision in an institutional setting opens a limited private practice. Although state statute requires licensure for counselors in independent practice, the counselor doesn't apply. He rationalizes that licensure is unnecessary in this situation because services won't be advertised and clients will be accepted only by personal referral.

− *F.7.(c)* State regulations require 1 year of postgraduate supervised practice in order to be licensed as a counselor. An AACD member arranges a sham supervisory relationship that does not entail any face-to-face supervision.

NOTE: Both the member seeking such nominal supervision and the practitioner colluding in such an arrangement would be in violation of this ethical principle.

F.8. It is unethical to use one's institutional affiliation to recruit clients for one's private practice.

+ *F.8.(a)* A counselor employed in a state rehabilitation agency is approached by a representative of a private hospital that offers occupational rehabilitation training. The representative asks the counselor to refer suitable clients and, in return, a referral fee will be paid. The counselor explains the ethical problems involved in this plan and refuses the offer.

+ *F.8.(b)*   An elementary guidance counselor maintains a part-time private practice with a specialization in family therapy. In working with a child at school, the counselor decides that a family intervention would be helpful. However, the counselor refers the family to another source.

− *F.8.(c)*   A counselor is employed as the coordinator for a rape crisis center to train and supervise volunteers as telephone hotline support staff. During an early training session, the coordinator invites trainees to see her in her private practice should they need personal counseling.

NOTE: In addition to the difficulty posed by recruiting clients through the counselor's institutional affiliation with the rape crisis center, she violates principle B.13—the ability to supervise and evaluate trainee effectiveness may be hampered by the counseling relationship.

− *F.8.(d)*   A graduate student discloses a personal problem during a counseling theories class. Later, the professor encourages the student to make an appointment for counseling in his private practice.

SECTION G: PERSONNEL ADMINISTRATION

It is recognized that most members are employed in public or quasi-public institutions. The functioning of a member within an institution must contribute to the goals of the institution and vice versa if either is to accomplish their respective goals or objectives. It is therefore essential that the member and the institution function in ways to (a) make the institutional goals specific and public; (b) make the member's contribution to institutional goals specific; and (c) foster mutual accountability for goal achievement.

To accomplish these objectives, it is recognized that the member and the employer must share responsibilities in the formulation and implementation of personnel policies.

NOTE: This section deals with professional relationships and practices between employers and employees rather than "personnel adminstration" in the traditional sense of the term.

G.1. Members must define and describe the parameters and levels of their professional competency.

+ *G.1.(a)* A counseling center at a university has just been assigned the additional functions of providing psychotherapy for students with eating disorders and establishing a suicide prevention program. No one on the staff has specific training in these areas. Therefore, the director appoints a search committee to recruit a counselor with the needed skills.

+ *G.1.(b)* The counseling office at an Army training facility installs a computer-assisted career information service. The counseling staff have no training in the new service. They enroll in an intensive inservice training program and visit other facilities with computer-assisted career information services already in operation.

− *G.1.(c)* A counseling intern is asked to do a psychological assessment of a new client including the use of projective techniques. Wanting the experience, the intern accepts the assignment and fails to disclose that she has no training in the use of projectives.

− *G.1.(d)* A residence hall director sets up growth groups to help freshmen make a smooth transition to college. These groups meet 2 hours per week over the course of the semester. Students are encouraged to self-disclose and get feedback. The director insists that each of the 16 resident advisers

65

lead a group. Neither the director nor the advisers have any background in group dynamics or training as group facilitators.

G.2.   Members must establish interpersonal relations and working agreements with supervisors and subordinates regarding counseling or clinical relationships, confidentiality, distinction between public and private material, maintenance, and dissemination of recorded information, work load, and accountability. Working agreements in each instance must be specified and made known to those concerned.

+ G.2.*(a)*   Counselors complete a weekly report form that identifies numbers and types of counseling contacts, workshops, and classroom presentations given, meetings attended, training activities, and supervision received and provided. The report is used to document counselor performance and to adjust equitably the workload among staff.

+ G.2.*(b)*   The head counselor at a high school regularly schedules supervisory sessions with his staff. In addition, he is readily available for consultation on an "as-needed" basis.

+ G.2.*(c)*   Rabbi Greenberg offers pastoral counseling to his congregation. He has trained his office staff in the methods of protecting client confidentiality. He knows that confidentiality can be easily breached through idle gossip or sloppy recordkeeping with disastrous results.

− G.2.*(d)*   Agency XYZ has never stated or circulated its ethical or personnel policies. The administration assumes that counseling staff understand organization polices and know about AACD's *Ethical Standards*. Actually, many breaches of the standards occur because of ignorance and misinterpretation.

− G.2.*(e)*   A contract between the university and the agency requires a weekly supervisory session between the practicum student and the field supervisor. Several weeks into the semester, the field supervisor stops scheduling supervision appointments. The student complains but neither the university practicum coordinator nor the agency director pursues the matter.

NOTE: The ethical problem occurs because the institution has an established policy that is disregarded without consultation or any effort to have the policy adjusted.

G.3.   Members must alert their employers to conditions that may be potentially disruptive or damaging.

+ G.3.*(a)*   Pedro tells the school counselor that Henry gave him a "diet" pill but that he didn't eat it. Henry maintains that he got the pill, only one, from a bottle in his parent's medicine cabinet. With Henry's permission, the counselor informs the principal. The principal interviews Henry's parents who agree to take stringent security measures at home. The principal has the school nurse brief each teacher about symptoms that could indicate diet pill ingestion.

+ G.3.(b) Several graduate students attend a party at which some of the professors openly use cocaine. The graduate students tell the department chairperson about the incident but do not disclose names. The chairperson issues a memo that such illegal activities will not be tolerated; furthermore, the statement declares that individuals involved in any such behavior in the future can expect to have their contracts with the department terminated.

− G.3.(c) A residence hall adviser learns from several independent sources that a student, disgruntled because he has been refused permission to move out, has bragged that he will set fire to the building. The adviser takes no action, assuming that the threat is not serious.

G.4. Members must inform employers of conditions that may limit their effectiveness.

+ G.4.(a) An employment counselor finds that so much staff time is needed to contact prospective employers and get information about job openings that there isn't enough time to update the files on the qualifications and interests of clients. The counselor's concern results in an increase in the placement fee in order to permit the hiring of clerical staff.

+ G.4.(b) A counselor is in the process of divorce proceedings and finds that she can't attend to clients during counseling interviews. She requests a temporary reassignment to noncounseling duties.

− G.4.(c) A counselor is being interviewed for a position at a high school that is the target of a highly publicized campaign to remove sex education from the curriculum, to take certain books off the school library's shelves, and to restrict the activities of the counseling staff to career guidance. This applicant is an active participant in this effort but does not mention this during the interview. He feels that his political activities have nothing to do with the practice of his profession and are, therefore, private and personal.

NOTE: The right to voice criticism of the school's policies and practices is the right of a private citizen. However, the principal has the responsibility to employ people who can effectively perform the duties for which they are hired. Because the applicant's views and activities could have a bearing on job performance, it is unethical to withhold the information.

− G.4.(d) A counselor's father has developed a terminal illness. She feels obligated to arrange for medical care and provide personal comfort during her father's last days. Consequently, she has to take time off from work. Instead of telling her supervisor the reason, she calls in "sick."

G.5. Members must submit regularly to professional review and evaluation.

+ G.5.(a) The director of the Office of Residence Life program meets once per year with each staff member. At this meeting an evaluation form is completed appraising the individual's performance. Discussion is encouraged. The evaluation form includes space for comments by both parties. The form is included in the staff member's personnel record.

− G.5.(b) A counselor considers himself in the vanguard of new practices in counseling with the elderly. He does not expect his supervisor to understand, much less be capable of evaluating his work. He describes his work in ambiguous terms and becomes irritable when asked for specifics. In truth, he considers evaluation to be personally demeaning and subverts the process in any way he can.

G.6. Members must be responsible for in-service development of self and/ or staff.

+ G.6.(a) The director of a rehabilitation counseling program requires that counselors who use state funds to attend professional growth conferences bring back information and present it at staff meetings.

+ G.6.(b) The director of guidance in a school system provides training in clinical supervision skills for secondary school head counselors. In addition, she reduces the head counselor work load. Subsequently, head counselors are expected to help their subordinates improve their counseling skills through ongoing clinical supervision.

− G.6.(c) The state licensing law requires counselors to get 75 hours of continuing education every 3 years. The director of a counseling agency believes that this requirement will be a strong incentive for staff to look after their own professional development. Therefore, the director does not provide inservice training opportunities.

− G.6.(d) A probation officer who is a member of AACD gets approval for funding to attend the annual AACD conference. The conference will be held in a city where the member has friends. Rather than attending the professional forums, the member registers for the meeting, attends only the opening session, and spends the remaining 2 days vacationing with friends.

G.7. Members must inform their staff of goals and programs.

+ G.7.(a) The director of a pastoral counseling center is required to submit an annual report. As part of this process, each staff member is asked to give input into departmental goals, concerns, and programs. This input is used in establishing plans for the coming year. Furthermore, staff members receive a copy of the center's annual budget.

− G.7.(b) The dean has become discouraged about the monthly staff meetings held to discuss policy, programs, and goals. Two argumentative staff members dominate the meetings and staff morale is in jeopardy. What's more, several staff members have complained that the dean is too autocratic in running the meetings. To solve the dilemma, the dean decides not to call additional meetings.

– *G.7.(c)* The university administration moves to consolidate the departments of counselor education and psychology. Plans for the merger are put into motion. However, faculty in neither department are consulted.

G.8. Members must provide personnel practices that guarantee and enhance the rights and welfare of each recipient of their service.

+ *G.8.(a)* The director of the college counseling service wants clients to be aware of policies on confidentiality. A copy of the policy statement is posted in the reception room. In addition, copies are distributed to each counselor and staff member.

+ *G.8.(b)* Student affairs staff are expected to implement an annual professional development plan. Money is budgeted to cover expenses for attendance at conferences and workshops.

– *G.8.(c)* The head of volunteer services at a telephone crisis "hotline" believes that individuals who volunteer as paraprofessional counselors are likely to be highly committed and reliable. Therefore, after the volunteers are trained and placed, there is no ongoing supervision.

G.9. Members must select competent persons and assign responsibilities compatible with their skills and experiences.

+ *G.9.(a)* The director of a counselor education program mandates standard policies for faculty hiring: (a) The search committee is composed of representatives of various university constituencies, (b) The committee is chaired by the faculty member who serves as the position's immediate supervisor, (c) Advertising is placed in national and local media, (d) Applicants must submit a resume, a letter of application, graduate transcripts, and three letters of reference directly to the search committee, and (e) A day-long interview process is scheduled for finalists, during which all search committee members meet with the candidates.

– *G.9.(b)* A substance abuse counselor is hired solely on the basis of a cursory interview and perusal of the applicant's vita. References are not checked. Official transcripts of graduate training are not required.

– *G.9.(c)* The director of a graduate program in counseling psychology ignores the recommendations of the faculty search committee and, instead, hires a personal friend who is not qualified for the position.

G.10. The member, at the onset of a counseling relationship, will inform the client of the member's intended use of supervisors regarding the disclosure of information concerning this case. The member will clearly inform the client of the limits of confidentiality in the relationship.

+ *G.10.(a)* A graduate program in counseling operates a clinical training facility. Clients are offered low-fee services that are provided by counselors-in-training. Clients are informed both verbally and in writing that interviews will be audio- or video-recorded and discussed in supervisory conferences.

− *G.10.(b)* A beginning counselor in the state rehabilitation agency doesn't tell clients that his cases are debriefed with a supervisor. He feels that clients would see him as a novice, which would only undermine his already fragile credibility. Furthermore, clients wouldn't want to "open up" if they knew that their most intimate secrets would be divulged.

G.11. Members, as either employers or employees, do not engage in or condone practices that are inhumane, illegal, or unjustifiable (such as considerations based on sex, handicap, age, race) in hiring, promotion, or training.

+ *G.11.(a)* The inspirational invocation that introduces an annual professional development conference concludes with, ". . . in the name of our Lord Jesus Christ." Subsequently, a resolution is introduced and passed that invocations at the annual conference must be nonsectarian.

+ *G.11.(b)* An elderly client tells his counselor that he was denied a promotion simply because of his age. The counselor becomes convinced that her client has reasonable cause for a complaint. She encourages him to pursue his complaint through normal channels and, ultimately, to consult an attorney.

− *G.11.(c)* Members of a search committee in a department of counselor education give perfunctory attention to the university's affirmative action policy. No genuine effort is made to recruit qualified minorities.

− *G.11.(d)* The director of a university residence hall is interviewing candidates for resident advisor positions in his residence hall. One of his top candidates, Lisa, discloses in her interview that she is a lesbian. Although she feels that her sexual orientation won't affect her job performance, she doesn't want to keep it a secret from her supervisor or co-workers. The director had been favorably impressed with Lisa and finds himself wishing that she hadn't told him the truth. He decides not to hire Lisa as an RA in order to protect the student residents.

SECTION H:
PREPARATION STANDARDS

Members who are responsible for training others must be guided by the preparation standards of the Association and relevant Division(s). The member who functions in the capacity of trainer assumes unique ethical responsibilities that frequently go beyond that of the member who does not function in a training capacity. These ethical responsibilities are outlined as follows:

H.1. Members must orient students to program expectations, basic skills development, and employment prospects prior to admission to the program.

+ *H.1.(a)*   The department of counselor education sends a descriptive brochure to each person who applies for admission to the master's degree program. Applicants to the doctoral program are sent a statistical breakdown of the types of position held by graduates of the program.

− *H.1.(b)*   In the brochure sent to prospective students by a counselor education department, two master's degree programs are outlined. Plan A describes an 18-month program. Plan B enables students to complete the program in 12 months by enrolling in a special summer practicum. After the students select their plan and arrive on campus, they learn from advanced students that plan A is preferable to B because of the lack of clients during the summer practicum. The faculty makes no attempt to increase the number of clients available for the summer practicum.

− *H.1.(c)*   A graduate student who has arrived on campus with the intention of specializing in rehabilitation counseling discovers that "rehab" has been dropped because of the loss of the professor who taught the necessary courses. His adviser suggests that he specialize in another area.

H.2. Members in charge of learning experiences must establish programs that integrate academic study and supervised practice.

+ *H.2.(a)*   Professor Chang, who teaches the introductory course in marriage and family therapy, wants her students to have an opportunity to translate theory into practice. She sets aside class time to have students deal with hypothetical cases using role play and discussion. In addition, students observe advanced practicum students working with actual clients at the university's clinical training facility.

71

– *H.2.(b)* Students in a counselor education program are permitted to waive practicum if they write a thesis. The practicum is the only course in the curriculum that provides opportunities for supervised practice.

– *H.2.(c)* A department offers a 2-year master's degree in marriage and family counseling. The department offers no didactic courses. Each student is assigned to a series of practicums in community agencies. The philosophy of the department is "learn by doing."

H.3. Members must establish a program directed toward developing students' skills, knowledge, and self-understanding, stated whenever possible in competency or performance terms.

+ *H.3.(a)* Skill in supervision is an objective of a doctoral program in counseling psychology. Therefore, the program requires PhD candidates to supervise master's level practicum students. This supervisory experience is, in turn, supervised by a professor. Doctoral students must demonstrate specific skills, such as being able to give accurate feedback to supervisees.

– *H.3.(b)* An instructor is assigned to teach a course entitled "Development of Counseling Skills." Class time is devoted to lectures and discussion of a variety of counseling theories. Grades are based on the degree of class participation and an essay examination. There are no opportunities for students to demonstrate and be evaluated on the performance of counseling skills.

H.4. Members must identify the levels of competencies of their students in compliance with relevant Division standards. These competencies must accommodate the paraprofessional as well as the professional.

+ *H.4.(a)* Faculty in a counselor education department are concerned about how much their students really know at the time they begin their practicum experience. The faculty design a qualifying examination covering counseling theory, tests and measurements, personality theory, and statistics. Students must pass this examination at a minimal competence level before they will be admitted to practicum.

+ *H.4.(b)* At a university, the women's center uses volunteer paraprofessionals to assist professional counseling staff. The director of the women's center is upset because the paraprofessionals are creating havoc. They come to the center mostly to sit, drink coffee, and gossip. The director and her professional staff develop the following plan to upgrade the performance of the paraprofessionals: (a) Job descriptions are written, (b) Paraprofessionals are invited and expected to attend staff meetings, and (c) Paraprofessionals receive performance evaluations after they have been "on the job" for 6 weeks.

– *H.4.(c)* A practicum instructor refuses to evaluate practicum students, claiming that evaluation destroys rapport and trust.

72

H.5. Members, through continual student evaluation and appraisal, must be aware of the personal limitations of the learner that might impede future performance. The instructor must not only assist the learner in securing remedial assistance but also screen from the program those individuals who are unable to provide competent services.

+ *H.5.(a)* As counselor education faculty observe a graduate student in role play and actual counseling sessions, they become alarmed about her lack of basic counseling skills. Despite feedback, the student fails to improve. She maintains rigid control of the interview while anger breaks through in the form of sarcasm. It seems that underlying hostility is getting in the way. In response to a suggestion from her supervisor that she explore these issues in counseling, the student becomes defensive and angry. Her faculty committee decides that the student must (1) demonstrate effective listening skills and (2) avoid sarcasm in role-played interviews and in sessions with real clients before being allowed to advance to practicum.

− *H.5.(b)* A counseling student tells one of his professors that he was once hospitalized for acute depression. The professor calls a meeting of the student's faculty committee to recommend that this student be dismissed from the program. His rationale is that an individual who has been hospitalized for psychiatric problems is a poor candidate for a career as a counselor.

− *H.5.(c)* A graduate program in counseling permits students to continue who can get satisfactory grades in the didactic coursework, but who do not show any evidence of a capacity to relate to clients.

NOTE: The U.S. Supreme Court case of the University of Missouri v. Horowitz *(1978) is relevant here. After a warning and a probationary period in which inadequate progress was made, Ms. Horowitz, a senior medical student with an excellent academic record, was dismissed for reasons of poor personal hygiene and poor peer and patient relations. The U.S. Supreme Court upheld the university's action of dismissing a student for inadequate performance in the supervised practice aspect of the program even though the student's performance in the academic aspect of the program was superior. The court also ruled that the procedures used in dismissing Ms. Horowitz did not violate her due process rights.*

H.6. Members must provide a program that includes training in research commensurate with levels of role functioning. Paraprofessional and technician-level personnel must be trained as consumers of research. In addition, personnel must learn how to evaluate their own and their program's effectiveness. Graduate training, especially at the doctoral level, would include preparation for original research by the member.

+ *H.6.(a)* A professor in an advanced counseling practicum helps students to evaluate the effect of their counseling. For example, clients are asked to complete a pre- and postevaluation form. In addition, a structured interview is scheduled 1 month after termination. This follow-up interview probes the ongoing impact of the counseling experience.

+ *H.6.(b)* A professor instructs doctoral students in publication techniques and encourages them to submit manuscripts to journals.

− *H.6.(c)* The research techniques course required for doctoral degree candidates is too large to be well taught. Advisers, therefore, are lenient in waiving this requirement for students who have already had any laboratory course (e.g., physics, chemistry, or computer science) or experience as research assistants.

− *H.6.(d)* Faculty decide that PhD candidates in counseling psychology should no longer be required to write dissertations. Instead, doctoral students can design and implement "projects." For example, one student sets up an innovative career counseling program at a high school. This project is accepted in lieu of a dissertation although it has no research component.

H.7. Members must make students aware of the ethical responsibilities and standards of the profession.

+ *H.7.(a)* Faculty in a counselor education program believe that professional ethics and malpractice issues should be infused throughout the curriculum. During the introductory course, 6 hours of class time are devoted to the AACD *Ethical Standards*. Furthermore, the courses in research methods, psychometric procedures, groups, and practicum also have units on ethics included in their syllabi.

+ *H.7.(b)* A faculty adviser discovers that one of her new master's degree candidates in counseling is engaged in private practice. The faculty adviser, believing the student is not qualified for independent practice, challenges the student. The student responds that he feels that he is a good enough counselor to justify being in private practice. Subsequently, the counselor education faculty develop a policy that a master's degree in counseling or a related field is the minimum credential for private practice and that degree-seeking students can practice only under supervision.

− *H.7.(c)* The instructor who teaches the introductory course in student personnel offers only superficial coverage of AACD's *Ethical Standards*. He does not include ethics material in his examinations because he considers the topic too subjective to lend itself to evaluation.

− *H.7.(d)* A female master's candidate is overjoyed when she learns she is to receive a graduate assistantship working with her major adviser on a research project. To her dismay, however, she finds she has little contact with the professor and is really supervised by a male PhD candidate. This supervisor makes her life miserable by demanding that she work 20 hours a week when the employment agreement was for 15 hours a week. Additionally, he makes sexual advances toward her. Finally, she complains to her major adviser.

Because of the potential for trouble, the major adviser never confronts the male doctoral student.

H.8. Preparatory programs must encourage students to value the ideals of service to individuals and to society. In this regard, direct financial remuneration or lack thereof must not be allowed to overshadow professional and humanitarian needs.

+ *H.8.(a)* The counselor education faculty want students to value the service component of the profession. Consequently, the faculty volunteer service to the community. For example, one professor serves as an adviser to a program for at-risk middle school students and works for free one evening per week at a United Way-sponsored mental health agency.

+ *H.8.(b)* An assistant professor has been hired by a small college to begin a master's program in counseling. The young man is rapidly winning a national reputation through his research efforts. Halfway through his second year, he is contacted by a prestigious university regarding an immediate opening for a position at a salary higher than what he is currently paid. Rather than leave his colleagues and students in the lurch, he insists on completing the current semester before accepting the new position.

− *H.8.(c)* A visiting faculty member teaches a summer institute course entitled "Career Exploration." However, his preoccupation with taking full advantage of recreational opportunities leads students and fellow faculty to feel that he is giving little of himself. He has cancelled several classes and told students they will all receive "A's". No objections are raised by the regular faculty.

H.9. Members responsible for educational programs must be skilled as teachers and practitioners.

+ *H.9.(a)* There are frequent complaints from students regarding the poor teaching of some faculty members. The department chairperson invites a professor from another discipline who is renowned as an excellent teacher to help faculty improve. Additionally, when a faculty position becomes open, the three finalists who are brought to campus are asked to present a 50-minute lecture on adult development.

+ *H.9.(b)* A professor of counseling psychology engages in private practice "on his own time"; that is, after fulfilling his obligations as an employee of the university. Consequently, he is able to share with his graduate students first-hand information about the ethical, legal, and financial challenges of private practice.

− *H.9.(c)* A professor is chosen to teach a course in student personnel administration because of his years of experience as a dean of students during the late '60s and early '70s. His lectures consist of "war stories" about student unrest and disruption. No attention is given to the characteristics and needs of the "typical" undergraduate student of the 90s.

− *H.9.(d)* A senior faculty member in a graduate department of counseling is chosen to teach an advanced course in research design because he has a strong background in mathematics. He is the least accomplished of all the faculty, however, in research and publication.

H.10. Members must present thoroughly varied theoretical positions so that students may make comparisons and have the opportunity to select a position.

+ *H.10.(a)* A professor regularly invites other professors and practitioners with differing theoretical approaches to lecture to her class in counseling methods in order to encourage students to adopt a broad perspective. The assigned text gives equal coverage to a wide variety of counseling theories. Students are required to write a term paper that compares and contrasts two of the major theories and sets forth the student's own theory of counseling.

− *H.10.(b)* A professor views behaviorism as mechanistic and dehumanizing and, therefore, excludes any consideration of behavior modification techniques from her course in counseling techniques.

H.11. Members must develop clear policies within their educational institutions regarding field placement and the roles of the student and the instructor in such placement.

+ *H.11.(a)* In order to improve the practicum experience, faculty in the counselor education department decide the following: A professor is appointed field placement director. This director personally talks with all people in charge of the placement sites to determine their willingness to properly supervise practicum students. When the students begin their placements, they meet with their field supervisors to develop a contract outlining goals, objectives, and strategies. The director follows through to make sure that supervisors adhere to the contract.

+ *H.11.(b)* A committee of counselor educators within a doctoral program in counseling psychology develops and publishes a set of guidelines for doctoral students that will help them apply for internship placements. A list of approved placements is included. Every effort is made to provide a wide range of quality internship placements.

− *H.11.(c)* A graduate student in counseling psychology spends a year working full time in a community counseling center. His major professor is unable to decide whether his work qualifies for internship credit because most internships are in the campus counseling center and there are no guidelines for outside internships.

− *H.11.(d)* A graduate student starts an internship at the university's career counseling center. Nobody seems to know what the student is supposed to

76

be doing; he is encouraged to "work up some goals" but there are no suggestions or structure. The student complains of the excessive ambiguity of the job to his university adviser, but the adviser does not feel comfortable about intervening. The student continues a futile search for a client population with which to work.

H.12. Members must ensure that forms of learning focusing on self-understanding or growth are voluntary, or if required as part of the educational program, are made known to prospective students prior to entering the program. When the educational program offers a growth experience with an emphasis on self-disclosure or other relatively intimate or personal involvement, the member must have no administrative, supervisory, or evaluating authority regarding the participant.

+ *H.12.(a)* Graduate students in counseling psychology are made aware before they enter the program that they need to have developed by the end of the program adequate psychological maturity and good interpersonal skills. Evaluation as to whether they meet this standard will be based primarily on their performance in practicum. They are made aware of growth groups and opportunities for personal counseling outside of the department that they may use at their discretion and in confidence.

+ *H.12.(b)* A staff counselor at the university's counseling center offers a growth group experience for graduate students in counselor education. The group facilitator is not a faculty member in the counselor education department and will give no feedback to the department about any individual in the group or about the group itself.

− *H.12.(c)* Students enrolled in a graduate course in group counseling are not informed in advance that the course really is designed as group therapy and that they are expected to discuss their personal problems in the group. If they do not reveal themselves fully, they are subjected to pressure for self-revelation from the instructor and may receive a lower grade.

H.13. The member will at all times provide students with clear and equally acceptable alternatives for self-understanding or growth experiences. The member will assure students that they have a right to accept these alternatives without prejudice or penalty.

+ *H.13.(a)* Professors in a counseling and guidance program encourage all of their students to voluntarily seek personal counseling. The assumption is that counseling can enhance their potential as helping professionals and that they should know how it feels to be on the "other side of the fence." Personal counseling is available free of charge at the university's counseling center. Client confidentiality is protected; that is, Counseling and Guidance Department professors are never told whether or not their students are seen in counseling.

− *H.13.(b)* Counselors-in-training enrolled in the group counseling course are required to attend a weekend self-growth "marathon" experience. One student asks the professor if he could substitute some other type of counseling experience. The request is denied on the grounds that the marathon is a course requirement for everyone and that no exceptions are made.

H.14. Members must conduct an educational program in keeping with the current relevant guidelines of the Association.

+ *H.14.(a)* The dean mandates that all graduate courses must have an enrollment of at least 15 students. The counseling psychology faculty argues that enrollment in practicum should be limited to 8 students to enable high-quality supervision.

− *H.14.(b)* The faculty of a counselor education program set a quota that limits the number of Asian-American students admitted to the doctoral program. Their position is that the Asian-American ethnic group is disproportionately represented.

CASE STUDIES

Examples in the previous section of the casebook illustrate the individual ethical standards. In actual practice, however, incidents are often more complex and involve several ethical standards as well as legal issues. In this section we present a series of case studies that are intended to: (1) portray these complex realities, (2) illustrate the functioning of the AACD Ethics Committee, and (3) provoke thought and discussion about current and emerging issues.

Although the incidents presented are fictional, they represent the types of cases the Ethics Committee typically receives and practitioners in the field encounter. We wrote some of the case studies, and other individuals contributed the rest. When case studies are based on an actual incident (or a combination of similar incidents), identifying particulars have been carefully disguised.

A COUNSELOR GOES TO COURT

*[Material for this case study was contributed by **Karen M. Smith**. Ms. Smith is a counselor with the Washoe County School District, Reno, Nevada.]*

On a Thursday morning, a high school freshman referred herself to her school counselor to discuss her experimentation with alcohol and drugs. During a second counseling session held the following Monday, the student revealed that on a single occasion over 4 years earlier, she had been sexually assaulted by her stepfather. At the present time, the stepfather was no longer in the student's home and was believed to be living in Mexico. The student expressed no fear that the abuse might reoccur.

The counselor informed the student that she was required to report the incident of sexual abuse to child welfare authorities. The student replied that her mother did not know about the incident, and because she enjoyed a close relationship with her mother, she wanted to tell her mother herself rather than have the counselor do it. Also, the mother spoke only Spanish and the counselor spoke no Spanish. The counselor agreed to the request and the student told her mother about the incident. The counselor continued to meet daily with the student, focusing on the drug and alcohol problem.

On Thursday of the following week, the student was taken from school to a hospital because of a suspected suicide attempt. The girl had swallowed a handful of over-the-counter stimulants, and the school nurse did not think there was serious danger to her health. Nonetheless, the counselor called the emergency room of the local hospital and was advised to bring the girl in. She remained at the hospital with the girl throughout the afternoon. That evening, she called child welfare authorities and discussed the student's case and the previous assault with a caseworker. The caseworker said that she would report the sexual abuse incident, and did report to her superiors and the police.

The police determined that the girl was in no immediate danger and took no action. They were powerless to prosecute the stepfather, even if he should return to the United States, because the statute of limitations had run out. The welfare department interviewed the family and also determined that there was no need for action.

These decisions by the authorities might have ended the incident, except that the child welfare caseworker believed that the school counselor had acted inappropriately. The caseworker filed a complaint with the district attorney's office, which brought charges against the counselor for failure to report suspected child abuse as required by law. After the case was adjudicated, the caseworker also filed a complaint with the AACD Ethics Committee, alleging that the counselor had violated standards B.4 and B.8.

Discussion

Because this incident has both ethical and legal ramifications, the ethical issues will be discussed first. Standard B.4 states that when the client's condition indicates that there is a clear and imminent danger to the client or others, the member must take reasonable personal action or inform responsible authorities. The Ethics Committee, in applying this standard to the complaint, focused on two considerations. Was the child in "clear and imminent" danger either through a potential repetition of the incident of abuse or through attempted suicide? If so, could the counselor have reasonably foreseen, and thus acted to avert, that danger? The counselor's professional judgment here was that there was no danger that the incident of abuse would be repeated because the perpetrator had left the country. The suicide attempt, if indeed it *was* a suicide attempt (and this is open to question), was not foreseen by the counselor because the client had given no indication of suicidal ideation.

Violation of standard B.8, which states that counselors are to protect minor clients' best interests, was also alleged. The Ethics Committee noted that the counselor, by allowing the client to divulge the incident of abuse directly to the mother, acted to preserve both confidentiality and the parent-child relationship. Her actions in working with the girl daily and accompanying her to the hospital indicated a sincere commitment to the client's well-being.

Conclusion

The AACD Ethics Committee dismissed the charges. The Committee found that this counselor, in exercising her professional judgment, acted well within the bounds of ethical behavior.

Whether the counselor acted within the constraints of the law is a separate issue. The school counselor was charged with a misdemeanor for failure to comply with the child abuse reporting statute, and was found guilty when the case went to court. The counselor appealed, pointing out that the court decision had reduced the counselor's role to mechanical reporting of all cases and left no room for professional judgment. The appeals court judge agreed with the counselor and overturned the conviction. The counselor, although ultimately exonerated, endured a most difficult experience that illustrates the hazards of professional practice in situations where professional judgment seems to conflict with the law.

Questions for Thought and Discussion

1. When law and ethics seem to conflict, which takes precedence? What are the risks inherent in either choice?

2. If this student had disclosed suicidal intentions during the counseling sessions, the counselor would have been obligated to breach confidentiality and exercise her "duty to warn and protect." Under what other circumstances are counselors obligated to breach confidentiality? (See essay by Stadler in the next section of the casebook.)

AIDS AND THE DUTY TO WARN

[*This case study was contributed by **Andrew A. Helwig**. Dr. Helwig is Associate Professor, School of Education, University of Colorado at Denver.*]

A counselor in a community mental health agency received a new client, a 29-year-old homosexual man. Throughout the first two sessions the client seemed to be reticent and slow to establish trust.

During the third counseling session, the client disclosed that he had just received laboratory evidence that he had the HIV (human immunodeficiency virus) but, as yet, no symptoms of AIDS. The client also stated that his partner of 2 years' duration did not know and that he was not going to tell him. For the rest of the session, the counselor and client discussed the client's fears, the seriousness of the situation, and the implications for both the client and his partner. The client remained adamant about not telling his partner because of his fear of losing him. He indicated that he had difficulty establishing long-term relationships with lovers and didn't want to risk this one.

The counseling session came to an end without any change in the client's willingness to inform his partner of the virus. Another appointment was scheduled for later that week. The client did not appear for this appointment. The counselor called the client's home and finally reached him several days later. An appointment was rescheduled but again the client did not appear. When the counselor called, the client stated that he did not intend to return for individual counseling. Instead, he had joined a support group for people with AIDS and ARC (AIDS-related complex) at a local hospital. The counselor took no further action.

A year later, the client's partner (now ex-lover) was diagnosed as having AIDS. As it turned out, the client had dropped out of his support group after attending only one meeting. He had not revealed his condition to his partner until the partner developed symptoms of AIDS. At that time the client also told his partner about his abortive attempts to seek counseling help.

The partner filed a lawsuit claiming civil damages against the counselor and also filed a complaint with the AACD Ethics Committee charging the counselor with violating standard B.4.

Discussion

Standard B.4 states that when the client's condition indicates there is a clear and imminent danger to the client or others, the member must take reasonable personal action or inform responsible authorities. Consultation with other professionals must be used where possible.

The Ethics Committee was required to inform the complainant that his complaint could not be processed until the civil suit was completed. The AACD Policies and Procedures for Processing Complaints of Ethical Violations specify that the Committee will not act on complaints currently under civil or criminal litigation.

Conclusion

This complaint remains pending and may never be resolved. The civil suit has not gone to trial and the complainant's physical condition continues to deteriorate. Readers are invited to deliberate, along with the Ethics Committee, on the difficult questions involved in attempting to apply the ethical "duty to warn" to cases in which AIDS is a factor.

Questions for Thought and Discussion

1. Is the danger "clear" and "imminent" in this case? On the one hand, the client was symptom-free and possibly would not have transmitted the virus to his partner. On the other hand, it was also possible for the client to transmit the virus but for the partner not to develop symptoms until many years later. In any event, a warning might well have been too late to be effective.

2. If the counselor was required to take "reasonable personal action," what should that action have been? Informing the partner? Informing medical authorities? Notifying the police? Who are "responsible authorities?" What is the counselor's responsibility if there are no established "authorities" to deal with AIDS-related issues in a particular community?

3. Given the seriousness of the situation, did the counselor have an ethical obligation to consult with other professionals to determine his best course of

action? Was he obligated to contact the hospital's support group sponsor to determine whether the client had informed his partner? Should the counselor be found in violation of standard B.4 on the basis that he failed to consult?

4. What steps can counselors take **now** to better prepare themselves for counseling an increasing number of clients who are at risk for AIDS, and for minimizing the ethical dilemmas in working with this population?

A "MYSTERIOUS" BREACH OF CONFIDENTIALITY

[*This case study was contributed by* **James P. Sampson, Jr.** *Dr. Sampson is Associate Professor and Co-Director of Center for the Study of Technology in Counseling and Career Development at Florida State University.*]

George, a college freshman working as a student assistant in the alumni relations office, was asked to print a set of computer-generated labels. Because the computer in the alumni office was being used, the director asked him to walk down the hall and see if it would be possible for him to use the computer in the counseling center. The counseling center secretary told him it would be no problem because she was just leaving to go to lunch. George then used the computer to print the labels.

George was taking a course in basic computer use and word processing. Because he was alone in the office, he decided to practice manipulating files on the fixed disk drive. He browsed through various counseling center directories and files, and noticed that it was not possible to access several of the files in a directory named "CLIREC" because a password was required. He noted that a word, which he thought might be the password, was taped to the side of the computer display terminal.

Trying the password and gaining access, George quickly read case notes on several counseling center clients. Discovering that one of the clients was a member of a sorority that often held social events with his fraternity, George read the case notes from her six counseling sessions. He learned that she was having difficulty in establishing interpersonal relationships and was experiencing sexual dysfunction.

Several weeks later George met the student client at a party. He introduced himself using only his first name. George was drunk and in an attempt to be funny, he asked her if her sex life had improved as a result of counseling. The woman became very upset at this invasion of her privacy and left the party. The next morning she appeared at the counseling center and asked her counselor how this could have occurred. The counselor had no explanation, although she was appalled at the breach of confidentiality. She could only assert that she had not discussed the student's case with anyone. The student then conferred with the director of the counseling center, who was equally bewildered. The director told the student that he would investigate the incident. The student was not satisfied with this outcome. Because the counselor and director were members of AACD, the student was informed of her right to file a complaint with the association.

The student sent a letter to the AACD Ethics Committee in which she described the incident with George and expressed her feelings of anger and betrayal. She stated that she was reluctant to file a complaint against the counselor, because the counselor had helped her in significant ways. She also believed that the counselor had not deliberately breached confidentiality. Her concern was to understand how the incident could have happened and to ensure that it would not happen again. The student sent copies of this letter to the counselor and the director.

The Ethics Committee responded to the student's letter. She was sent copies of the AACD *Ethical Standards* and Policies and Procedures for Processing Complaints of Ethical Violations so that she could file a formal complaint if she so chose.

Discussion

The case continued to evolve. The counseling center investigated the incident and discerned George's identity. George admitted his involvement and described to the director how the events had occurred. The counseling center professional staff developed and implemented a policy requiring that: (1) case notes be stored on floppy disks only and locked in counselors' office files, (2) only counseling center staff have access to computers in the counseling center, and (3) all password data in written form be kept by the director only. Inservice training was given to all secretarial and clerical staff, emphasizing the confidentiality of the counseling relationship and counseling records.

Although no formal complaint was filed, the counselor and director wrote to the Ethics Committee and explained how the incident had occurred. They acknowledged that the ethical standards had been violated, most notably standard B.6 (confidentiality of computer-maintained data) and G.6 (responsibility for staff inservice development). They expressed their regret that the incident had happened, enclosed a copy of their new policy, and described the steps they had taken to rectify the situation.

Conclusion

The counselor and director met with the student and told her of the actions they had taken to secure the confidentiality of records. The student found them acceptable and decided not to pursue the complaint. The case was resolved at this point.

Questions for Thought and Discussion

1. Computer use in counseling has evolved—and will continue to evolve—at a rapid pace. What steps can counselors take to ensure that ethical practices keep pace with advancing technology?

2. Who should have access to counselors' case notes? When computers, tape recordings, and other technologies are used, what additional safeguards are needed?

3. What other ethical concerns are raised by the use of computers in counseling? (See essay by Sampson in the next section of the casebook.)

A DUAL RELATIONSHIP

[*This case study was contributed by* **Virginia B. Allen**. *Dr. Allen is Associate Professor of Counselor Education at Idaho State University.*]

Sandra Smith was admitted to a master's degree program in counseling. Unbeknownst to the faculty, Sandra had a number of personal and family problems. During her first semester she was encouraged in several of her classes to come to understand herself better and resolve any personal issues that might hinder her ability as a counselor.

As the first semester progressed, Sandra was having academic difficulties, which she attributed to her personal problems. She realized that unless she got help in resolving them she probably wouldn't be able to pass her classes and continue in the program.

Another requirement of the program was that each student be responsible for obtaining the support of a major adviser. Sandra made appointments and talked to each of the faculty members. She found herself drawn to one faculty member in particular. She was currently taking a class from him, enjoyed visiting with him, and generally found him to be supportive of her.

Several of their initial appointments were spent in guidance activities such as determining which classes to take, what the counseling profession had to offer, what kinds of jobs were available, and how to better prepare for classes and thus improve her grades. As Sandra felt increasing rapport with this faculty member, she finally disclosed that her life was filled with problems and that her marriage was slowly crumbling. She and the faculty member discussed several options that were available to her and set a weekly appointment schedule to continue to discuss her problems. These appointments and discussions lasted throughout the first semester.

During the second semester, Sandra enrolled in this professor's practicum section and saw him weekly for supervision. The professor realized that her marital problems and unhappiness were hindering her work as a counselor. He continued to work with her during supervision hours to resolve these problems and make choices that would promote her personal happiness and improve her counseling skills.

When the counseling program's faculty met to review the progress of first-year students, Sandra was mentioned as having academic difficulties. The faculty member who had been seeing her for supervision disclosed to his colleagues that she was having personal problems. He also stated that resolution was close at hand and he thought that once these concerns were resolved she would do fine in the program and become a good counselor.

During the second year of her program Sandra continued to have regular meetings with the professor and was beginning to make slow progress in overcoming her academic and personal problems. At this time she decided to apply for candidacy that required, among other things, the support and signature of the primary adviser. She took the form to the professor to ask for his signature.

The professor told Sandra that he couldn't support her candidacy at this time because of her unresolved problems. He would sign the form and support her at a later date if she continued to meet with him and show progress toward resolving her personal issues. She continued to meet with him regularly to fulfill this requirement.

The following semester Sandra again asked the professor for his support and signature and was again turned down for the same reasons. At this time she filed a complaint with the AACD Ethics Committee charging the professor with violating standards H.12, H.13, H.14, and B.2.

Discussion

Standard H.12 states that when educational programs require growth experiences with an emphasis on self-disclosure or other intimate or personal involvement, the supervisor must have no administrative, supervisory, or evaluating authority regarding the participant. Supervisors must avoid dual relationships with their supervisees.

Standard H.13 states that members will provide students with clear and equally acceptable alternatives for self-understanding or growth experiences. The member will assure students that they have the right to accept these alternatives without prejudice or penalty. H.14 states that members conduct an educational program in keeping with the ethical guidelines of the association. B.2 states that information resulting from a counseling relationship must be kept confidential.

In considering the charge that standard H.14 had been violated, the Ethics Committee reviewed the philosophy, goals, and actual working procedures of the program. The Committee found that this standard had not been violated.

Documentation related to standard H.12 included the professor's appointment calendars and his own admission that the majority of the appointments over the course of the 2 years were spent in discussing the student's personal problems. The faculty member was found in violation of standard H.12 for promoting a dual relationship with a student over whom he had supervisory, administrative, and evaluating authority.

Standard H.13 required more deliberation by the Ethics Committee. The faculty member reported that the university counseling center was mentioned to the student as an appropriate place to receive counseling. The student admitted that she knew of the counseling center's existence and the services it provided, but didn't feel she could have gone there and still have received the professor's support for candidacy. The Ethics Committee found the professor in violation of H.13 because he did not clearly promote this alternative and left the impression that there could be prejudice or penalty on his part if the student had accepted this alternative.

The professor did divulge to his colleagues that this student was having personal problems. By establishing a dual relationship with the student, the faculty member put himself in a double-bind situation. He couldn't maintain confidentiality and carry out his role as a professor. As a faculty member he had to divulge information about a student when it could have affected the program and perhaps ultimately the counseling profession. The Ethics Committee found him to be in violation of B.2 because he did break the confidentiality of a counseling relationship regardless of his rationale in doing so.

Conclusion

The AACD Ethics Committee found the member in violation of standards B.2, H.12, and H.13. The Committee imposed a 2-year suspension from membership coupled with a probationary period during which the faculty member would be closely supervised. With the Ethics Committee's concurrence, the professor asked his department chairperson to provide this supervision. The chairperson submitted semiannual reports concerning the supervisory period as required by the Ethics Committee.

Questions for Thought and Discussion

1. The potential for role conflicts always exists when counselor educators deal with personal dimensions of student growth along with the cognitive elements of counselor training. How might a counseling program be set up to avoid dual relationships between faculty and students? What safeguards should be included?

2. This case study highlights several ethical pitfalls that can occur when professors counsel their students. For instance, confidentiality can be compromised. What other ethical violations could potentially result from a dual relationship? (See essay by Kitchener and Harding in the next section of the casebook.)

A SEXUAL ATTRACTION

During a counseling session, a client revealed that she was attracted to the counselor and desired a personal and sexual relationship with him. The counselor, aware at that moment that the attraction was mutual, shared his feelings but went on to explain that dual relationships are unethical. He also stated that he did not think he could continue to counsel with her effectively. The client agreed, and he terminated the counseling relationship and offered to refer her to another counselor. The client asked for time to think it over and left the office.

The next day the client telephoned, stating that she wanted to resolve the incident and discuss a referral. The counselor agreed to meet her that evening at a restaurant. That night, they began a sexual relationship. The counselor did not pursue the question of referral to another counselor, although he was aware of the client's unresolved therapeutic issues. He was afraid that the other counselor might learn of his sexual relationship with the former client.

The counselor experienced increasing guilt and remorse, and ended the relationship after 1 month. He took several steps to attempt to rectify the situation. He made arrangements for the former client to see another counselor, offered to pay for her counseling, and sought counseling for himself. He informed his employer of his actions and agreed to work under supervision, accepting only those clients who would pose no danger that such an incident might reoccur.

The former client filed a complaint with the AACD Ethics Committee, charging the counselor with violating standards A.8, B.12, and B.14.

Discussion

Standard A.8 states that members must avoid engaging in activities that meet their own personal needs at the client's expense. Standard B.12 states that when a member determines an inability to be of professional assistance to the client, the member must suggest an appropriate referral. Standard B.14 states that sexual relationships with clients are unethical.

In considering this case, the Ethics Committee noted that, technically, the counselor was not in violation of standard B.14 because the counseling relationship was terminated before the counselor entered into a sexual relationship with the client. Although some helping professionals believe that ethical codes should prohibit sexual relationships with **former** clients, the AACD *Ethical Standards* are silent on this issue.

The counselor's behavior was in partial compliance with standard B.12, in that he terminated the professional relationship at the time he became aware of his feelings. At issue is whether he had an obligation to attempt to refer the client at that same time. Her unresolved therapeutic issues were not addressed for 1 month.

Did the counselor violate standard A.8 by meeting his own needs at the client's expense? His actions in entering into a personal and sexual relationship despite his knowledge that it was improper, and then severing that relationship after 1 month, were bound to cause the client considerable emotional pain.

Conclusion

The Ethics Committee did not find the counselor to be in violation of standard B.14 as it is written. However, the Committee did consider the counselor's **purpose** in terminating the counseling relationship, and found that his actions violated the spirit if not the letter of this standard. The Committee found that the counselor's failure to pursue the issue of referral constituted a breach of standard B.12. The Committee also found that the counselor had violated standard A.8 by meeting his own needs at the client's expense.

In determining the most appropriate sanctions, the Committee considered the counselor's good faith efforts to rectify the situation. These factors mitigated against an extreme sanction such as permanent expulsion. The Committee imposed a 2-year suspension of membership coupled with a probationary period during which the counselor's work was closely supervised, with periodic reporting to the Committee.

Questions for Thought and Discussion

1. Helping professionals have debated the question of whether ethical codes should prohibit sexual relationships with former clients. What is your stance toward this issue?

2. Sexual relationships with clients are a frequently claimed violation against helping professionals. Because the counseling relationship is inherently an intimate one, counselors may be in a more vulnerable position than professionals in other fields. How can counselors protect themselves from such vulnerability?

ADJUSTMENT VERSUS ADVOCACY

[*This case study was submitted by* **Jesse Zapata**. *Dr. Zapata is Associate Professor of Counseling and Guidance at the University of Texas at San Antonio.*]

Frank Wilson was a counselor in a school whose student population had changed rapidly from predominantly White and middle class students to 30% Hispanic students who were primarily from working-class families. The principal perceived that some of the teachers were having difficulty adjusting to the school's new population. In addition, some of the Hispanic students seemed to be having difficulty adjusting to the school. The principal asked Mr. Wilson to identify and provide group counseling to some of the Hispanic students who seemed to be having behavioral difficulties in their classes.

Mr. Wilson met with a group of 10 students for 8 weekly sessions. Several months after the group terminated, the AACD Ethics Committee was contacted by the parents of the students who had participated in the group. They contended that Mr. Wilson had violated AACD's ethical standards by his failure to act on information that he possessed regarding discriminatory and harmful treatment of their children. Letters submitted by the parents and by Mr. Wilson are produced below.

The Parents' Formal Complaint

"Our children were asked to participate in group counseling in order to help them do better in school, and we gave our permission for them to participate. We believed that they would be helped and were very happy that they would get that opportunity. The counseling did seem to help in most of the classes, but problems continued in Mrs. Martin's class. At the same time, several of our children began cutting Mrs. Martin's class and telling us that they did not want to go to school any more. In time they told us that Mrs. Martin was calling them 'dirty Mexicans' and making fun of their English. We did not believe them at first but eventually they were able to convince us. They also told us that they had talked with Mr. Wilson about the problem but that he had not believed them at all. Several of us went to talk to the principal and demanded that Mrs. Martin be fired. We also demanded to know why Mr. Wilson had not done anything about the problem when he found out about it.

Our children placed their trust in the adults in the school, and they were let down. We understand that the teacher, Mrs. Martin, has been transferred to another school in the district. But Mr. Wilson, who was aware of what was happening in Mrs. Martin's classroom and did nothing, is still a counselor in the school.

We believe that counselors are in the school primarily to help the children and that Mr. Wilson failed to do his job right. Following the guidelines you sent us, we are filing a formal complaint against Mr. Wilson and we charge him with violating standards A.10 and B.1 of the AACD *Ethical Standards*."

Mr. Wilson's Response

"The principal of my school asked me to provide group counseling to Hispanic students who were acting out in their classes. I asked teachers to refer students to me who they thought were having academic difficulty but who they also believed had some potential for good work. Teachers referred 30 students, and after initial screening and brief interviews, I decided to work with 10 of those students in a group. I worked with the 10 students for eight sessions for the purpose of helping them understand their problems and to help them bring about meaningful change.

About the third session, one of the students reported that one of his teachers, Mrs. Martin, had called him an animal. Other students picked up on this and reported that the same teacher had called them names, including 'dirty Mexicans,' and that this teacher also made fun of the way they mispronounced certain words in English.

In my years as a teacher and counselor, I have never discriminated. I see all students as being the same regardless of their ethnicity. I have also learned to question students carefully because they sometimes misinterpret or exaggerate events. After careful questioning, I believed that some of what the students were reporting might be occurring, but I also believed that the students were triggering some of the teacher's responses through their behavior. I chose to focus on helping the students improve their behavior in that teacher's classroom and to give them some ideas about how to communicate with the teacher. Neither I nor the students brought up the issue again.

I don't know what else I could have done. It would not have been at all appropriate for me to have taken sides with the students against the teacher. Also, I'm not Mrs. Martin's supervisor, so I had no control over her behavior."

Discussion

Standard A.10 states, in part, that "Through awareness of the negative impact of both racial and sexual stereotyping and discrimination, the counselor guards the individual rights and personal dignity of the client in the counseling relationship." Standard B.1 informs members that their "primary obligation is to respect the integrity and promote the welfare of the client(s), whether the client(s) is (are) assisted individually or in a group relationship."

In this case, Mr. Wilson believed that he had handled the group properly when Mrs. Martin's behavior was raised as a topic for discussion. Mr. Wilson felt that it would not have been appropriate or productive for him to have colluded with the students in their anger against the teacher. It may well have been a useful counseling goal to attempt to teach the students some strategies for succeeding in that teacher's class. On the other hand, the students apparently felt that Mr. Wilson discounted their stories and devalued their feelings when they discussed the problems they were having with Mrs. Martin. Mr. Wilson's view was that he was simply attempting to question them carefully, based on his awareness that junior-high-age students are sometimes quite dramatic and prone to exaggeration. The Ethics Committee determined that it would be impossible, without having been present in the group when the incident occurred, to judge which view best represented the reality of the situation.

The Ethics Committee determined that the ethical issues involved in the case extended beyond the question of Mr. Wilson's behavior within the group. Was it sufficient for him to attempt to teach students "adjustment" to the situation? Or did he have an obligation to take an "advocacy" role when he learned or suspected that the students were being treated with prejudice? The Committee felt that, given the extreme nature of the teacher's behavior as described by the students, and given Mr. Wilson's own statement that he believed that "some of what the students were reporting might be occurring," he had an ethical obligation to investigate the situation further. Although he had no supervisory relationship to Mrs. Martin, options available to him included discussing the situation with her directly (with the students' permission), or if Mrs. Martin was unresponsive and uncooperative, discussing the situation with the principal. His failure to take any action constituted a breach of standard A.3, which states that "Ethical behavior among professional associates, both members and nonmembers, must be expected at all times. When information is possessed that raises doubt as to the ethical behavior of professional colleagues, whether Association members or not, the member must take action to attempt to rectify such a condition."

It was more difficult to assess whether standards A.10 and B.1 had also been violated. However, the Committee decided that the counselor had demonstrated a lack of sensitivity to student needs and concerns, as evidenced by his failure to follow up and his assumption that the issue had been resolved, especially in light of the fact that some of the students began to be truant from Mrs. Martin's class.

Conclusion

The Ethics Committee sent a letter to Mr. Wilson informing him that he had been found in violation of standards A.3, A.10, and B.1. To Mr. Wilson's credit, he responded in a proactive manner. He enrolled in a course in multi-cultural education at a local university to enhance his self-awareness. He worked closely with the principal to arrange for the school's staff to receive extensive inservice education aimed at helping them deal with the changing student population.

Questions for Thought and Discussion

1. How can counselors, in schools and in other settings, determine whether their proper role is one of facilitating "adjustment" to society versus serving as advocates for clients who receive unfair treatment by the dominant society?
2. How can counselors prepare themselves to serve a variety of clients in a multicultural society?

GENETIC COUNSELING AND INFORMED CONSENT

[*This case study was contributed by* **J. Melvin Witmer** *and* **Betty Black**. *Dr. Witmer is Professor of Counselor Education, Ohio University. Ms. Black is Coordinator, Genetic Services of Southeastern Ohio, College of Osteopathic Medicine, Ohio University.*]

When Suzanne was 10 years old she was diagnosed as having tuberous sclerosis. Although Suzanne had a very mild expression of the disease, most affected individuals have a degree of mental retardation and hard-to-control seizures and follow a progressive downhill course with increasingly severe symptoms. Frequent outcomes include further brain damage, severe behavioral problems, institutionalization, and early death. At the initial diagnostic interview the doctor told Suzanne that when she grew up she should never have children because they could have a severe form of the disease. Tuberous sclerosis is an autosomal genetic disease, which means that any child of Suzanne's would have a 50/50 chance of getting the defective gene and having the disease.

At age 17 Suzanne was a senior in high school, maintaining a 2.5 grade point average and leading a typical teenager's life. Her seizures were well controlled with daily medication. However, Suzanne was having bouts of depression and began seeing her school counselor. She was uncertain of her future plans, whether to get a job or go on to school. She was also in conflict with her mother. Because Suzanne and her boyfriend were discussing marriage, her mother was insisting that she get a tubal ligation before they married. The family physician supported the mother's views, but Suzanne's boyfriend was uncertain about a tubal ligation. The school counselor, feeling limited in time as well as expertise for dealing with the depression, genetically related problems, and family conflicts, referred her to the community mental health center.

When the school counselor discussed this referral with the mother, the mother agreed that Suzanne was experiencing depression related to her post-high school plans, but denied that family conflict was a contributing factor. The mother reluctantly took Suzanne to the community mental health center, still believing that her daughter's stress was related to a decision about college versus getting a job after high school. The mother signed the consent form for the mental health agency to provide counseling to Suzanne and for the school counselor to release information.

By the third session it was apparent to the mental health counselor that the major factors in Suzanne's depression were her genetic disease, the doctor's directive, and her mother's insistence on a tubal ligation before marriage. Her mother was opposed to abortion. Suzanne seemed to perk up when the counselor suggested they might explore alternatives to tubal ligation.

The mental health counselor contacted a local genetics counselor about Suzanne's case without disclosing her name. The genetics counselor discussed the options of in vitro fertilization, using an egg donor, and methods of early prenatal diagnosis that would allow the termination of an affected pregnancy. Concurrent multiple birth control measures were suggested.

During the next counseling session Suzanne affirmed her decision to get married. She stated that she wanted to get married first and then decide with her husband what to do about having or not having children. The counselor affirmed this as a right she would have, but also suggested a joint session with her fiancé to discuss these matters. When Suzanne asked how she could deal with her mother's insistence on a tubal ligation, the counselor discussed assertive communication, and then he and Suzanne role-played talking with her mother. Suzanne left the session saying that she would discuss her feelings with her mother.

When Suzanne told her mother about the alternatives discussed in counseling, the mother became very angry and said she didn't want to hear any more. She immediately called the mental health counselor, stating, "I agreed for you to counsel my daughter to get rid of her depression. I don't see why you had to get into these things. It just complicates her life. I did not consent to your telling her she could have an abortion or use birth control pills. You had no right to talk to her about these things. You went against medical advice given by our family physician. I'm going to do something about this." She then hung up.

Several hours later the counselor called the mother and invited her and Suzanne to come to the agency for a conference, hoping they could still work out the misunderstanding as well as Suzanne's problems. The mother seemed to have calmed down a bit and said she would think it over.

The counselor also talked with his supervisor. They decided to contact the AACD Ethics Committee for an opinion on what "consent" should include and the implications of consent for a parent who gives legal permission for a minor to receive counseling.

Discussion

Upon receiving the information provided by the community counseling center, the Ethics Committee reviewed the case, focusing on three issues that seemed pertinent: (1) Was an appropriate procedure used to obtain the mother's consent? (2) Did the counselor act in the best interests of the client? (3) Did the counselor practice beyond his competence by providing information about options related to childbearing to a person with tuberous sclerosis?

The Ethics Committee found the first issue the most difficult one to assess. The concept of "informed consent" requires that the client give consent voluntarily, be mentally competent to make the decision, and understand the information provided by the counselor about counseling as a treatment modality. Because Suzanne was 17 years old, the mother was required to give consent. The mother's signature on the consent form was evidence that she had given permission for her daughter to be counseled. Presumably, she did so voluntarily and was mentally competent to do so. The question in this case was: To what did she believe she was consenting in giving the counselor permission to help her daughter overcome depression? Did she have adequate information to give informed consent?

Informed consent is problematic in counseling. Because of the nature of the counseling process, it is difficult and sometimes impossible to inform the client of all the possible goals, procedures, and limitations that might be relevant to the client's presenting problem. Yet, standard B.8 requires that counselors inform clients of "the purposes, goals, techniques, rules of procedure, and limitations that may affect the relationship at or before the time that the counseling relationship is entered." Because consent is a process rather than an event that occurs only at the first contact, the critical issue is what one should (or must) disclose at the time of the initial contact.

In this case, also at issue is what a counselor needs to disclose to a parent who gives consent to work with a minor. The information sent by the mental health center indicated that in the intake session the mother and daughter did discuss the daughter's depression and uncertainty about whether to go to college or get a job. Suzanne had also mentioned that she was thinking about getting married, and her genetic disease was disclosed. The counselor's information shows only that he told the mother they would review these concerns to determine whether they were related to the depression and, if so, would work toward a resolution.

The Ethics Committee's opinion was that the counselor did provide sufficient information for the mother to give her consent. Because the counselor was not familiar with the genetic disease, he was not able to anticipate what implications there might be in exploring alternatives. The Committee noted, however, that the counselor might have arranged for a joint session with the mother when he saw the necessity to contact a genetics counselor to understand the options available to a person with tuberous sclerosis.

In considering the second issue, the Ethics Committee agreed that the counselor did act responsibly in serving the best interests of the client. No evidence was found that the counselor had violated the portion of standard B.8 that states, "When working with minors or persons who are unable to give consent, the member protects these clients' best interests," or standard B.1, which notes that

94

the member's "primary obligation is to respect the integrity and promote the welfare of the client."

Regarding the third issue, the Ethics Committee did not see any evidence of incompetence in the counselor's reported professional conduct. Although the information about tuberous sclerosis and its genetic implications was beyond his knowledge, he very appropriately consulted a specialist in this area. His actions were in compliance with standard B.11, which states that "The member may choose to consult with any other professionally competent person about a client."

Conclusion

The AACD Ethics Committee agreed that the counselor had met the minimum criteria for consent, and that although he might have had further contact with the mother, he was not negligent in keeping the client informed of his procedures. A responsibility of a mental health counselor is to assist the client in resolving emotional issues related to personal conditions and choices. To do so requires information regarding options and their implications, and integrating this information with former perceptions and emotions. No evidence was presented that would suggest that the counselor did not act in the best interests of the client. One might question whether a counselor should provide information in an area for which he has had little or no formal training or experience. However, the information provided was appropriate and accurate.

The Committee's conclusion regarding the three issues in this case was based only on information from the service provider. An inquiry that included information provided by the client and her mother might have influenced the Committee toward a different conclusion.

Questions for Thought and Discussion

1. What elements should "informed consent" include in order for the consent process to be ethically appropriate and legally defensible?

2. Counselors who work with minor clients encounter special ethical issues, such as distinguishing between the rights of the minor client and the rights of the parent or guardian. In this case, did the mother have the right to insist that tubal ligation was the best solution? Was the family physician professionally responsible in recommending that procedure without considering other options with Suzanne?

3. This case highlights some of the issues involved in genetic counseling. What other ethical issues might a counselor face in working with clients who have genetic conditions?

UNPREPARED FOR PRIVATE PRACTICE

For 11 years, John Jones had enjoyed his work as a career and vocational counselor with a state agency in an eastern seaboard city. His wife received a promotion that required the couple to move to a small town in a southern state. After the move, John was unable to find a position as a career/vocational counselor. He secured a part-time position as an instructor at a local community college. He decided to open a private practice operating out of a home office to supplement his part-time income. He determined that he would specialize in career counseling to draw on his experience and expertise.

To advertise his private practice, John created a brochure that was headed:

SUBURBAN CAREER COUNSELING CENTER
Member, American Association for Counseling and Development
10 Oak Street   Anytown, U.S.A.
JOHN JONES, M.A.
is a counselor with over a decade of experience
in helping individuals make career decisions . . .

The brochure went on to outline the types of services provided, fees, and other information.

John made plans to join the chamber of commerce and distribute his brochure through its membership list. To get started in business immediately, he passed out the brochure to students in his classes at the community college. One of the community college students took the brochure to a counselor at the community college counseling center and asked for advice on whether she should use this service at the fees charged. Because a similar service was offered to students through the counseling center at no charge, the community college counselor went to John and objected to his distributing brochures in his classes. John replied that he saw no conflict of interest because he was not employed as a **counselor** at the community college and that his actions represented only fair competition in a free marketplace. The community college counselor filed a letter of complaint with the AACD Ethics Committee and enclosed a copy of John's brochure.

Discussion

The community college counselor, in her complaint, charged John with violating standard F.8, which states that it is unethical to use one's institutional affiliation to recruit clients for one's private practice. John's argument that he was employed as a teacher rather than a counselor at the community college indicated a misunderstanding of this standard. John, in his response to the charge, also raised the point that community college students might receive his brochure through means other than his direct distribution in class, and that they had the right to free choice regarding the career counseling services they wanted to receive. He believed that he was innocent of any wrongdoing.

Conclusion

The Ethics Committee, in reviewing the case, noted that the format of John's brochure was misleading in that it implied that his "Suburban Career Counseling Center" was a member of AACD. The association has only individual members; it does not offer membership to organizations or institutions. Thus, standard F.4, which states that members do not present their affiliation with any organization in such a way that would imply inaccurate sponsorship or certification by that organization, was also pertinent to this case.

The Ethics Committee found that John was in violation of standards F.8 and F.4, and requested that he cease and desist practices that attempted to directly recruit community college students for his private practice. He was reminded of his ethical obligation to inform any prospective clients who were also community college students that a similar service was available to them at no fee at the community college counseling center. Finally, the Committee asked him to cease distribution of his brochure until it could be redesigned to eliminate the misleading reference to AACD.

John replied to the Ethics Committee, agreeing that he would cease distributing his brochures at the college and would redesign them.

Questions for Thought and Discussion

1. When members are simultaneously employed by institutions or agencies and in private practice, how can they avoid conflict-of-interest situations?

2. What are the limits to advertising within ethical bounds? (See essay by Fong and Sherrard in the next section of the casebook.)

INTERNATIONAL CONSULTING

[*This case study was contributed by* **Ajit K. Das** *and* **Farah A. Ibrahim**. *Dr. Das is Associate Professor at the University of Minnesota, Duluth, and Dr. Ibrahim is Associate Professor at the University of Connecticut, Storrs.*]

Dr. Stout was a faculty member in the college of education at a large state university. His doctorate was in counseling and guidance, and he taught courses in career guidance and group procedures and supervised some counseling practica. Although his university had a long-standing contract with several developing countries in Africa to provide consulting services, Dr. Stout had not taken any particular interest in these projects. However, he had recently talked to some of his colleagues who had been involved in overseas assignments, which he learned they had found rewarding. He also learned that some faculty had been rewarded with merit increases and promotions following their international assignments. Dr. Stout decided that an overseas assignment might be advantageous to his own professional development.

Before he had taken any steps to pursue this option, his dean called and asked him if he had any interest in international education. If so, would he consider going to Nigeria for a year to work with the faculty there to develop a counselor education program? Dr. Stout did not want to miss this opportunity. He told the dean that he was very interested in international consultation and had kept himself informed about the university's projects in Africa.

The next year he was sent to Nigeria to work with the faculty of the Institute of Education to develop a counselor education program. All of the faculty members at the Institute had been trained in the United States or England. They had serious reservations about transplanting an American or British model to their country. They wanted to do a needs assessment and design a long-term research and development project to provide a database. Then, a counselor education program could be developed that would train personnel to work in an emerging vocational guidance program serving Nigerian youth. They expected Dr. Stout to help them in planning such a project but found that he did not have much to contribute. He had only superficial knowledge of the Nigerian school system and little understanding of Nigerian society or its social, political, and economic history. Furthermore, he believed that the counselor education curriculum should focus on counseling and communication skills and not be overburdened with academic studies, which he regarded as irrelevant to the essential nature of counseling.

Dr. Stout's Nigerian colleagues were puzzled and frustrated with his attitude. They felt that instead of helping them with their project, he was actually hindering them. They tried several times to confront him directly, but backed off when it created bad feelings. They asked their project director to write to the dean of Dr. Stout's college to replace him. After 2 months, they received a reply from the dean saying that Dr. Stout was one of his most competent faculty members and he regretted that things were not working well for them. They were discouraged by this reply and wanted to take some action that would lead to better screening of foreign consultants. They reviewed the AACD *Ethical Standards* and filed a formal complaint charging Dr. Stout with violating standards A.7, E.1, E.2, and E.4.

Discussion

Because Dr. Stout was an AACD member, the Ethics Committee accepted the complaint and notified Dr. Stout of the charges. He responded with a long letter in which he explained his views that counseling skills are transcultural and that a skills-based curriculum would be appropriate in any setting. Upon request of the Ethics Committee, he also supplied his vita, which did not reflect any particular expertise in international education or consultation.

Standard A.7 states that "members recognize their boundaries of competence and provide only those services and use only those techniques for which they are qualified by training or experience." It further states that "members

98

should only accept those positions for which they are professionally qualified." In reviewing the case, the Committee felt that Dr. Stout had willingly accepted a position for which he had no special competence. An extenuating circumstance was that he honestly believed that a counselor training model developed in the United States could be transplanted to another country regardless of cultural differences between the two countries.

Standard E.1 states that a "member acting as a consultant must have a high degree of self-awareness of his/her own values, knowledge, skills, limitations, and needs in entering a helping relationship that involves human and/ or organizational change." The Committee agreed that Dr. Stout had shown a lack of self-awareness in accepting an assignment for which he had no particular expertise. He did not act as if he were aware of his culture-bound values.

Standard E.2 states that "there must be understanding and agreement between member and client for the problem definition, change of goals, and prediction of consequences of interventions selected." It was clear from the complaint that the consultant and his clients looked at counselor training for Nigerian schools from very different perspectives. The Nigerian faculty thought it was necessary to generate a database about the forces that influence the development of Nigerian youth and to adapt counseling techniques developed elsewhere to make them consistent with Nigerian cultural values. The consultant held the view that counseling skills are transcultural and can be used in any culture, no matter how different outwardly. It seemed that Dr. Stout tried to impose his own assumptions and did not make a genuine effort to work out a clear definition of the problem or goals with the Nigerian faculty. Again, the extenuating circumstance was that he genuinely believed in his own viewpoint and failed to see any reason for a compromise.

Standard E.4 states that "the consulting relationship must be one in which client adaptability and growth toward self-direction are encouraged and cultivated. The member must maintain this role consistently and not become a decision maker for the client or create a future dependency." The Committee felt that, although Dr. Stout did not seem to encourage client self-direction and decision making, it was not because he wanted to create a future dependency. His behavior was dictated by his view that counseling techniques developed in the West could be taught to people anywhere in the world, without need to adapt these techniques to fit local cultural values. The Committte felt it was a naive view that would be difficult to defend, given the current knowledge of cross-cultural communication and counseling.

Conclusion

The Committee concluded that the primary issue involved in this case was that of recognizing the limits of one's competence, which is addressed in standard A.7. Dr. Stout was not equipped either by training or experience to serve as a consultant to an educational institution in a country about which he had no special knowledge. Even after he accepted the position, he seemed to have made little attempt to familiarize himself with social, cultural, and economic institutions in Nigerian society that might require different strategies for facilitating human development. Instead, he adhered to a particular theoretical view of counseling that made it difficult for him to collaborate with his Nigerian colleagues and reduced his effectiveness as a consultant. This stance also resulted in his inability to meet some of the ethical criteria for consulting as described in Section E of the *Ethical Standards*.

The Committee considered the fact that standards specifically addressing international consulting have not been delineated. It was decided not to censure Dr. Stout for having accepted the assignment. The Committee did, however, write him a letter informing him of their findings and asking him not to do further work in international consulting until he could develop expertise.

Questions for Thought and Discussion

1. Does international consulting require any special competencies beyond those needed for consulting within one's own culture? If so, what are these competencies and how can they be developed?

2. What criteria should counselors use in determining where their boundaries of competence lie?

ESSAYS ON ETHICS IN PROFESSIONAL PRACTICE

This section of the casebook presents nine essays on a variety of topics that raise ethical concerns for counselors.

- Confidentiality creates ethical dilemmas more frequently than any other issue in counseling. The first essay, **Confidentiality**, defines the scope of confidentiality, presents its philosophical underpinnings, frames issues, and discusses implications for practice.
- **Ethics Curricula for Counselor Preparation Programs** will be of special interest to counselor educators who wish to develop ethics curricula or to evaluate existing ones. The authors present suggestions for infusing ethics into the entire curriculum.
- A complex interplay of clinical, ethical, legal, and entrepreneurial acumen is needed when private practitioners market their services. **Ethical Dilemmas in Marketing Counseling Services** addresses specific ethical concerns and presents useful recommendations.
- The United States is home to an increasing diversity of races, cultures, and languages. Unfortunately, counselors are as capable of subtle forms of discrimination as are any other Americans. **Ethical Issues in Multicultural Counseling** addresses this concern.
- **Dual Role Relationships** explores the ethical traps inherent in the temptation to mix incompatible roles. Distinctions are drawn between potentially problematic dual role relationships and those that may be ethically acceptable.
- Child abuse is a social illness; it also presents counselors with excruciating dilemmas. **Ethical Conflicts in Cases of Suspected Child Abuse** will help counselors make informed decisions in such cases.
- **Counseling Records: Legal and Ethical Issues** discusses ways counselors can keep useful records and appropriately document their actions so as to avoid ethical and legal problems.
- Computers have become a ubiquitous tool in counseling. **Ethical Use of Computer Applications in Counseling** investigates this new technology and its potential for misuse.
- Although counselors, like other health care professionals, are susceptible to a range of disorders, they are obligated to provide competent service. **Counselor Impairment** discusses ethical issues involved when counselors are unable to function adequately.

CONFIDENTIALITY

Holly A. Stadler

Counselors encounter dilemmas of confidentiality more frequently than other types of ethical dilemmas, and counselors find them the most difficult dilemmas to resolve (Hayman & Covert, 1986). In addition to the frequency of these dilemmas and the difficulty in resolving them, some particular problems related to confidentiality (i.e., client suicidal statements) are also the most stressful events mental health practitioners encounter (Farber, 1983; Deutsch, 1984). These factors highlight the importance of understanding the concept of confidentiality, its basis in moral philosophy, and its relevance to a range of counselor activities and responsibilities. I will begin this discussion by clarifying the scope of confidentiality, differentiating it from other similar concepts. Then I will present philosophical ideas that are the underpinnings of confidentiality and frame the confidentiality conflicts that arise in counseling. The discussion will close with implications for counselor practice.

Privacy, Confidentiality, and Privileged Communication

Before proceeding any further, the domain of confidentiality must be differentiated from similar domains—those of privacy and privileged communication. These three terms all too frequently are used interchangeably in professional communication. Although each term is founded on respect for a person's right to determine the contexts in which personal information may or may not be revealed, such respect has different manifestations.

Privacy—This term is derived from moral philosophy. It identifies the right of persons to choose what others may know about them and under what circumstances. The central notion here is the freedom to determine the disposition of personal information. Some (Caplan, in Beauchamp & Childress, 1983) see privacy as even more basic than the right to self-determination. According to this author, a privacy right is derived from a universal human need for privacy common in some way to all cultures.

Confidentiality—The right to privacy in general contexts is otherwise known as confidentiality in the context of professional relationships. Confidentiality highlights a professional ethical responsibility to respect a client's right to control personal information and access to it. This right creates a strong duty on the part of the professional to protect confidentiality.

Holly A. Stadler, PhD, is Associate Professor in the Division of Counseling Psychology and Counselor Education, University of Missouri-Kansas City.

Privileged communication—This term connotes a "legal right which exists by statute and which protects the client from having confidences revealed publicly from the witness stand during legal proceedings without his permission" (Shah, in Corey, Corey, & Callanan, 1988, p. 177). In statutes such as licensing laws, clients in relationships with certain types of professionals are said to have privilege. In some states clients of counselors have privileged communication. Clients may waive this right and personal confidences may be revealed in legal proceedings.

Ethical Underpinnings of Confidentiality

Why is confidentiality such a strong moral force in the lives of so many professionals, including counselors? Why do professionals go to great lengths to protect clients' personal secrets, the secrets that are at the heart of confidentiality? Response to questions such as these can be found in an illuminating argument put forth by Sissela Bok (1983). She contended that professional confidentiality is based on four premises, the last of which speaks to professional confidentiality in particular. If we examine the first of these premises, we find the frequently cited principle of autonomy invoked. This principle calls on us to respect others as capable of controlling various aspects of their lives (including their personal information) and the secrets they hold. Counseling is directed toward freeing clients from the emotional constraints that prevent them from exercising control over their lives. Counselors work to enhance client autonomy. Thus, one tenet upon which confidentiality as well as counseling is based urges us to respect our clients' decisions about who knows what about them, when, and for how long.

A second premise that Bok (1983) identified as underlying confidentiality is respect for human relationships, and for the secrets that certain types of relationships entail. This includes respecting client secrets shared in counseling relationships. She contended that human relationships could not endure without secrets. Counseling is certainly one form of relationship in which disclosure of secrets is essential. The intimate context of these disclosures is seen as essential to the success of counseling and, by its very nature, worthy of respect. Thus the respect for relationships and their secrets underlies both confidentiality and counseling.

Beyond the obligations created under the first and second premises, an additional duty is created (according to Bok) by a pledge of silence—the offer of confidentiality extended from counselor to client. This pledge to safeguard client information incurs allegiance to it as well as the expectation that the counselor will actively protect that information. So the counselor is bound to the pledge, in word and deed. Of course, in serious dilemmas a counselor might ask, "Should I have entered into this pledge? Can I be justified in overriding it? Does this pledge bind me to confidentiality when a client's secrets include actions that might endanger others?"

The final premise underlying confidentiality relates to its utility. Confidentiality is useful to both individuals and society. Clients who fear the revelation of their personal secrets can find refuge in the confidentiality of the counseling relationship. Some might delay or forego help they desperately need without the assurance of confidentiality. Society accepts the risks of not knowing about specific problems and dangers in society so that those in trouble can receive assistance. Confidentiality is seen as a socially useful assurance.

The duties to respect autonomy, respect relationships, keep a pledge of silence, and reinforce its utility are *each* of great importance in counseling. When they are combined in support of the principles of confidentiality, they develop a powerful moral claim on counselors' actions. I believe the power of that claim makes confidentiality a compelling duty for counselors, more compelling than each of the duties taken separately.

There is a clear congruence between the premises underlying confidentiality and basic counseling assumptions. This congruence and the compelling nature of the duties evoked answer the questions posed at the beginning of this section. This is why confidentiality is considered such a strong moral force in professional life. It may also explain the lengths to which counselors go to protect client secrets.

Typical Dilemmas of Confidentiality

Ethical dilemmas that hinge on confidentiality usually arise when the limits of confidentiality are called into question. Conflicts occur when other duties (e.g., protecting others from harm) seem to justify setting aside the duty to protect client confidentiality. Because confidentiality is such a strong moral force in counseling, situations in which that duty may be superseded by other more compelling duties evoke tension and distress in counselors. This may explain why counselors find dilemmas of confidentiality the most difficult to resolve (Hayman & Covert, 1986). The compelling nature of adherence to the duty to protect confidentiality is also reflected in the moral tension of counseling potentially dangerous clients.

The mandated reporting of child abuse and the duty to warn endangered third parties are the most frequently encountered exceptions to the general duty of confidentiality in counseling. Conflicts about these exceptions turn on contradictory ethical duties, one arising out of the principle of autonomy and the other out of the principle of beneficence. We have discussed earlier the principle of autonomy—respect for persons' control over their lives. This is presented in the foreword to section B of the AACD *Ethical Standards*: "The member must recognize the need for client freedom of choice." The relevance of a second principle, the principle of beneficence, to the work of counselors is readily apparent. This principle guides us to do good and prevent harm. As counselors we hope that all the work we do with clients is to promote their well-being. This can be noted in section B.1 of the *Ethical Standards*: "The member's primary obligation is to respect the integrity and promote the welfare of the client(s) . . . ." We also hope that counseling helps prevent the harm that might befall clients had their circumstances deteriorated without the benefit of counseling. This second duty arising from the principle of beneficence—to prevent harm— is the one that most regularly comes into play when counselors have conflicts about confidentiality.

The courts, professional societies, and federal and state governments have identified some duties that may override the duty to protect confidentiality. For example, counselors are mandated by state statute to report suspected abuse or neglect of children (usually under the age of 18). The Family Educational Rights and Privacy Act (P.L. 94–142) (1976) allows parents access to some educational information about their children. Alcohol and drug abuse clients (U.S. Department of Health and Human Services, 1987) have a great deal of control over access to their records. Minors in some states may receive substance abuse counseling or may discuss pregnancy or sexually transmitted diseases with a counselor without a legal requirement of parental notification. AACD's *Ethical Standards* (1988) respect a client's control over confidential information but regard a client dangerous to him- or herself or to others as an exception to this general rule. Court rulings, in particular the landmark *Tarasoff v. University of California Board of Regents* (1974) case, have identified a duty to warn and protect parties endangered by a client's potential violence. We will look at each of these issues more closely, keeping in mind that we will focus solely on ethical (not legal) considerations.

Child Abuse and Neglect

This topic is discussed more fully in another essay. Briefly, from an ethical standpoint, the duty to prevent the future harm of continued abuse or neglect, and to protect children who are insufficiently autonomous to act on their own behalf is a socially useful and justifiable role for counselors. In such situations the principle of beneficence overrides the principle of autonomy, and confidential information is disclosed to child protective service agencies. The AACD *Ethical Standards* (standard B.4) speak to this concern for harm to an abused or neglected client or the child of an abusive client.

Student Records

The essay by Remley discusses the legal aspects of P.L. 94–142. By distinguishing behavioral or counseling records from a student's other academic records, the law supports client confidentiality. In this situation the benefit of a parent knowing or having access to counseling information is insufficient to override confidentiality. Respect for the child's autonomy, for the counseling relationship, for the pledge of silence, and for the utility of confidentiality is upheld by this law. However, if a counselor violates confidentiality by showing the records to another, the parent is then allowed access to the counselor's records. If a counselor keeps records truly confidential, confidentiality can be maintained *even* when parents request counseling information.

Substance Abuse

Since 1975 the federal government has regulated the conditions of disclosure of the records of clients who are in treatment for substance abuse or who have participated in prevention or referral activities. In general the government has prohibited disclosure and protected confidentiality. There are, however, certain exceptions. Although some of these include auditing and research, I will elaborate only on those most relevant to client behavior. Exceptions to the general duty of confidentiality identified by the U.S. Department of Health and Human Services (1987) are those situations in which the benefit to be produced or the harm to be prevented is so compelling as to justify overriding client autonomy and confidentiality. Occurrences such as medical emergencies, child abuse or neglect, and third-party endangerment are ones in which severe consequences would likely develop if client information was not revealed. Confidentiality is overriden in these situations. It is important to note that only information relevant to the problem at hand should be revealed.

With regard to minors in substance abuse treatment, or prevention or referral programs, federal regulations permit notifying of parents of their child's involvement but bow to state laws when those laws are more restrictive. Some states require and others prohibit notification. Counselors should be familiar with their state laws in this regard, as well as with laws governing counseling of minors regarding pregnancy or sexually transmitted diseases.

Suicide

A problem that occurs with unfortunate frequency in counseling is a client's verbalization about thinking or attempting to end his or her life. The AACD *Ethical Standards* (section B.5) consider this an occasion that warrants unusual intrusion into a client's life by a counselor, including the possible disclosure of confidential information. The ethical theory supporting the standard is that the grave harm to be prevented and the good of continued existence supersede a duty to protect private confidences.

If suicide problems were as easily reckoned with as the ethical analysis would have us believe, counselors might not experience stress with suicidal clients. However, emotions rise when such life-threatening topics are discussed. Determining the lethality of client threats and appropriate methods of intervention is stressful for counselors. In general, though, as the lethality of a client's threats increases, so does the gravity of the harm to be prevented as well as the justification for intrusion. There is little justification for divulging information about a client who threatens suicide by overdosing on vitamin C. On the other hand a client who has developed an operational plan to shoot himself in the head at a time and place where he won't be interrupted has a plan high in lethality, high in gravity of harm, and high in justification for intrusion. I will leave it to the reader to ponder the counselor's duty in this last circumstance if the client is also imminently terminally ill and living a life of overwhelming physical pain. Is intrusion warranted? Most would say that counselors should at the very least not assist in putting a plan into operation.

Duty to Warn

Until the late 1970s the subject of client dangerousness to others received little attention in the counseling literature. This situation changed abruptly after a California court took up the issue of the responsibilities of psychologists and psychiatrists who know of a client's plan to murder another person.

106

The court case known as *Tarasoff v. Regents of University of California* is well known today. Though it applied only to psychologists and psychiatrists in the state of California, it is the concern of many counselors. To summarize, a graduate student named Poddar at the University of California in Berkeley told his psychologist at the university counseling center that he planned to murder Tatiana Tarasoff. The psychologist informed the supervising psychiatrist and the campus police. After detaining Poddar, the campus police determined that he was not dangerous and released him. The psychiatrist concluded that the matter should be dropped and any records pertaining to it be destroyed. Several months later Poddar did kill Tarasoff, and her parents brought suit against the University of California. Several appeals of verdicts were made. In the end, a second ruling by the California Supreme Court found the psychologist and psychiatrist had a duty to use reasonable care when they determined that a patient presented a serious danger of violence to another. They had a duty to protect the intended victim against such danger. Warning the intended victim is one form of protection. Some in the mental health professions (Stone, 1976) have argued that this ruling is faulty in that it erroneously assumes therapists can accurately predict client violence. Stone believes that following the ruling will result in more violence in society as dangerous persons no longer will have a confidential refuge where violent tendencies can be discussed without threat of disclosure.

The subject of the spread of communicable diseases, in particular acquired immune deficiency syndrome (AIDS), has aroused considerable discussion about the duty to warn. State statutes that address this issue will usually identify a duty on the part of a physician who has conducted or interpreted the appropriate medical tests. Responsibilities of other health care professionals are not discussed in these statutes.

Mental health care providers will wonder if a duty to warn potential victims of client violence as enumerated in the Tarasoff decision can be extended to cover AIDS. Legal experts are best consulted in these matters. With regard to ethical considerations, good ethics begin with good facts. Counselors should know the dangers and incidence of disease transmission associated with positive testing for the human immune virus (HIV), AIDS-related complex (ARC), and AIDS. Different duties could be identified based on the danger a client's disease status and transmission behaviors present.

These issues are much too complex to be discussed fully here (see Melton, 1988, for a full discussion). Many considerations must be evaluated in order to justify a duty to warn. The psychological devastation that accompanies any of these medical conditions and rampant discrimination against infected persons warrant extreme caution in these dilemmas. Confidentiality concerns turn on the balance between public welfare and individual privacy.

Implications for Counselors

Some conclusions can be drawn from the previous discussion to direct the work of ethically sensitive counselors.

Informing Clients

As clients begin counseling, they should be apprised of what counseling is all about, the importance of confidentiality, and the limits of confidentiality. To demonstrate respect for clients' decision-making capacity, counselors let clients know what to expect so that clients can decide if they wish to engage in counseling. When apprised of the counselor's responsibility to report suspected child abuse or neglect and a counselor's duty to warn potential victims of client violence, some clients might choose to exercise their right to forego counseling. Those who choose counseling do so with an understanding of the protections afforded their private information.

Clients in marital, family, or group counseling must know that very limited confidentiality is available to them. Once a counseling session includes more than one client, the confidentiality safeguards are diminished. Although counselors protect client confidentiality because of a professional obligation to do so, other clients have no such obligation. This should be made known to individuals prior to group or marriage and family counseling.

Releasing Information

We also might conclude from the discussion in previous sections of this essay that counselors should be aware of procedures for obtaining consent for release of confidential client information. Fully informing clients includes telling them who is requesting to disclose information (e.g., a client's school or agency), the type of information to be disclosed (e.g., results of career evaluation), and the duration of the consent (e.g., 6 months from current date). A client must be of sufficient maturity and rationality to be able to comprehend what is being requested in a consent for disclosure. The client must also be able to make a decision based on rational reasons. If these conditions are not met, valid consent cannot be given, but proxy consent can be sought from a parent or guardian. A guideline to follow here is this: If clients do not seem to understand the concepts of informed consent or disclosure of private information, they cannot give valid consent. (See Faden & Beauchamp, 1986, for additional information.)

Counselors whose work includes diagnosis, referral, or treatment of clients with alcohol or drug problems should have a copy of the federal regulations (U.S. Department of Health and Human Services, 1987) readily available. Responding to requests by outside parties for any information about these clients must be met with denial of any knowledge of the clients. The exception in this case occurs when clients consent to disclosure of information to outside parties. For example, if a telephone caller should request to speak with a client in a treatment program, a proper reply would be, "Due to confidentiality regulations, I am unable to tell you whether a person by that name has ever been associated with this program." Clients who do wish to speak with outside callers can make this known to the staff by signing a disclosure form.

Substance abuse programs that encourage recovering community members to attend support group meetings (e.g., Alcoholics Anonymous, Narcotics Anonymous) that are held on treatment units may compromise client confidentiality. Community members can readily identify clients by seeing them in the treatment environment. Holding meetings in areas not frequented by clients or securing client consent for these disclosures can help avoid confidentiality dilemmas.

These hints may help counselors develop or reinforce habits that protect confidential information. It is also important that counselors be prepared for situations in which confidentiality may be overridden.

Exceptions to Confidentiality

We have seen that situations arise in which the duty of confidentiality ethically may be superseded by a more stringent duty. In those cases, such as suspected child abuse, the burden of proof is on the counselor to show that a stronger duty is being fulfilled. This means that the counselor must adequately justify a decision to override confidentiality. Earlier discussion focused on possible justifications. Counselors should be familiar with the general exceptions to confidentiality and their justifications.

Fostering a Confidential Work Environment

Counselors employed in agencies and educational institutions frequently complain of the difficulty in creating an ethic of confidentiality in the work environment. Teachers reveal private student information in the teachers' lounge, secretaries talk openly about interesting or noteworthy clients, and counselors talk about clients over lunch at a local restaurant. Because confidentiality is such a compelling moral force in counseling, these types of revelations of private information are unacceptable. Clients or potential clients who witness the cavalier way in which private information is treated may rightfully mistrust counselors. Idle discussion about client information sets a bad tone for clients, counselors, and staff.

Direct confrontation of breaches of confidentiality may be the clearest way for counselors to demonstrate their respect for clients and the counseling relationship. Confrontation sends a message to other professionals and non-professionals that counselors are not tolerant of a work standard that discourages confidentiality. In addition managers of counseling services may wish to develop employee contracts that include a confidentiality clause.

Counselors are advised to begin an ethical dialogue with employers prior to accepting a job and to continue that dialogue throughout their employment. In the final analysis, it is the counselor's responsibility to foster an ethical environment. School principals, teachers, business managers, and other related professionals are not familiar with the AACD *Ethical Standards*. They will continue to encourage or even demand unethical counselor behavior if they are ignorant of the counselor's ethical obligations.

Conclusion

By preparing for typical ethical dilemmas, counselors can reduce the stress associated with these problems. Thoughtful deliberation based on ethical reasoning can help counselors resolve the dilemmas they find most troublesome.

References

Beauchamp, T., & Childress, J. (1983). *Principles of biomedical ethics.* New York: Oxford.

Bok, S. (1983). *Secrets: On the ethics of concealment and revelation.* New York: Vintage Books.

Corey, G., Corey, M., & Callanan, P. (1988). *Issues and ethics in the helping professions.* Pacific Grove, CA: Brooks/Cole.

Deutsch, C. (1984). Self-reported sources of stress among psychotherapists. *Professional Psychology, 15,* 833–845.

Faden, R., & Beauchamp, T. (1986). *A history and theory of informed consent.* New York: Oxford.

Family Educational and Privacy Rights Act (Buckley Pell Amendment), 20 U.S.C. & 1232g (1976).

Farber, B. (1983). Psychotherapists' perceptions of stressful patient behavior. *Professional Psychology, 5,* 697–705.

Hayman, P., & Covert, J. (1986). Ethical dilemmas in college counseling centers. *Journal of Counseling and Development, 64*(5), 315–317.

Melton, G. (1988). Ethical and legal issues in AIDS-related practice. *American Psychologist, 43,* 941–947.

Stone, A. (1976). The Tarasoff decisions: Suing psychotherapists to safeguard society. *Harvard Law Review, 90,* 358–378.

Tarasoff v. Regents of University of California, 13c.3D 177; 529 p. 2D553; 118 California Reporter, 129 (1974).

U.S. Department of Health and Human Services. (1987). Confidentiality of alcohol and drug abuse patient records; Final Rule. *Federal Register,* 42 CFR Part 2.

ETHICS CURRICULA FOR COUNSELOR PREPARATION PROGRAMS

Dennis Engels, Bobbie L. Wilborn, and Lawrence J. Schneider

Ethical issues permeate all aspects of life. Ethical guidelines are essential for all professions, and particularly for helping professions, to protect the public and govern professional behavior. Ethical concerns cover the entire continuum of professional choice and behavior, from matters of life and lethality to issues such as integrity and responsibility.

Even seemingly innocent missteps, such as revealing a client's identity, can have a monumental impact on public opinion of and confidence in mental health care. In 1972, for example, U.S. Senator Thomas Eagleton was for a short time a vice presidential candidate. Once "informed sources" revealed that Eagleton had received psychiatric assistance for depression, his candidacy was doomed. The stigma the public attached to mental health care persists, as evidenced by former President Reagan's pejorative reference to presidential candidate Michael Dukakis as disabled following a rumor that Dukakis had sought mental health assistance.

Unfortunately, the public has no monopoly on misperceptions and ignorance of mental health ethics and ethical standards. Evidence suggests that mental health providers regularly violate, ignore, and are unfamiliar with their own profession's ethical codes and related legal strictures (Allen, 1986; APA Ethics Committee, 1987; APA, 1988; Boyd, Tennyson, & Erickson, 1973, 1974; Golden & O'Malley, 1979; Holroyd & Brodsky, 1977; Jagim, Wittman, & Noll, 1978; Kibler & Van Hoose, 1981; Sanborn, 1975; Tymchuck, Drapkin, Ackerman, Major, Coffman, & Baum, 1982).

Because circumstances requiring moral and ethical choice pervade our increasingly complex society, it is clear that ethics needs to be overtly and deliberately taught in any counselor education program. Moreover, it makes good sense to stimulate students to become familiar with ethical issues and to engage in ethical decision making in the relative safety and calm of a counselor preparation program *before* they enter practice. This essay will focus briefly on historical and general concerns regarding professional ethics and then proceed to

Dennis Engels, PhD, is Professor, Bobbie L. Wilborn, PhD, is Professor, and Lawrence J. Schneider, PhD, is Associate Professor in the Department of Counselor Education at the University of North Texas.

program and curriculum issues, infusion of ethics into all courses, and specific components of an ethics course.

Background and History

Although attention to professional ethics is found in the works of Confucius, Plato, Canon Law, and other philosophical, legal, and religious sources (Mann & Kreyche, 1966), it is striking to note the relative recency of published ethical standards in the American Association for Counseling and Development (formerly American Personnel and Guidance Association). Although AACD was founded in 1913 (as the National Vocational Guidance Association), AACD's first ethical standards were not published until 1959, following APGA President Donald Super's 1953 charge to develop a code of ethics (Allen, 1986; Engels, 1981b; Super, 1953). Since its origin, this code has undergone periodic revision, most recently in 1988.

Specific attention to ethics by the Council for the Accreditation of Counseling and Related Educational Programs (CACREP, 1988) and the publication of ethical standards by several AACD divisions, related mental health professions, and credentialing and regulatory bodies bespeak the importance of ethical guidelines in the development and maturing of professional practitioners. AACD members need to know the letter and spirit of the AACD *Ethical Standards* and would do well to have an appreciation for the ethical codes of related professions.

Legal issues also deserve increased attention in this era of frequent and extensive litigation, more and varied forms of professional counselor credentials, especially licensure, the growing numbers of laws aimed at protecting the public (e.g., the Buckley Pell Amendment to "The Educational Rights and Privacy Act"), and judicial decisions directly related to the helping professions (e.g., *Tarasoff*, 1976).

Personal and Normative Definitions of Ethics and Accountability

Definitions of ethics range from abstract concepts of virtue and goodness to the situationally pragmatic, with an overt emphasis on consensus and individual values, especially moral values. Values are the counselor's beliefs about what is good, what is good for clients, and how those goals should be achieved. How the counselor responds to professional ethics and any conflict between ethics and the law will be related to the individual's values. According to research, ethics is more concerned with the process of deciding than with the outcome of ethical decisions. Yet, ethical and legal accountability will more likely be judged in terms of counselor behavior and client outcome (Eberlein, 1987; Fine & Ulrich, 1988; Hartz, 1973; Sanders, 1979). Whereas the legal process can focus on intent, an ethics committee or jury would most likely emphasize and evaluate an individual's behavior and its impact rather than intent.

Programmatic and Curricular Attention to Ethics

Because ethics preparation is essential for aspiring professionals, it is incumbent on educators to develop an ethics curriculum or curricula in a counselor education program. As a point of departure, however, it is essential to see curriculum as a subset of the total program. Herr and Cramer (1988) emphasized the importance of overt attention to philosophy, goals, specific objectives, and related programmatic considerations. Without careful program planning and implementation, separate courses or units on ethics are at risk of being ignored or otherwise diminished in effectiveness.

Faculty and student educational and experiential backgrounds are vital factors in developing an ethics course for aspiring counselors. Fine and Ulrich (1988), Golightly (1971), and Kitchener (1986) advocated exposing students to fundamental underpinnings of ethics, most notably philosophical bases and applications. Welfel and Lipsitz (1983) also considered this attention to philosophical and moral ethical principles as necessary over the long term. However, faculty and student readiness for engaging in ethics study focused on philosophical principles may vary greatly among and within programs, departments, and institutions.

Stadler and Paul (1986) found that only 23% of their national sample of counselor educators had coursework in ethics in their own preparation. Notwithstanding an appreciation of Stadler and Paul's cautions about generalizing from their findings, the fact that over three fourths of their 115 respondents reported no formal graduate-level coursework in ethics suggests that it might be highly unrealistic to expect those with no formal education in ethics to present moral and philosophical principles effectively. Although Fine and Ulrich (1988) and Kitchener (1986) addressed this obstacle and suggested appropriate sources of renewal in ethics education, it seems unlikely that educators will devote ample time to acquire needed expertise, especially in the face of the knowledge explosion that makes it demanding simply to stay abreast in one's area of specialization.

Just as faculty may not be ready to present philosophical constructs, students who lack formal education in philosophy may not be ready to benefit from such instruction. Hence, counselor educators need to assess their own and students' readiness, with consideration to short- and long-term means of providing ethics education. As a near-term option, exploiting faculty experience in addressing ethical issues might be appropriate, with a long-term departmental commitment to seek new faculty with formal preparation in ethics as a means to eventual ascendence to a program with a decided philosophical base. As a middle ground, pragmatic aspects of works such as those by Abeles (1980), Beck (1971), Fine and Ulrich (1988), Golightly (1971), Kitchener (1986), Pelsma and Borgers (1986), and available models and textbooks (e.g., Corey, Corey, & Callanan, 1988; Keith-Spiegel & Koocher, 1985; Rest, 1984; Van Hoose & Paradise, 1979) could constitute potentially strong resources for programmatic and curricular ethics preparation.

In line with a purposeful focus on ethics as part of the overall counselor preparation program, a faculty might do well to identify general programmatic and curricular goals such as the following: (1) to facilitate student self-awareness, with attention to personal assumptions, values, biases, strengths, and limitations; (2) to facilitate student awareness of the pervasive nature of ethical issues in life and society, including attention to new issues that arise daily from scientific breakthroughs, cultural changes, and other phenomena (e.g., surrogate mothers and their parental rights); (3) to foster commitment to personal and professional ethical action and responsibility for action; (4) to facilitate broad ethical knowledge and reasoning skills that students can adapt to a range of issues and settings; (5) to heighten student appreciation for the complexity and ambiguity of ethical principles and standards (e.g., conflicts among and between ethical principles and respective ethical standards of different helping professions and between ethical standards and laws); and (6) to foster sensitivity to cultural and other issues native to a geographical region as well as national concerns (e.g., consideration of English as the official language of a state or the role of ethnic factors in various subcultures' use of mental health services). Delineating such broad goals can be an important first step to specifying goals and objectives for ethics components in all courses and for pointed attention to a separate ethics course.

Because the AACD *Ethical Standards* (1988) presume that *all* members will maintain the highest standards of professional conduct, it is imperative that both master's and doctoral students receive extensive ethics education and, optimally, be required to participate in an ethics course with no discernible distinctions between levels of content or expected mastery of course content. From this perspective, one course could serve students at both levels.

Infusion

Engels (1981a, 1981b) saw conscious formal infusion of ethics into each course by each faculty member and supervisor as necessary for students to recognize the pervasive status of ethical issues in all aspects of counseling instead of seeing ethics as separate from the overall counseling process. With one exception (Welfel & Lipsitz, 1983) in the literature we examined, those few who addressed infusion tended to focus on it as isolated to supervision or as a form of abdicating ethical education responsibilities, yielding little concentrated attention to ethics (Eberlein, 1987; Fine & Ulrich, 1988; Handelsman, 1986a, 1986b).

Some external standards (e.g., CACREP, 1988) do not mandate a separate course. Hence, although the mandate to include ethics is clear, how counselor educators will facilitate that competence is not clear. Given the pervasive nature of ethics in all aspects of counseling, conscious overt infusion seems essential, with a concomitant need to seriously consider including a specific course in ethics or, minimally, dedicating a major segment of a professional orientation course to ethics.

Advocacy of a separate ethics course in addition to infusion will be reflected in the next sections of this essay. Although ethical issues and principles abound, six points of focus have been selected for inclusion in the balance of the essay.

Faculty Characteristics

Rousseve (1969) believed it important that counselor educators and supervisors be open and whole people and thus serve as professional role models. Seen in this light, it is imperative that professionals engage in ongoing self-examination regarding personal and professional values, ethics, competence, dedication, and the modeling of these characteristics, with special sensitivity to and awareness of their positions of authority and the special trust students place in faculty and supervisors. These professionals should be prepared and willing to explicate their ethical perspectives and reasoning and to be open about the assumptions on which their positions rest. It seems unrealistic to expect aspiring counselors to take the risks involved in good learning or good counseling practice if professors and supervisors are not prepared or willing to do so.

A major ethical crucible for both faculty and students rests in the supervisory relationship. Ethical issues related to supervision, especially those related to dual relationships in supervision, seem to have received little attention in the literature. Beyond the strong modeling potential of the supervisory relationship, Upchurch (1985) noted the major power and status differences between supervisor and supervisee, and Reid (1986) underscored this element of vulnerability in responding to a report of a survey on sexual intimacy between educators and students (Glaser & Thorpe, 1986). Students have the right to understand how ethical standards apply to their supervision (Upchurch; Cormier & Bernard, 1982).

Students must also become aware of the purpose of the training standards that apply to them. Issues that students and faculty should define clearly include what relationships are appropriate for faculty to maintain with students, whether faculty should serve as counselors for students, what is a conflict of interest situation, and what credit is due a student who conducts research under the direction of faculty (Glaser & Thorpe, 1986; Roberts, Murrell, Thomas, & Claxton, 1982).

Ethical Standards

To help aspiring counselors understand ethical behavior that will guide their professional lives, they need to be exposed to ethical standards developed by AACD and other professional counseling associations, to understand the relationship of ethics to established law, to examine conflicts between laws and ethics, and to explore how the differences may be resolved. How ethical codes and laws individually and jointly affect counselors, clients, and society are major topics for study (Bailey, 1980; Stude & McKelve, 1979; Talbutt, 1983).

Ethical codes serve to protect members of the profession from practices that could result in public condemnation, provide a measure of self-regulation for the profession, and provide clients some degree of protection from incompetents (Van Hoose & Paradise, 1979). However, the standards present only a rationale for ethical behavior that can be difficult to apply to specific situations. Opportunities to discuss, interpret, and apply the guidelines to practical examples through case studies must be provided to enhance students' decision-making processes. Case studies may be developed by the instructors or students, obtained from editions of *The Ethical Standards Casebook* (Callis, 1976; Callis, Pope, & DePauw, 1982; Herlihy & Golden, 1990), current textbooks (Corey, Corey, & Callanan, 1988; Keith-Spiegel & Koocher, 1985; Van Hoose & Kottler, 1985), special features in journals such as the "getting down to cases" section of the *Career Development Quarterly*, special issues of journals (Hennessey, 1980; Larrabee & Terres, 1985; Stadler, 1986), or virtually any counseling case information.

Confidentiality

Confidentiality is a central dimension of counselor-client relationships and a major ethical concern that is closely intertwined with legal issues. Review of confidentiality should cover both professional and legal perspectives. It is important to emphasize that confidentiality is a right belonging to the client rather than to the counselor, to clarify distinctions between the concepts of confidentiality (grounded in ethics) and privileged communication (grounded in law), and to study requirements for breaking confidentiality when third parties are at risk. Coverage of this topic should include review of relevant legal statutes, which are not uniform across all states (Herlihy & Sheeley, 1987). Because state statutes differ, counselors are apt to give incorrect assurances to clients that what they say during counseling will not be revealed to anyone.

Reporting abuse and the duty to warn/protect are two issues related to confidentiality that merit comprehensive coverage. All states have now enacted legislation concerning the reporting of child abuse (Vandecreek & Knapp, 1984). However, many professionals seem unaware of child-abuse reporting statutes, and many who are aware choose to ignore or break the statutes (Swoboda, Elwork, Sales, & Levine, 1978). Although child abuse receives considerable media attention, students should also know that in many states, duties to inform authorities now include instances of abuse to the handicapped and the elderly (Fitting, 1986).

Another major issue related to confidentiality involves the "duty to warn" and the "duty to protect," which have evolved from *Tarasoff v. Regents of University of California* (1976). (See Herlihy & Sheeley, 1988, and Fulero, 1988, for a summary and discussion of this landmark case and closely related cases.) The concepts of the "duty to warn/protect" hold that, in certain circumstances, therapists have some obligation to break confidentiality to notify or take "reasonable care to protect" (Fulero, p. 184) third parties who are at risk of harm from imminent client behavior. Determination of the imminent harm to third parties involves many parameters that vary with the particulars of the case as well as the specific jurisdiction (Fulero; Herlihy & Sheeley, 1988). The "duty to warn" has been incorporated in AACD's *Ethical Standards* (1988), which direct that counselors take reasonable personal action when the client poses clear and imminent danger to self or others. The "duty" also raises related ethical concerns—counselors may resist working with clients perceived as potentially dangerous, thus closing doors to those most in need of help. Another concern arises in that pointing out the limits of confidentiality at the start of counseling may interfere with establishing a trusting relationship and could discourage potential clients from pursuing counseling. Confidentiality, privilege, and record keeping all merit inclusion in ethics courses (Baird & Rupert, 1987; Fulero & Wilbert, 1988; Handelsman & Galvin, 1988; and Jagim et al., 1978).

Legal Issues

As students start to apply ethical standards to practice, they become aware of conflicts between ethical standards and legal statutes. Knowledge of and strict compliance with a professional ethical standard offers no certainty of freedom from legal difficulties (Mappes, Robb, & Engels, 1985).

Courses in ethics need to attend to some major legal concepts and the interaction of ethical standards and legal principles as they affect counselors. Particularly germane are topics of professional disclosure, informed consent, and contracts (Gill, 1982; Hare-Mustin, Marcecek, Kaplan, & Liss-Levenson, 1979), confidentiality and privilege (Hopkins & Anderson, 1985; Knapp & Vandecreek, 1983; Schultz, 1982; Vandecreek & Knapp, 1984; Herlihy & Sheeley, 1987), duty to warn (Gehring, 1982; Fulero, 1988; Herlihy & Sheeley, 1988; Kermani & Drob, 1987; Snider, 1985), civil and criminal liability (Hendrickson, 1982; Herlihy & Sheeley, 1988; Hopkins & Anderson, 1985; Lovett, 1980a, 1980b; Snider, 1985; Wright, 1981), the minor client (Chaney, 1985; Clark & Bingham, 1984; Klenowski, 1983; Long, 1981; Zingaro, 1983), and the suicidal client (Fujimura, Weis, & Cochran, 1985; Hipple & Cimbolic, 1979; Ray & Johnson, 1983; Schultz, 1982). Court testimony (Dorn, 1984; Edenfield, 1985; Howe, 1980) and use of psychotherapeutic drugs (Ponterotto, 1985; Walker, 1986) are also important issues for the counselor in training.

In teaching an ethics course, some attention should be given to basic legal underpinnings. Five considerations seem practical and crucial. First and foremost, it is a legal maxim that ignorance is no excuse before the law. Therefore, it is vital to instill in students an inquisitive and assertive attitude toward discovering what federal and state regulations apply to the location in which they counsel. Although professional ignorance has served as an adequate legal defense in the past (e.g., *Bogust v. Iverson*, 1960), Van Hoose and Kottler (1985) noted that it is doubtful that ignorance would be tolerated in the litigious climate of our current culture.

Second, aspiring counselors need a "legal mentality." That is, they must comprehend that the epistemological foundations of law give a perspective on reality and human behavior that tends to be quite different from the focus of the mental health disciplines. The law holds reasoned, precedent-based, due process as appropriate procedure. In legal thinking, fairness is considered to inhere in stable and uniform procedures that afford all individuals equality under the law. The philosophy of law purports that for every difference or wrong, there is a remedy (e.g., imprisonment, compensation). When questions arise over differences or equality, the law presumes that the adversarial process ensures that the truth will win out. The explicit form this takes is for one side to defeat the other. Furthermore, the law adopts the position that each side acting out of self-interest will do the best possible job of elucidating different facets of the case from which the court will extract and establish a fair compromise for both sides. Criteria exist for legal proof (e.g., reasonable doubt, preponderance of evidence), and these criteria commonly differ from those used in counseling and social science research (e.g., statistical probability). Thus, philosophical differences between legal proof and scientific validity may be meaningful.

Students also need clarity about conflicts between ethics and law. Any counseling issue can be conceptualized along two dimensions of lawfulness and professional appropriateness as depicted in the following figure:

	Professional Appropriateness	
Lawfulness	A Ethical/Legal	B Unethical/Legal
	C Ethical/ Illegal	D Unethical/ Illegal

In our experience, aspiring counselors feel a sense of certitude and have greater consensus about behaviors that fall in the categories of legal-ethical (A) or illegal-unethical (D). However, behaviors classified in the illegal-ethical (C) or legal-unethical (B) quadrants arouse considerable anxiety. These latter two categories present opportunities for misjudgment and poor practice when counselors fail to appreciate distinctions between the lawful and ethical dimensions.

To illustrate, consider sexual issues in counseling. A client may present a sexual problem (e.g, impotence), which is ethical and legal (quadrant A) for the counselor to discuss with the client. If, during the course of treatment, a counselor engages in sexual relations with a married client, the counselor would be violating not only AACD's ethical standards but in some jurisdictions would also be breaking the law (quadrant D). An ethical-illegal dilemma may arise when a counselor feels that sufficient reason exists to advise and assist a young teenager in obtaining birth control (quadrant C). Finally a perfectly legal but possibly unethical situation (quadrant B) arises when a counselor initiates a sexual relationship with a previous client after termination of counseling. The "lawfulness-professional appropriateness" schema used with examples often helps students clarify legal and ethical issues and typically generates considerable debate.

Because ethics and law are intertwined in so many counseling issues, a fourth course component that seems worth including is development of rudimentary skill in the use of legal materials. Researching and referencing legal literature and court cases can give students positive experience and knowledge in reviewing and summarizing court decisions and legal conceptions of related professional issues in law journals. Typically, legal reporters give sufficient details about case particulars so that students' interest in professional-lawful issues is enhanced. As a teaching tool, the reports can be rich sources of case examples to use in class discussions. Court reports and many law journals are available in university or public libraries or in local county law libraries.

A final component is to have an attorney speak to the class. After attending to the philosophy of law, students are in a better position to formulate questions about the legal aspects of counseling matters. Opportunity to hear how attorneys think and conceptualize the same issues that concern counselors can enlighten students and frequently leads to spirited debate. It is one matter to understand that the law has differing perspectives on mental health issues but quite another to comprehend and experience others' perspectives firsthand.

Accreditation, Credentialing, and Professional Organizations

Students' knowledge about the organization and structure of their professional associations can be vital in establishing a career identity and socialization into their profession. Examining by-laws and governing structures can help students understand how, for example, AACD arrives at positions on issues and how, as concerned individual professionals, counselors can influence positions and directions their association takes. One function of a professional organization is to establish ethical standards and mechanisms for handling complaints about members. Students need to know the rationale for such mechanisms (e.g., education and self-policing to protect the profession from government control), procedures for making complaints, and degrees of ethical sanctions (Levenson, 1986).

Students also need to be familiar with certification and licensure requirements. At the beginning of the course, students can be encouraged to contact the relevant board(s) in the state(s) where they eventually intend to work and request applications for certification/licensure. This provides students with direct knowledge about requirements, information, and the documentation they will need to complete applications later. Contact with the National Board for Certified Counselors can achieve similar ends.

Although trainees may view state and professional regulations as restrictions and impediments to achieving their altruistic goals, they need to be aware that state and other credentialing bodies have a vested interest in and are legally charged with protecting the public by certifying that the credentialed professional possesses a minimal level of competence. State regulatory bodies often rely on professional associations to identify what constitutes the minimal level of competence.

Self-Awareness and Ethical Decision Making

Value-influenced decisions affect both specific and general aims of counseling (Bergin, 1985; Stein, 1985; Weiner & Boss, 1985), and each counselor should understand the explicit values that guide professional decisions. Mann and Kreyche (1966) noted that one's personal moral values and moral decision making are at the very heart of ethics, and those values provide the basis for evaluating right and wrong, with dominant concern for what one *should* do. Although codes of ethics can provide some useful directions, only the individual can make ethical choices (Van Hoose & Paradise, 1979). A major implication of this attention to personal values is that a counselor must continuously work on a clear knowledge of self, especially of personal values and how those values relate to professional issues and to clients and clients' rights to choice. Intensive self-assessment and faithfulness to personal, societal, and professional ethical standards can strengthen counselor competence and confidence in making ethical decisions.

It seems essential that counselors in preparation continuously strive for self-awareness and self-understanding, with full awareness of personal assumptions, biases, strengths, and limitations as an essential first step in the preparation process. We have found that a required self-study in written or media form can

119

be very effective, albeit with minimal focus on grades and maximal focus on student insights regarding personal and professional development in the past, present, and future. Faculty modeling of self-awareness and empathy toward student introspection and growth also could be facilitative for student development in this area. Counselors may rely upon personal utilitarian ethical principles that attempt the greatest possible balance of good consequences or the least possible balance of bad consequences in the world as a whole. Because of this, counselors ascribe to many differing values that may lead to more than one justifiable course of action when confronted with a situation not directly addressed by ethical codes or legal statutes.

Van Hoose and Paradise believe that the underlying reasoning for counselor judgments may be attributed to five qualitatively different ethical orientations, and they developed the Ethical Judgment Scale (1979). They contended that use of the scale to explore one's rationale for ethical judgments is a first step in synthesizing a personal ethical system. Van Hoose and Kottler (1985) listed additional questions that can be useful in understanding one's moral rules. Kibler and Van Hoose (1981) warned, however, that an awareness that the individual's ethical decisions are along the lower or middle continuum of moral development will not ensure a positive morality. "Individuals who are seldom analytical in their thinking are not inclined to work through their personal style of ethical choice" (p. 222). They urged that training programs put a major emphasis on the development of moral theory so that counselors can learn to personally weigh their moral decisions rather than depend on external mandates.

Van Hoose and Paradise's (1979) model for ethical decision making includes: (a) identification of the problem or dilemma, (b) identification of any rules or guiding principles that exist to help solve the dilemma, (c) generation of possible and probable courses of action, (d) consideration of potential consequences for each course of action, and (e) election of the best course of action. Eberlein (1987) noted that, ironically, most problem-solving and decision-making models omit a fundamental step that the Canadian Psychological Association included in its 1986 ethical code, namely, assuming responsibility for the consequences of one's chosen behavior. It is imperative in mature decision making that one be aware of and accept responsibility for the obligation or possibility of choice. Moreover, acceptance of responsibility for consequences of choice needs to both precede and follow choice (accepting responsibility for *possible* consequences as well as actual consequences). Van Hoose and Paradise offered case summaries of ethical dilemmas to work through. Working through a hierarchy of dilemmas and determining a plan of action can provide the opportunity to systematically assess the individual's decision-making processes and develop an awareness of one's style of dealing with moral issues.

Expanding on the centrality of personal moral and ethical values in ethical choices, Engels (1981a) and Kelly (1972) discussed a concept of maximal ethics that holds that consensus ethical standards constitute the least one must do, and maximal ethics requires the counselor to consider the most one can ethically do for maximal client benefit. This is essentially a form of client advocacy. Other writers (Eberlein, 1987; Tennyson & Strom, 1986; Van Hoose & Paradise, 1979;

Welfel & Lipsitz, 1983) discussed related ideas for simultaneously complying with and transcending published standards.

Related Issues

Admission criteria and procedures, assessment, client values, counseling theories, group counseling, involuntary clients, normality-abnormality, para-professionals, referral, research, setting-specific standards and policies, technology, and many other issues could be addressed in an ethics course (Engels, Caulum, & Sampson, 1984; Goodyear & Stinnett, 1984; Sampson & Pyle, 1983).

Space limitations require merely listing general issues that merit attention. (We reiterate our suggestion that instructors consider topics germane to their particular region.) Our suggestions include coverage of the importance of net-working with other mental health providers in the community to become aware of resources that may benefit one's clients. Related to this, counselors should be familiar with the local mental health code. Counselors frequently need to refer to state agencies. If clients cannot afford needed help from the private sector, or in the case of emergency situations, it becomes crucial to know whom to contact and how to obtain services from the public sector.

In this same vein, counselors need to establish good working liaisons with appropriate mental health and legal authorities and be able to obtain help with potential and probable ethical and legal issues *before* crises arise. Many counselors work with children in school settings. Understanding issues related to counseling minors, confidentiality of school records, testing, and educational rights of the handicapped is imperative for these settings (Talbutt, 1983). Because of the increasing complexity of ethical and legal issues, obtaining informed consent from clients both for treatment and research purposes has grown in importance. Students need to comply with institutional committees charged with overseeing human subjects in research and be exposed to methods of obtaining client consent for therapeutic interventions (e.g., Handelsman & Galvin, 1988). The pamphlet prepared by the National Board for Certified Counselors (1987) presents an active way to promote clients' awareness of their rights and responsibilities. Because many counselors will work with couples, families, and groups, ethical issues involved in these modes of delivering services merit discussion. With burgeoning numbers of cultures and subcultures in the United States, counselors must become better versed in ethical issues related to cultural diversity and socioeconomic variables (Corey, Corey, & Callanan, 1988; Ibrahim & Arredondo, 1986).

Summary, Conclusions, and Implications

Ethical behavior evolves from a matrix of experience, good judgment, personal maturity, awareness of values, counseling skill, and knowledge about principles and codes. We believe that ethics education must be ongoing and be infused in every aspect of the counselor preparation program. However, inclusion of a didactic course in ethics and professional issues has merit both for providing a focal point for pulling together threads from many diverse aspects of training and for presenting aggregate information in a systematic and formal way. Such a course should not merely examine philosophical underpinnings but should also hone appreciation for ethical conflict and foster competence for ethical decision making.

A specific course in the curriculum in combination with planned integration of ethics into every part of the program and curriculum can be an excellent means to students' ethical maturation. We suggest providing such a course toward the end of the formal program when students have a broader base of knowledge, skill, and experience to which they can relate more abstract ethical principles. Without such an experiential base, beginning students might have difficulty making and understanding necessary distinctions (e.g., between ethical and legal concepts).

Despite all the knowledge of ethical principles and legal obligations that educators and supervisors communicate to students, in the face-to-face counseling situation counselors must grapple with their own values. Counselors in training need to be made aware that no escape is possible from this struggle. In reality, counselors would limit their effectiveness if they were to be merely zealous and legalistic in following ethical and legal requirements. Codes and procedures for practice point the way and attempt to ensure that counselors adhere to the highest standards, but those in training need to know that exceptions occur in everyday practice, that exceptions may be warranted, and that counseling in everyday life is never completely without risk of acting unethically or unlawfully. However, aspiring counselors need to be aware that although extenuating circumstances may require violating one ethical guideline for the sake of another, in a final case adjudication a counselor's behavior will be externally measured against professional codes and legal statutes and internally evaluated in the counselor's personal and professional conscience.

References

Abeles, N. (1980). Teaching ethical principles by means of value confrontations. *Psychotherapy: Theory, Research and Practice, 17*, 384–391.

Allen, V.B. (1986). A historical perspective of the AACD Ethics Committee. *Journal of Counseling and Development, 64*, 293.

American Association for Counseling and Development. (1988). *Ethical standards.* Alexandria, VA: Author.

American Psychological Association. (1988). Trends in ethics cases, common pitfalls and published resources. *American Psychologist, 43*, 564–572.

American Psychological Association. Ethics Committee. (1987). Report of the Ethics Committee: 1986. *American Psychologist, 42*, 730–734.

Bailey, J.A. (1980). School counselors: Test your ethics. *The School Counselor, 27*, 285–293.

Baird, K.A., & Rupert, P.A. (1987). Clinical management of confidentiality: A survey of psychologists in seven states. *Professional Psychology: Research and Practice, 18*, 347–352.

Beck, C.E. (Ed.). (1971). *Philosophical guidelines for counseling.* Dubuque: W.C. Brown.

Bergin, A. (1985). Proposed values for guiding and evaluating counseling and psychotherapy. *Counseling and Values, 20*, 99–116.

Bogust v. Iverson, 10 Wisc. 2d 129, 102 N.W.2d 228 (1960).

Bongar, B. (1988). Clinicians, microcomputers, and confidentiality. *Professional Psychology: Research and Practice, 19*, 286–289.

Boyd, R.E., Tennyson, W.W., & Erikson, R. (1973). Counselor and client confidentiality. *Counselor Education and Supervision, 12*, 278–288.

Boyd, R.E., Tennyson, W.W., & Erikson, R. (1974). Changes in counselor disclosure of data from 1962 to 1970. *Measurement and Evaluation in Guidance, 7*, 32–38.

Callis, R. (Ed.). (1976). *Ethical standards casebook.* (2nd ed.). Washington, DC: American Personnel and Guidance Association.

Callis, R., Pope, S.K., & DePauw, M.E. (1982). *APGA ethical standards casebook.* (3rd ed). Falls Church, VA: American Personnel and Guidance Association.

Chaney, S. (1985). Reporting child abuse—the legal implications. *Texas Psychologist, 37*, 10–12.

Clark, A., & Bingham, J. (1984, August). The play technique: Diagnosing the sexually abused child. Fort Worth, TX: *Tarrant County Physician*, pp. 54–57.

Corey, G., Corey, M.S., & Callanan, P. (1988). *Issues and ethics in the helping professions.* (3d. ed.). Pacific Grove, CA: Brooks/Cole.

Cormier, L, & Bernard, J. (1982). Ethical and legal responsibilities of clinical supervisors. *Personnel and Guidance Journal, 60*, 486–491.

Council for the Accreditation of Counseling and Related Educational Programs. (1988). *Accreditation procedures manual and application.* Alexandria, VA: Author.

Dorn, F. (1984). The counselor goes to court. *Journal of Counseling and Development, 63*, 119–120.

Eberlein, L. (1987). Introducing ethics to beginning psychologists: A problem-solving approach. *Professional Psychology: Research and Practice, 18*, 353–359.

Edenfield, W. (1985). Courtroom common sense for the mental health expert. In D.L. Avila & A.W. Combs (Eds.), *Perspectives on helping relationships and the helping professions* (pp. 114–134). Boston: Allyn & Bacon.

Engels, D.W. (1981a). Maximal ethics in counselor education. *Counseling and Values, 26*, 48–54.

Engels, D.W. (1981b). Timely and timeless ethical issues and considerations in counselor education. In M. Altekruse, J. Eddy, & G. Pitts (Eds.), *Counseling practicum: Developing counselors* (pp. 118–136). Carbondale: Southern Illinois University Press.

Engels, D.W., Caulum, D., & Sampson, D.E. (1984). Computers in counselor education: An ethical perspective. *Counseling and Supervision, 24*, 193–203.

Fine, M.A., & Ulrich, L.P. (1988). Integrating psychology and philosophy in teaching a graduate course in ethics. *Professional Psychology: Research and Practice, 19*, 542–546.

Fitting, M.D. (1986). Ethical dilemmas in counseling elderly adults. *Journal of Counseling and Development, 64*, 325–327.

Fujimura, L., Weis, D., & Cochran, J. (1985). Suicide: Dynamics and implications for counseling. *Journal of Counseling and Development, 63*, 612–615.

Fulero, S.M. (1988). Tarasoff: 10 years later. *Professional Psychology: Research and Practice, 19*, 184–190.

Fulero, S.M., & Wilbert, J.R. (1988). Record-keeping practices of clinical and counseling psychologists: A survey of practitioners. *Professional Psychology: Research and Practice, 19*, 638–660.

Gehring, D. (1982). The counselor's "duty to warn." *Personnel and Guidance Journal, 61*, 208–212.

Gill, S. (1982). Professional disclosure and consumer protection in counseling. *Personnel and Guidance Journal, 60*, 443–446.

Glaser, R.D., & Thorpe, J.S. (1986). Unethical intimacy: A survey of sexual contact and advances between psychology educators and female graduate students. *American Psychologist, 41*, 43–51.

Golden, L., & O'Malley, P. (1979). Unethical practice as perceived by mental health professionals. *Counseling and Values, 23*, 194–197.

Golightly, C. (1971). A philosopher's view of values and ethics. *Personnel and Guidance Journal, 50*, 289–294.

Goodyear, R.K., & Stinnett, R.E. (1984). Current and emerging ethical issues for counseling psychology. *The Counseling Psychologist, 12*(3), 87–98.

Handelsman, M.M. (1986a). Ethics training at the master's level: A national survey. *Professional Psychology: Research and Practice, 17*, 24–26.

Handelsman, M.M. (1986b). Problems with ethics training by "osmosis." *Professional Psychology: Research and Practice, 17*, 371–372.

Handelsman, M.M., & Galvin, M.D. (1988). Facilitating informed consent for outpatient psychotherapy: A suggested written format. *Professional Psychology: Research and Practice, 19*, 223–225.

Hare-Mustin, R., Marcecek, J., Kaplan, A., & Liss-Levenson, N. (1979). Rights of clients, responsibilities of therapists. *American Psychologist, 34*, 3–16.

Hartz, J. (1973). *A cross-historical comparison of ten year follow-up studies of talented young people.* Unpublished dissertation, Madison: University of Wisconsin-Madison.

Hendrickson, R. (1982). Counselor liability: Does the risk require insurance coverage? *Personnel and Guidance Journal, 61*, 205–207.

Hennessy, T.L. (Ed.). (1980). Special issue: Values and the counselor. *Personnel and Guidance Journal, 58*, 557–639.

Herlihy, B., & Golden, L. (1990). *AACD ethical standards casebook.* (4th ed.). Alexandria, VA: American Association for Counseling and Development.

Herlihy, B., & Sheeley, V. (1987). Privileged communication in selected helping professions: A comparison among statutes. *Journal of Counseling and Development, 65*, 479–483.

Herlihy, B., & Sheeley, V. (1988). Counselor liability and the duty to warn: Selected cases, statutory trends, and implications for practice. *Counselor Education and Supervision, 27*, 203–215.

Herr, E.L., & Cramer, S.H. (1988). *Career guidance and counseling through the lifespan.* (3d. ed.). Boston: Scott Foresman.

Hipple, J., & Cimbolic, P. (1979). *The counselor and suicidal crisis.* Springfield, IL: Charles C Thomas.

Hopkins, B., & Anderson, B. (1985). *The counselor and the law.* Alexandria, VA: AACD Press.

Howe, D. (1980). Court testimony in child custody suits. *Texas Psychologist, 32*, 8.

Holroyd, J., & Brodsky, A. (1977). Psychologists' attitudes and practices regarding erotic and nonerotic physical contact with patients. *American Psychologist, 32*, 843–849.

Ibrahim, F.A., & Arredondo, P.M. (1986). Ethical standards for cross-cultural counseling: Counselor preparation, practice, assessment and research. *Journal of Counseling and Development, 64*, 349–352.

Jagim, R.D., Wittman, W.D., & Noll, J.O. (1978). Mental health professionals' attitudes toward confidentiality, privilege, and third-party disclosure. *Professional Psychology, 7*, 459–466.

Keith-Spiegel, P., & Koocher, G.P. (1985). *Ethics in psychology: Professional standards and cases.* New York: Random House.

Kelly, E. (1972). The ethics of creative growth. *Personnel and Guidance Journal, 51*, 171–176.

Kermani, E., & Drob, S. (1987). Tarasoff decision: A decade later dilemma still faces psychotherapists. *American Journal of Psychotherapy, 41*, 271–285.

Kibler, R., & Van Hoose, W. (1981). Ethics in counseling: Bridging the gap from theory to practice. *Counseling and Values, 25*, 219–226.

Kitchener, K.S. (1986). Teaching applied ethics in counselor education: An integration of psychological processes and philosophical analysis. *Journal of Counseling and Development, 64*, 306–311.

Klenowski, J. (1983). Adolescents' rights of access to counseling. *Personnel and Guidance Journal, 61*, 365–367.

Knapp, S., & Vandecreek, L. (1983). Privileged communications and the counselor. *Personnel and Guidance Journal, 62*, 83–85.

Larrabee, M.J., & Terres, L.K. (Eds.). (1985). Special focus on ethical and legal issues. *Elementary School Guidance and Counseling, 19*, 170–216.

Levenson, J.L. (1986). When a colleague practices unethically: Guidelines for intervention. *Journal of Counseling and Development, 64*, 315–317.

Long, T. (1981). Ethical issues in counseling children. *Counseling and Values, 26*, 243–250.

Long, T., & Impellitteri, J. (Eds.). (1971). Special issue: Ethical practice: Preserving human dignity. *Personnel and Guidance Journal, 50*, 245–330.

Lovett, T. (1980a). Exploring potential counselor liability in civil, criminal actions: Personal, professional protection. *ASCA Newsletter*, February, pp. 3–4.

Lovett, T. (1980b). Exploring potential counselor liability in civil, criminal actions: Criminal law as it relates to counselor conduct. *ASCA Newsletter*, May, pp. 3–4.

Mann, J., & Kreyche, G. (1966). *Reflections on man: Readings in philosophical psychology from classical philosophy to existentialism*. New York: Harcourt, Brace & World.

Mappes, D., Robb, G., & Engels, D. (1985). Conflicts betwen ethics and law in counseling and psychotherapy. *Journal of Counseling and Development, 64*, 246–252.

National Board for Certified Counselors. (1987). *Your consumer guide to counseling services . . . Client rights and responsibilities*. Alexandria, VA: Author.

Pelsma, D.M., & Borgers, S.B. (1986). Experience-based ethics: A developmental model of learning ethical reasoning. *Journal of Counseling and Development, 64*, 314–331.

Ponterotto, J. (1985). A counselor's guide to psychopharmacology. *Journal of Counseling and Development, 64*, 109–115.

Ray, L., & Johnson, N. (1983). Adolescent suicide. *Personnel and Guidance Journal, 62*, 131–135.

Reid, P.T. (1986). Unethical intimacy: Don't blame students. *American Psychologist, 41*, 1175.

Rest, J.R. (1984). Research on moral development: Implications for training counseling psychologists. *The Counseling Psychologist, 12*(3), 19–29.

Roberts, G., Murrell, P., Thomas, R., & Claxton, C. (1982). Ethical concerns for counselor educators. *Counselor Education and Supervision, 22*, 8–14.

Rousseve, R. (1969). Counselor know thyself. *Personnel and Guidance Journal, 47*, 628–633.

Sampson, J., & Pyle, K.R. (1983). Ethical issues involved with the use of computer-assisted counseling, testing, and guidance systems. *Personnel and Guidance Journal, 61*, 283–287.

Sanborn, M.P. (1975). What about your ethics? In P. Wolleat (Ed.), *Contemporary perspectives on group work in the schools* (pp. 45–51). Madison: University of Wisconsin-Madison.

Sanders, J.R. (1979). Complaints against psychologists adjudicated informally by APA's Committee on Scientific and Professional Ethics and Conduct. *American Psychologist, 34*, 1139–1144.

Schultz, B. (1982). *Legal liability in psychotherapy*. San Francisco: Jossey-Bass.

Snider, D. (1985). The duty to warn: A potential issue of litigation for the counselor supervisor. *Counselor Education and Supervision, 25*, 66–73.

Stadler, H. (Ed.). (1986). Special issue: Professional ethics. *Journal of Counseling and Development, 64*, 291–351.

Stadler, H., & Paul, R.D. (1986). Counselor educators' preparation in ethics. *Journal of Counseling and Development, 64*, 328–330.

Stein, H. (1985). Therapist and family values in a cultural context. *Counseling and Values, 30*, 35–46.

Stude, E., & McKelve, J. (1979). Ethics and the law: Friend or foe? *Personnel and Guidance Journal, 57*, 453–456.

Super, D. (1953). APGA: Promise and performance. *Personnel and Guidance Journal, 31*, 496–499.

Swoboda, J.S., Elwork, A., Sales, B.D., & Levine, D. (1978). Knowledge of and compliance with privileged communication and child-abuse-reporting laws. *Professional Psychology, 9*, 448–457.

Talbutt, L.C. (1983). Recent court decisions: A quiz for APGA members. *Personnel and Guidance Journal, 61*, 355–357.

Tarasoff v. Regents of University of California et al. 551 P.2d 334, 13 Cal, 3d 177, 529 P.2d 553 (1974), 17 Cal 3d 425, (1976).

Tennyson, W.W., & Strom, S.M. (1986). Beyond professional standards: Developing responsibleness. *Journal of Counseling and Development, 64*, 298–302.

Tymchuck, A.J., Drapkin, R.S., Ackerman, A.B., Major, S.M., Coffman, E.W., & Baum, M.S. (1982). Ethical decision-making and psychologists' attitudes toward training in ethics. *Professional Psychology, 13*, 412–421.

Upchurch, D. (1985). Ethical standards and the supervisory process. *Counselor Education and Supervision, 25*, 90–98.

Vandecreek, L., & Knapp, S. (1984). Counselors, confidentiality, and life-endangering clients. *Counselor Education and Supervision, 24*, 51–57.

Van Hoose, W., & Kottler, J. (1985). *Ethical and legal issues in counseling and psychotherapy*. (2nd ed.). San Francisco: Jossey-Bass.

Van Hoose, W., & Paradise, L. (1979). *Ethics in counseling and psychotherapy: Perspectives in issues and decision-making*. Cranston, RI: Carroll Press.

Walker, J. (1986). Reply to Ponterotto. *Journal of Counseling and Development, 64*, 662.

Weiner, J., & Boss, P. (1985). Exploring gender bias against women: Ethics for marriage and family therapy. *Counseling and Values, 30*, 9–23.

Welfel, E.R., & Lipsitz, N.E. (1983). Wanted: A comprehensive approach to ethics research and education. *Counselor Education and Supervision, 22*, 320–332.

Wright, R. (1981). What to do until the malpractice lawyer comes: A survivor's manual. *American Psychologist, 36*, 1535–1541.

Zingaro, M. (1983). Confidentiality: To tell or not to tell. *Elementary School Guidance and Counseling, 17*, 261–267.

ETHICAL DILEMMAS IN MARKETING COUNSELING SERVICES

Margaret L. Fong and Peter A.D. Sherrard

Counselors in private practice are not only trained mental health professionals but also business persons; they have services to offer and they sell these services using marketing approaches. Until recently, professional counselors promoted business mainly by communicating to referral sources, not the public, about the availability and quality of services offered. A shift in public policy spurred by legal cases involving attorney advertising (e.g., *Bates v. State Bar of Arizona*, 1977) supports the professional's right to advertise as long as the advertisement is not false, deceptive, or misleading. This shift is based on the recognition that professional practice is a business and is entitled to use strategies such as "social marketing" that are relevant to sound business practice. Social marketing is defined by Kotler (cited in Woody, 1988) as the use of marketing approaches to increase the acceptability of a social idea, cause, or practice in target groups so as to maximize the target group response. Marketing techniques include market segmentation, consumer research, concept development, communications, facilitation, and incentives.

The availability of potent marketing tools and support for their use have changed the climate of professional practice, a change that is reflected in the revised *Ethical Standards* (American Association for Counseling and Development, 1988). The *Ethical Standards*, although not organized around the topic of social marketing specifically, address aspects of marketing in sections A, E, and F. The entire section F: Private Practice, is relevant, as are standards A.4, A.7, A.11, E.3, and E.4. These standards provide a base, a professional code, to direct counselors' behavior while engaging in activities of marketing such as advertisement of services. These specified behaviors, directly addressed in standards, are binding on AACD members and are often referred to as mandatory ethics (Corey, Corey, & Callanan, 1984). These standards are likely to be weighted heavily in any regulatory or legal proceeding even for practitioners who choose not to belong to AACD (Woody, 1988).

Frequently, similar standards have been adopted by state licensure boards, and thus become *legally* binding on professional counselors. Each state, in exercising its

Margaret L. Fong, PhD, is Associate Professor and Peter A.D. Sherrard, EdD, is Assistant Professor in the Counselor Education Department, University of Florida.

authority in disciplining licensees, attempts to balance the individual's right to free speech (i.e., advertising) against the public interest. For example, the Florida Mental Health Counseling Act (1987) prescribes discipline for (a) false, deceptive, or misleading advertising that beneficial results from any treatment will be guaranteed, (b) paying a kickback, rebate, or other remuneration for receiving a client or referring a client, (c) making misleading or deceptive representations of the practice of mental health counseling, and (d) soliciting clients personally or through an agent by the use of fraud, intimidation, or undue influence.

To what extent do counselors engaged in the marketing of counseling services violate mandatory ethics? After a review of the ethics literature, Welfel and Lipsitz (1983) concluded that the figure of 5% represents a fair estimate of the number of practitioners who seem substantially insensitive to any of the ethical dimensions of counseling. Herlihy, Healy, Cook, and Hudson (1987) reported a survey of the type and frequency of complaints to the licensure boards of the seven states that at the time of their study had established professional counselor licensure long enough to have data on violations. Directly related to the standards that address marketing, inaccurate representation of title or credentials was the most commonly reported type of claim. Another frequent complaint was practicing beyond professional competence or scope of license. Of particular note is that these violations were reported but none were reported for those mandatory ethical and legal concerns frequently discussed in counselor education programs and the journals, such as the breach of confidentiality and failure to report child abuse. It could be concluded that counselors do not widely understand or use the ethical and legal standards that guide the use of marketing strategies when they make decisions in everyday attempts to persuade people to buy counseling services.

The exercise of professional judgment today involves clinical, ethical, legal, and entrepreneurial acumen. Woody (1988) emphasized these interrelated spheres of judgment in asserting that a practitioner who recognizes the forces at work in today's mental health environment should have a "firm allegiance to professional ethics, realize that ethics are superseded by governmental regulation, and accept the fact that survival in the business world requires a contemporary strategy for service delivery" (p. 40).

The complex interplay of these spheres of judgment may partially explain why counselors have problems in being ethical when marketing counseling services. The AACD *Ethical Standards* are only a part of the basis for explicating professional responsibility. In fact most scholars of ethical behavior would argue that ethical codes are not designed to serve as blueprints for solving all ethical problems the counselor confronts because of the complexities inherent in actual counseling practice (Welfel & Lipsitz, 1983). Mabe and Rollin (1986) noted that the really difficult ethical decisions occur in issues that limit the use of the ethical code, when the code is silent, or when there are conflicts between the code and values or between two possibly relevant codes. Such conflicts are called ethical dilemmas (Pope & Bajt, 1988).

A key concern or issue when considering the application of professional ethics for marketing counseling services is that the counseling profession, the legal system, and the field of business are based on different value systems.

When counselors, who are guided by the values of the human services professions that emphasize enhancing the public welfare, attempt to use marketing approaches that are grounded in an entirely different value system—that of exchange of goods—many ethical conflicts or dilemmas can and do occur (Fong-Beyette, 1988; Stadler, 1988).

What counselors must do to assess ethical issues in the marketing of counseling services is to apply not only the available standards or *mandatory ethics* but also to carefully consider the complex influences on judgment in professional practice. Tennyson and Strom (1986) called this *responsibleness*, the use of critical reflection and dialogue to make an ethical decision. In a similar vein Corey et al. (1984) described *aspirational ethics* as general sensitivity to the broad effects of each counseling interaction on the client and society. Aspirational ethics come from a moral base that society accepts as supreme or overriding in judgments about actions. Kitchener (1984) offered higher level norms called principles, which are the foundation of moral codes. These principles include autonomy, nonmaleficence, beneficence, justice, and fidelity.

The concept of autonomy includes both freedom of action (freedom to do what one wants as long as it does not interfere with similar freedoms of others) and freedom of choice (freedom to make one's own judgments). Nonmaleficence charges that above all we do no harm; in fact "all other things being equal, not harming others is generally a stronger ethical obligation than benefitting them" (Kitchener, 1984, p. 47). Beneficence urges that we contribute to the health and welfare of those served; for example, standard E.4 of the *Ethical Standards* states that client adaptability and growth toward self-direction are encouraged and cultivated. Justice means fairness and suggests that persons have the right to be treated equally unless an inequality is relevant to the issue in question. Finally, fidelity implies faithfulness, promise keeping, and loyalty; in this case, counselors are faithful to their clients.

Whereas the ethical codes of professional associations emphasize the responsibility of the professional *for* the client, the introduction of business values adds issues of *mutual* responsibility. In any business such as a counseling practice the integrity of these principles rests in a mutually reciprocal relationship between service provider (counselor) and consumer. Rubright and MacDonald (1981) rooted this doctrine in exchange theory and asserted a value-for-value exchange as fundamental to a business contract. Client rights imply professional obligations and professional rights (e.g., fee for service) imply client obligations. Thus, the higher level moral guides apply to both counselor and client; for example, the principle of autonomy refers to both parties, and either party has cause for complaint when autonomy is violated, such as when clients do not receive promised services or when counselors do not receive the agreed-upon fee for services provided.

Specific Ethical Dilemmas

Having established a framework for dialogue on ethical dilemmas when marketing counseling, we will discuss in detail four areas of particular concern. These are dilemmas that can occur when using standard marketing approaches for (1) creating a product, (2) positioning in the marketplace, (3) promoting counseling services, and (4) obtaining payment for services.

Creating a Product

When generating a good marketing plan, careful consideration is given to the product to be offered, in this case to the counseling services the counselor will offer. Traditional marketing practice begins with some form of marketing research to determine the potential users of a service and what particular services they desire (Wittman, 1988). In contrast, ethical standards direct counselors to offer only those counseling services that they have the training and experience to offer. If the counselor's areas of expertise match the needs revealed by market research, no dilemma occurs as the two value orientations are not in conflict. For example, however, what if there is a great need in the community for disability evaluations and the counselor, with only a general testing course and no supervised experience in assessment, realizes that if he or she does not move quickly to take the contracts someone else will? Marketing principles would lead the counselor to take the risk and accept the contract to enhance market growth, whereas counseling ethics would lead the counselor to reject or at least postpone the offer. This is a true dilemma with potential long-term economic implications for the counselor and long-term effects on the clients who might end up poorly served by someone even less competent.

The *Ethical Standards* provide clear direction here. Counselors cannot agree to provide or advertise the provision of services beyond their scope of training. However, there is nothing to prevent the counselor, once aware of a market need, from seeking specialized courses and supervised training to become fully qualified to offer that counseling service. Counselors must exercise professional judgment as to when they have achieved competence by balancing judgments of expertise with the principles of nonmaleficence and beneficence. An example of poor judgment is evidenced by a psychologist who advertised himself as an expert in neuropsychology on the basis of attending two 1-day workshops and independent reading in neuropsychology. He was censured by the Ethics Committee of the American Psychological Association and mandated to cease and desist advertising as a neuropsychologist and engaging in the practice of neuropsychology (American Psychological Association, 1987).

From a purely marketing stance, when marketing research indicates a need for a counseling service, considerations of product effectiveness, potential harm, and the abilities of the producer (counselor) are a part of this research only in terms of how they may affect the sale of the product if known by the consumer. By contrast the ethical principle of nonmaleficence can be interpreted as requiring counselors to ignore public demand for counseling services or techniques that are not supported by empirical research. For example, a counselor who operates a smoking cessation clinic adds the aversive procedure of rapid smoking to the treatment package because several local physicians who make frequent referrals request it. If the counselor has expertise in smoking cessation and habit change, how can the counselor justify using a dramatic and demonstrably hazardous behavioral technique?

A less clearly resolved dilemma related to marketing a product is the request on one hand by an agency or family for the counselor to disguise the intent of counseling services, and the requirement by the *Ethical Standards* to respect the need of the client for informed consent (freedom of choice). For example, the administrative officer of a corporation believes that his employees are under much stress. However, he refuses to have the programs the counselor will offer called stress management because he believes that employees will see their participation as an admission of weakness and inability to handle the job. How can these employees/clients freely choose when they are not fully aware of the intent of the counseling services and their supervisor's judgment? What is to be gained if they attend and receive disguised stress management? Will the counselor lose the contract if he or she insists on full disclosure? Will the counselor without disclosure lose the trust of the workshop recipients? Will the recipients lose potential benefit? What are the considerations of harm versus benefit, the promotion of autonomy and fidelity, and the implementation of justice? Counselors can resolve these dilemmas through critical reflection on these and other questions and through dialogue with professional peers. Tennyson and Strom (1986) recommended that counselors in private practice regularly engage in such problem-posing dialogue with other professionals.

Positioning in the Marketplace

Positioning starts with a product, in this case a particular counseling service. Positioning is not what you do to a product but rather what you do to the mind of the prospective consumer (Ries & Trout, 1986). By asking how counseling is positioned in the consumer's mind, clues can be gathered for developing an effective marketing plan. "The basic approach of positioning is not to create something new and different, but to manipulate what's already up there in the mind, to retie the connections that already exist" (Ries & Trout, p.5).

To effectively position counseling services requires that distinctions be drawn as to what is unique about counseling and what is unique about the specific counseling services being offered. When using a marketing perspective, the counselor considers only what can be stated in 25 words or less that is "(1) roughly right, (2) enduring, (3) succinct, (4) memorable, (5) believable, and (6) energizing to all" (Peters, 1987, p. 142). But can the counselor be "roughly right" and accurate at the same time when describing professional competence? By concentrating on the perceptions of the prospect (client) rather than the reality of the product (counseling service) the counselor may create distinctions that have no substance and thus be unethical.

Consider the distinctions that some mental health professionals make to suggest differences in the practice of counseling. In our local Yellow Pages can be found advertisements for marriage counseling and divorce counseling, for transitions counseling and growth counseling, for child counseling and child behavior counseling, for relationship mediation and divorce mediation, and many more. Do real distinctions exist between these pairs of counseling services, as required by ethical standards that prohibit any deception and distortion about the actual service being offered or the credentials of the counselor? Henry, Sims, and Spray (1975) asserted that distinctions among the mental health professions in the practice of individual psychotherapy are illusory, that the substantive differences are in the other activities besides psychotherapy. To hint otherwise to gain a positioning edge could be seen as a betrayal of the ethical injunction concerning accurate representation.

A further example is the frequent practice of professional counselors who offer a multitude of different services to corner a percentage of the overall community market and then develop actual expertise in these services as the demand for services builds; for example, child custody evaluations. Ethical conscience is thus compromised by entrepreneurial intiative and the market creates the expertise. The obligation to seek specialized training and supervision is fulfilled as the market creates the need for that advertised service. The ethical tests of nonmaleficence and beneficence should be carefully applied to such cases.

Promotion of Services

Advertising and public relations are the promotion or communication part of a marketing plan. From a marketing standpoint the criterion for effective promotion is the amount of the product—in this case counseling services—that is sold. Indeed, the media regularly carry accounts of unscrupulous advertisements that sell unneeded or harmful products. Ethical standards F.2, F.3, and F.4 specify what a counselor may state in an advertisement and caution that the information may not be misleading, partial, or out of context. Yet, advertising is the medium for positioning oneself in the public mind, and often a particular packaging of services and credentials appeals to the market desired. For example, two professional counselors offering "astrological counseling services" may be an embarrassment to other professional counselors, but if they have earned appropriate credentials in this "specialty" are they operating unethically or illegally? This question requires thoughtful dialogue with professional peers.

Two other promotional strategies that present ethical issues are the creation of a public fear in order to sell services and the creation of dependency in clients to encourage continual use of services. A national chain of adolescent treatment centers regularly runs television and radio ads asking if your adolescent is moody, irritable, apathetic, and reclusive and if you, the parent, realize these symptoms are not just growing pains. Your child needs help and help is available by calling the treatment center. What are the ethics of this promotional campaign? How easy is it to assess whether a teenager has problems of normal adolescence or needs immediate psychiatric treatment? Does the ad inform parents in a useful manner or does it sell services by building worry? Again, this ethical question must be settled by careful reflection and dialogue. Similarly, widely accepted business promotional practices such as routinely scheduling intermittent "follow-up" visits may give clients the impression that their counselor thinks they are unable to cope fully, thereby maintaining dependency in clients who really are coping on their own and ready to terminate. Standard E.5 clearly states that client adaptability and growth toward self-direction must be cultivated and creation of future dependency avoided.

Payment for Services

Third party reimbursement generates a complex set of issues for the professional counselor. Third party reimbursement entails a client purchasing an insurance policy to cover specific medical or psychiatric conditions. Payment is made to eligible service providers designated by the company. These providers diagnose the client using a designated system, usually the *Diagnostic and Statistical Manual of Mental Disorders* (American Psychiatric Association, 1987). Once a provider makes a diagnosis, it becomes part of the client's permanent medical record, available to anyone authorized to look at that record (Richards, 1988). By accepting third party reimbursement, providers (counselors) also agree to provide whatever documentation an insurance company deems necessary to substantiate treatment.

Beck (1988) raised critical ethical questions concerning counselors' acceptance of third party reimbursement. Does the provider's scope of practice, training, certification, and license give authority to offer services that require making diagnoses? Are providers really helping clients when they establish a psychiatric diagnosis only for the purpose of insurance reimbursement, particularly when the diagnosis given is part of the client's life-long health history? Do cooperation with and concession to the demands of the health care industry undermine investment in more comprehensive prevention and counseling services for the community? Clearly, third party reimbursement undermines both client and counselor autonomy, offers the possibility of harm to the client (balanced against the immediate good of services received), supports an unjust system (as not all clients can afford insurance), and raises questions about counselor fidelity (i.e., faithful to whom and under what circumstances). Counselors who accept third party reimbursement need to form a personal perspective on these ethical questions.

Implications for Counselors

The previous sections have included examples of the application of both mandatory ethical standards and aspirational ethics, based on critical reflection and dialogue for resolution of ethical dilemmas in marketing counseling. To further illustrate the ethical use of marketing practices this section will present a case study of marketing approaches in conflict with ethics.

The Case of the Defective Product

Counselor M, a graduate of a CACREP-approved program in community counseling, is a licensed professional counselor. As part of her graduate training she co-led a stress management group and used relaxation tapes. Counselor M becomes aware of an open bidding period for a long-term contract with a local military facility to provide stress management services on an individual and group basis for all noncommissioned officers. This contract specifies that the contractor must have advanced training and expertise in stress management. Counselor M takes out her old group notes, purchases a popular stress management guide at the local bookstore, and designs a six-session stress management group. The group activities encourage participants to be aware of their life change events, other stressors at work and home, and the potentially negative effects of stress on the body. Stress management techniques emphasize deep relaxation and controlled breathing. On her bid Counselor M notes that she is an experienced counselor with coursework and training in stress management. Counselor M wins the bid and begins the groups, assuring the local commanding officer that great reductions in personnel stress will be seen within 6 months. The self-referred individual clients receive client centered counseling and are encouraged to explore stressful feelings and experiences.

In the authors' experience this case is not unusual despite the numerous unethical marketing practices it illustrates. Major ethical concerns include using ineffective and outdated techniques (standard A.11), providing unsupportable claims of treatment outcome (standard F.2), misrepresenting qualifications (standards A.4, E.3, and F.3), and exceeding boundaries of competence (standard A.7). In addition, some might see the need to promote client self-direction (standard E.4) also violated as no needs assessment procedure is utilized and the more proactive stress management techniques available are not being provided in the group sessions. Counselor M violated these standards while attempting to win a lucrative military contract. Her good intentions, or beneficence, are countered by the threat of harm, or nonmaleficence, to the employees. However, it is quite possible for her to correct these practices. Each violation will now be discussed, highlighting potential changes.

The stress management approaches offered emphasize life change units (a weak predictive factor in stress), failing to reflect recent research on the role of cognitive and life-style factors in stress and stress resistance. Counselor M seems unaware of empirically supported methods (as required in standard A.1) or the need to explain the limitations of the methods chosen. Thus the product is defective and offered in a potentially unethical manner. This could have been avoided if Counselor M had conducted a thorough search of the professional literature prior to creating her package. When counselors are in solo practice, this regular review and self-study are crucial due to the lack of exchange of ideas with peers.

Counselor M told the commanding officer that there would be substantial improvement in 6 months. On what did she base this claim? Certainly the research on stress management does not support such claims. It is understandable that the officer wanted to know that the money spent would result in improvement, but Counselor M needed to have an honest discussion about possible outcomes and what would be reasonable measures of improvement. By making such a discussion part of the initial negotiation phase with a client, counselors can establish reasonable expectations and avoid violation of standards.

Note that Counselor M is a qualified professional counselor. However, she misrepresented her qualifications by not clearly stating her very limited experience with stress management. Then, once she obtained the contract, she was caught in providing services to individuals despite a lack of supervised training in this specialty area. She needed to refrain from bidding on such contracts until she was reasonably certain she had the necessary competencies, or to use the services of a counselor with more expertise and training. For example, part of the contract could have been a referral service rather than direct services for individual counseling, or she could have collaborated on the bid with a more experienced counselor.

It is also essential to avoid such future violations of exceeding competence. Counselor M needs to make a strong commitment to a goal-directed program of continuing education throughout her career. She also needs to become involved in some form of peer supervision (Remley, 1988) that would help her recognize similar situations and resolve the many ethical decisions related to private practice.

In fact, these two recommendations are the best methods available to avoid making unethical decisions about marketing practices. Continuing education and peer supervision provide the essential ingredients for the critical reflection and dialogue necessary for ethical responsibleness. As noted earlier, the counselor needs both awareness of the ethical standards *and* a commitment to ethical responsibleness to resolve the many ethical dilemmas of marketing.

References

American Association for Counseling and Development. (1988). *Ethical standards.* Alexandria, VA: Author.

American Psychiatric Association. (1987). *Diagnostic and statistical manual of mental disorders* (3rd ed., revised). Washington, DC: Author.

American Psychological Association. (1987). *Casebook on ethical principles of psychologists.* Washington, DC: Author.

Bates v. State Bar of Arizona, 433 U.S. 350, 1977.

Beck, E.S. (1988). Ethical questions to consider for third party reimbursement. *Private Practice News, 2,* 8–9.

Corey, G., Corey, M.S., & Callanan, P. (1984). *Issues and ethics in the helping professions* (2nd ed.). Monterey, CA: Brooks/Cole.

Florida Mental Health Counseling Act, FL Stat. 491.009, Vol. 2 (1987).

Fong-Beyette, M.L. (1988). Do counseling and marketing mix? *Counselor Education and Supervision, 27,* 315–319.

Henry, W.E., Sims, J.H., & Spray, S.L. (1975). *The fifth profession: Becoming a psychotherapist.* San Francisco: Jossey-Bass.

Herlihy, B., Healy, M., Cook, E.P., & Hudson, P. (1987). Ethical practices of licensed professional counselors: A survey of state licensing boards. *Counselor Education and Supervision, 27,* 69–76.

Kitchener, K.S. (1984). Intuition, critical evaluation and ethical principles: The foundation for ethical decisions in counseling psychology. *The Counseling Psychologist, 12,* 43–55.

Mabe, A.R., & Rollin, S.A. (1986). The role of a code of ethical standards in counseling. *Journal of Counseling and Development, 64,* 294–297.

Peters, T. (1987). *Thriving on chaos: Handbook for a management revolution.* New York: Knopf.

Pope, K.S., & Bajt, T.R. (1988). When laws and values conflict: A dilemma for psychologists. *American Psychologist, 43,* 828–829.

Remley, T.P. (1988, October). *Peer supervision.* Paper presented at the meeting of the Association for Counselor Education and Supervision, St. Louis, MO.

Richards, D.L. (1988). Third party reimbursement: Big brother is watching. *Private Practice News, 2,* 1–4.

Ries, A., & Trout, J. (1986). *Positioning: The battle for your mind*. New York: Warner.

Rubright, R., & MacDonald, D. (1981). *Marketing health and human services*. Rockville, MD: Aspen Systems.

Stadler, H.A. (1988). Marketing counseling: Caveat emptor. *Counselor Education and Supervision, 27*, 320–322.

Tennyson, W.W., & Strom, S.M. (1986). Beyond professional standards: Developing responsibleness. *Journal of Counseling and Development, 64*, 298–302.

Welfel, E.R., & Lipsitz, N.E. (1983). Wanted: A comprehensive approach to ethics research and education. *Counselor Education and Supervision, 22*, 320–332.

Wittman, P.P. (1988). Marketing counseling: What counseling can learn from other health care professions. *Counselor Education and Supervision, 27*, 308–314.

Woody, R.H. (1988). *Protecting your mental health practice: How to minimize legal and financial risk*. San Francisco: Jossey-Bass.

ETHICAL ISSUES IN MULTICULTURAL COUNSELING

Farah A. Ibrahim and Patricia Arredondo

This essay offers suggestions for expanding the *Ethical Standards* (1988) of the American Association for Counseling and Development (AACD) to more fully address needs of diverse cultural groups, including linguistic minority clients. These client groups share similarities with mainstream culture; however, they do have unique belief systems, values, assumptions, modes of coping, decision making, problem solving, and life-styles that do not reflect the values, assumptions, and modes of coping and communicating of mainstream society.

The latest revision of the AACD *Ethical Standards* was recently reviewed in the *Journal of Counseling and Development.* Although the new standards are properly credited for nine statements related to computer use and applications (Allen, Sampson, & Herlihy, 1988), and although they have incorporated some of the recommendations offered since 1978 regarding multicultural issues, we are concerned that they fall short in addressing the needs of diverse cultural groups. We laud AACD for expressing concern for client protection regarding technology issues. However, we are concerned that the needs of historically disenfranchised groups persist in being overlooked. We would like AACD to work proactively to create access to the new technology for these populations (Ibrahim, 1985).

This is a lamentable situation in light of the facts about the population of the United States: "22% are Black, Hispanic, Asian, and Native American," and that ". . . by the end of the century, half of the work force will be Black and Hispanic" (Jackson, 1988, p. 29). New immigrant minority groups are entering the United States in large numbers. According to Kellogg (1988), since 1979 the latest waves of immigrants have been from Latin America (42%) and Asia (41%). Counselors in the schools, community agencies, private practice, and industry are already meeting with these publics and are forced to "fly by the seat of their pants," providing services that may be meaningless, at a minimum, or highly injurious at a maximum.

Farah A. Ibrahim, PhD, is Associate Professor in the Department of Educational Psychology, University of Connecticut, Storrs. Patricia Arredondo, EdD, is Director of Empowerment Workshops, Brookline, Massachusetts. The authors wish to express appreciation to Martha McNulty for her support and assistance.

As the profession attempts to move forward, it is leaving behind a large percentage of the population. Position statements and research that would guide counseling professionals still lag behind good intentions (Casas, Ponterotto, & Gutierrez, 1986). Psychological research has failed to expand the cultural pluralism of psychological theories to make them relevant to culturally diverse groups (Kagehiro, Mejia, & Garcia, 1985; Ibrahim, 1989). Theories remain uninformed, yet they serve as frameworks for assessment, research, and practice. Although training programs realize the importance of understanding the needs of culturally diverse groups, they often are geared to educating professionals to provide services to an amorphous middle class, mainstream population. (Bernal & Padilla, 1982; Ibrahim & Arredondo, 1986; Ibrahim, Stadler, Arredondo, & McFadden, 1986; Wyatt & Parham, 1985).

The Problem

The preamble of the 1988 AACD *Ethical Standards* says that the "Association is an educational, scientific, and professional organization whose members are dedicated to the enhancement of the worth, dignity, potential, and uniqueness of each individual and thus to the service of society" (p. 1). However, the preamble does not address cultural factors or recognize the sociocultural nature of human behavior. Cultural factors are specifically addressed in section A: General (10); section B: Counseling Relationship (19); and section C: Measurement and Evaluation (1 & 12). However, these standards do not explain how counselors can implement the charge—there is no reference to the need for further training or education, a need that has been articulated repeatedly in the literature (Casas et al., 1986; Cayleff, 1986; Ibrahim & Arredondo, 1986; Irving, Perl, Trickett, & Watts, 1984).

Commitment to Multiculturalism

Counselors must embrace the concept of cultural pluralism. The first step for all counseling professionals, whether they consider themselves members of the mainstream culture or a minority group, is to enhance their own multiculturalism (Ibrahim & Schroeder, 1987).

A declaration of multicultural interest does not automatically enhance counselor sensitivity and effectiveness; professionals must have awareness, knowledge, and skills. This stance is especially important for individuals who are from minority or oppressed groups because membership in such groups does not magically enhance multiculturalism, nor does it ensure the awareness, knowledge, or skills required to overcome the negative effects of racism or cultural oppression.

Monoculturalism is a form of maladjustment in a pluralistic society (Szapocznik, Santisteban, Kurtines, Perez-Vidal, & Hervis, 1983); it is *unethical* for professionals to remain monocultural and practice in this society. We propose that a minimum goal for every professional should be to become biculturally effective.

A Proposed Systems Change. The centrality of cultural factors in counseling should be incorporated in every core course, rather than relegated to an overburdened survey course. We want to incorporate multicultural factors at the core of the *Ethical Standards*, rather than on the periphery.

The American Psychological Association (APA) declared counseling practice with a culturally unfamiliar group without *competence* (appropriate education and training) as unethical at the APA's 1973 Vail Conference. Both the AACD and the APA *Ethical Standards*, however, fail to define competence in the multicultural domain. The references made pertain to racial and ethnic minority groups, women, and lower social classes, as if cultural factors are their domain only. The standards make no reference to language differences. Historically, individuals and groups who are different from the mainstream have been characterized as "deprived" or "disadvantaged" (Sue, 1981; Atkinson, Morten, & Sue, 1983), and have been separated and isolated, rather than valued for the diversity and enrichment they bring to this society.

We support a culturally determined and wholistic world view that incorporates values, belief systems, life-styles, and modes of problem solving and decision making. Theoretically, and programmatically, this world view applies to all people in the universe. It is a perspective that views each individual as a unique human being with values, beliefs, and assumptions that are conditioned by the cultural context of a primary environment, with influences from secondary environments (whether a majority group or numerous minority groups), all embedded in the larger context defined by national or geographic boundaries. The concept of mental health services in a cultural context of varying sociocultural environments is now accepted by the Association for Counselor Education and Supervision (ACES) in its educational guidelines (Corey, Corey, & Callanan, 1988).

Recommendations for Expanding the Applicability of the Current Standards

The following guidelines and illustrative cases are intended to expand the current AACD standards to apply to multicultural encounters. As noted earlier, the preamble statement needs to be clarified in sociocultural terms as "enhancing the worth and dignity, potential, and uniqueness of each individual . . . " (*Ethical Standards*, AACD, 1988, p. 1). In section A: General, in the first statement in A.1, the member must be charged to improve practice, teaching, services, and research in a culturally pluralistic society.

Case Illustrating Standard A.1

A certified counselor (an Anglo-Saxon Protestant) who was educated in the 1960s, considers himself to be a liberal (concerned about social justice issues), competent, and ethical professional. However, he is being sued by a Black female client who is unemployed and very depressed. She charges that the counselor was inflicting "White, male standards of behavior and goals on her," which led to feelings of "despair and failure as she examined her job-seeking behavior in the light of these standards and assumptions." Furthermore, she charges that the counselor "chose to not understand her oppressions, feelings, and attitudes, and kept admonishing her to pull herself together . . . . " The counselor is confused by the charges and feels victimized by the client. Furthermore, he is upset because in the last 20 years he has made an effort to "grow professionally" by taking continuing education workshops on new approaches. He never took a course or workshop on multicultural counseling, however, because he believes "people are people" and that he is not biased.

Standard A.7 needs to be expanded to specifically address cultural factors. Standard A.9 should say that, in various subcultures in this society, mainstream modes of relating across genders may be perceived as sexual harassment.

In Section B: Counseling Relationship, a critical variable has been overlooked—the language of communication. Both spoken and written language are factors in the counseling relationship.

Case Illustrating Standard B.1

A Chinese immigrant woman asserted that her inability to speak English resulted in a lost opportunity for her child. Her daughter was not allowed to participate in a program that promised scholarships to students who complete high school. This was a special program targeted for inner-city first graders. Due to language differences, the English-speaking counselor could not properly explain the essential facts of the program or understand the child's mother. Because time was a factor, the counselor crossed the child's name from the list. The mother told the school principal, "My child does speak English; why should she be penalized because of me?"

In section B: Counseling Relationship, the opening statement should say that client freedom of choice has different meanings for individuals based on their cultural background and ethnicity, and this needs to be clarified with the client. Furthermore, section B.1 needs to be expanded to address cultural and social factors to truly convey respect for the client. Counseling services should be empowering to the client.

The controversy about whether universal or culture-specific approaches are most effective has overlooked a key variable: the individual client, and specifically, that client's worldview. This critical variable helps the counselor to decide what goals, processes, and strategies would be therapeutic for the client (Ibrahim, 1988). This is the mediating variable that can lead to effective interventions (Sadlak & Ibrahim, 1986; Cunningham-Warburton, 1988).

Standard B.8 says that the member must tell the client about the counseling techniques that will be used and their limitations. Sundberg (1981) noted that along with informing, the counseling professional has a responsibility to enhance communication skills of culturally diverse clients if they are to be capable of rejecting an offensive technique. This information would be particularly useful for clients who come from lineal-hierarchical social systems and do not give themselves permission to confront authority. In Standard B.10, a statement is made regarding self-disclosure without clarifying that culturally diverse clients and students may have different modes of expression, different levels of language competence, and different goals for self-disclosure. It is important that the group leader not demand the same level of self-disclosure from all individuals in a group.

Case Illustrating Standard B.2

A female group facilitator of a professional support group for men and women has had difficulty with a member's apparent unwillingness to "open up" in the group. The facilitator has gently encouraged this person to self-disclose; now the group has picked up the theme and the member is beginning to feel harassed. He has missed the last two meetings. He returns only to encounter a great deal of hostility regarding his "lack of self-disclosure." The client is of German-English extraction and has recently moved from a small community to a large city. At the session the client responds to the group by saying that he was offended by their constant demands for self-disclosure and upset with their disclosures, which seemed to be disclosure for its own sake, and finally, that he could see no connection between whining about personal disasters and professional development. Then he announces that he is leaving the group and walks out. The facilitator and the members are shocked by the response.

An expanded view of section B.12 would encourage the member to refer a prospective client when the member has no training or experience in working with the client's cultural group. Furthermore, the standards should state that most theories of counseling were developed in a specific context and may not apply to individuals who do not live within that context. Corey et al. (1988) expressed concern regarding the goal of "self-actualization" and trust in counseling relationships. The understanding of both these variables needs to be moderated by the counseling context and the counselor and client dyad. Additionally, the standards should explicitly state that people from diverse backgrounds may send and receive verbal and nonverbal messages differently (Wolfgang, 1985).

Section C: Measurement and Evaluation, recognizes sociocultural variables in C.1 and C.12. However, the counselor must first understand the client's cultural identity and worldview before any other assessment is undertaken. This can be accomplished ascertaining the client's beliefs, values, assumptions, and modes of problem solving and decision making, or by assessing the client's worldview (Ibrahim & Kahn, 1987) and then comparing the client's individual worldview to his or her primary identification group to see if that norm group can be used to make judgments about this person.

Olmedo (1981) recommended that both psychological and educational assessment should take into account the social, political, and economic realities minorities face. Furthermore, a movement away from fixed response formats and preselected vocabularies is recommended, and the use of multimethod, multilevel assessments is encouraged, including free response formats, open-ended interviews, and participant-observer techniques (Goldstein, 1981; Ibrahim, 1986; Ibrahim & Arredondo, 1986). Bilingual assessment or testing in the client's primary language is one means of providing fairness while addressing differences. However, in no way should results of translated versions of tests be interpreted as providing appropriate data. Despite translation, these tests are still based on culture-specific theories, and interpretations of their results are therefore limited.

Section D: Research and Publication, recognizes the responsibility of the researcher regarding the welfare of research subjects. Sociocultural factors are not explicitly addressed, however. The standards seem difficult to implement unless counselors have been specifically educated regarding different value structures. Otherwise, the danger exists that incorrect conclusions will be drawn from the data, as has been the case in the past (Hernandez, 1974). The standards need to consider the subject's language and sociocultural experiences, researcher bias, and how consultation from experts in the culture under study can be obtained (Caplan & Nelson, 1973; Ibrahim, 1986; Tapp, Kelman, Triandis, Wrightsman, & Coelho, 1974).

Section E: Consulting, and section F: Private Practice, should specify that members who do not have the skill to conduct counseling or consulting relationships with diverse populations should *not* undertake these relationships. Furthermore, in advertising, there should be a statement of competence (training and experience) to work with ethnic, cultural, gender, sexual preference, and social class variables (Ibrahim, 1986).

Case Illustrating Standard F.1

A psychologist advertised herself as being competent in working with women, specifically minority women. A peer familiar with her lack of training and experience confronted her and asked how she had acquired her competencies. The psychologist responded that it was from personal knowledge of being a woman and a minority group member (Ibrahim, 1986, p. 12).

As noted earlier, membership in a certain group does not guarantee that one has the awareness, knowledge, and skills to be effective with that group. As Corey et al. (1988) observed, counselors not educated in understanding their own values and assumptions about various groups will perpetuate their own tunnel vision in their clients.

With reference to standard G.1, administrators should recognize that people from different sociocultural backgrounds will have different moral-ethical assumptions (Davidson & Thomson, 1980; Ibrahim, 1986; Osgood, May, & Miron, 1975). Administrators should learn about cultural relativity in order to become more comfortable with cultural differences.

Standard G.10 makes reference to confidentiality. Confidentiality, also, should be discussed in sociocultural terms, and its meaning to the individual client should be clarified. Again, in this context, the language of communication becomes a factor.

With regard to section H: Preparation Standards, counselor education programs should respond to cultural diversity in their policies, procedures, and curricula, and recognize the cultural diversity among students, faculty, and clients. Faculty should ensure a comprehensive curriculum, with stated objectives about cultural competence for each course (Arredondo, 1983; Ibrahim & Arredondo, 1986; Ibrahim et al., 1986). Furthermore, H.5 should stress that cultural differences not be confused with "personal limitations" of the learner.

Cases Illustrating Section H

An international student from southern Asia charged that her practicum supervisor had unjustly graded her practicum work because they had not been able to agree on the issue of when to maintain and when to break eye contact with the client. Her position was that the clients, who were all inner-city Black teenagers, responded positively to her nonverbal expression.

A Black student charged that her faculty had oppressed her during her training by constantly criticizing her lack of use of "affective terms." She was able to cite research studies in support of her position that the expression of affect was a cultural variable and not a universal constant.

Standard H.9 should be expanded to include a statement regarding the role of educators' personal values and how these may influence the selection and presentation of instructional material. Standard H.10 should address the issue of the limited generalizability of current theories of counseling and psychology (Kagehiro et al., 1985).

Challenge

It is imperative in the counseling process that practitioners recognize the sociocultural nature of human behavior and the cultural context of each encounter. Kenneth Clark (1972) noted that the mental health professions cannot be immune to the forces of racism in our society, and that racism may be reflected in diagnosis, assessment, and treatment. Counselors and those who train and supervise counselors should expand upon the literal limitations of the AACD *Ethical Standards* so that they are relevant to all the clients they serve.

References

Allen, V.B., Samson, J.P., & Herlihy, B. (1988). Details of the AACD ethical standards. *Journal of Counseling and Development, 67*, 157–158.

American Association for Counseling and Development. (1988). *Ethical standards.* Alexandria, VA: Author.

Arredondo, P.M. (1983). Professional responsibility in a culturally pluralistic society. In G.R. Walz & L. Benjamin (Eds.), *Shaping counselor education programs in the next five years: An experimental prototype for the counselor of tomorrow* (pp. 91–106). Ann Arbor, MI: ERIC/CAPS.

Atkinson, D.R., Morten, G., & Sue, D.W. (1983). *Counseling American minorities.* Dubuque, IA: Brown.

Bernal, M.E., & Padilla, A.M. (1982). Status of minority curricula and training in clinical psychology. *American Psychologist, 37*, 780–787.

Caplan, N., & Nelson, S. (1973). On being useful: The nature and consequence of psychological research on social problems. *American Psychologist, 28*, 199–211.

Clark, K.B. (1972). Foreword. In A. Thomas & S. Sillen (Eds.), *Racism and psychiatry* (pp. 11–13). New York: Brunner/Mazel.

Corey, G., Corey, M.S., & Callanan, P. (1988). *Issues and ethics in the helping professions.* Pacific Grove, CA: Brooks/Cole.

Casas, J.M., Ponterotto, J.G., & Gutierrez, J.M. (1986). An ethical indictment of counseling research and training: A cross-cultural perspective. *Journal of Counseling and Development, 64*, 347–349.

Cayleff, S.E. (1986). Ethical issues in counseling: Gender, race, and culturally distinct groups. *Journal of Counseling and Development, 64*, 345–347.

Cunningham-Warburton, P. (1988). *A study of the relationship between cross-cultural training, the scale to assess world views, and the quality of care given by nurses in a psychiatric setting.* Unpublished doctoral dissertation. University of Connecticut, Storrs.

Davidson, A.R., & Thomson, E. (1980). Cross-cultural studies of attitudes and beliefs. In H.C. Triandis & R.W. Brislin (Eds.), *Handbook of cross-cultural psychology: Social psychology* (pp. 25–71). Boston: Allyn & Bacon.

Goldstein, A.P. (1981). Evaluating expectancy effects in cross-cultural counseling and psychotherapy. In A.P. Marsella & P.B. Pedersen (Eds.), *Cross-cultural counseling and psychotherapy* (pp. 85–101). New York: Pergamon.

Hernandez, D. (1974). *Mexican American challenge to a sacred cow.* Los Angeles: University of California Press.

Ibrahim, F.A. (1985). Human rights and ethical issues in the use of advanced technology. *Journal of Counseling and Development, 64*, 134–145.

Ibrahim, F.A. (1986, August). *Reflections on the cultural encapsulation of the Ethical Principles: Recommendations for revisions.* Paper presented at a roundtable, Chair P.B. Pedersen, at the 94th annual meeting of the American Psychological Association, Washington, DC.

Ibrahim, F.A. (1988). *Multicultural counseling: An existential world view perspective.* (Book chapter under review).

Ibrahim, F.A. (1989). Response to psychology in the public forum on socially sensitive research. *American Psychologist, 44*, 847–848.

Ibrahim, F.A., & Arredondo, P.M. (1986). Ethical standards for cross-cultural counseling: Counselor preparation, practice, assessment, and research. *Journal of Counseling and Development, 64*, 349–351.

Ibrahim, F.A., & Kahn, H. (1987). Assessment of world views. *Psychological Reports, 60*, 163–176.

Ibrahim, F.A., & Schroeder, D.G. (1987, October). *Effective communication with multicultural families.* Paper presented at the annual meeting of the Connecticut Association for the Education of Young Children, Storrs.

Ibrahim, F.A., Stadler, H.A., Arredondo, P.M., & McFadden, J. (1986, April). *Status of human rights issues in counselor preparation: A national survey.* Paper presented at the annual meeting of the American Association of Counseling and Development, Los Angeles, CA.

Irving, J., Perl, H., Trickett, E.J., & Watts, R. (1984). Minority curricula or a curriculum of cultural diversity? Differences that make a difference. *American Psychologist, 38*, 320–321.

Jackson, D. (December 16, 1988). In toy box America, minorities snowed over by images of White. *The Boston Globe*, p. 29.

Kagehiro, D.K., Mejia, J.A., & Garcia, J.E. (1985). Value of cultural pluralism to the generalizability of psychological theories: A reexamination. *Professional Psychology, 16*, 481–494.

Kellogg, J.B. (1988). Forces of change. *Phi Delta Kappan, 70*, 199–204.

Olmedo, E.L. (1981). Testing linguistic minorities. *American Psychologist, 36*, 1078–1085.

Osgood, C.E., May, W.H., & Miron, M.S. (1975). *Cross-cultural universals of affective meaning.* Urbana: University of Illinois Press.

Sadlak, M.J., & Ibrahim, F.A. (1986, August). *Cross-cultural counselor training: Impact on counselor effectiveness and sensitivity.* Paper presented at annual meeting of the American Psychological Association, Washington, DC.

Sue, D.W. (1981). *Counseling the culturally different.* New York: Wiley.

Sundberg, N.D. (1981). Cross-cultural counseling and psychotherapy: An overview. In A.J. Marsella & P.B. Pedersen (Eds.), *Cross-cultural counseling and psychotherapy.* New York: Pergamon.

Szapocznick, J., Santisteban, D., Kurtines, W., Perez-Vidal, A., & Hervis, O. (1983, November). *Bicultural effectiveness training: A treatment intervention for enhancing intercultural adjustment in Cuban American families.* Paper presented at the Ethnicity, Acculturation, and Mental Health Among Hispanics Conference, Albuquerque, NM.

Tapp, J.L., Kelman, H.C., Triandis, H.C., Wrightsman, L.S., & Coelho. G.V. (1974). Continuing concerns in cross-cultural ethics: A report. *International Journal of Psychology, 9*, 231–249.

Wolfgang, A. (1985). The function and importance of nonverbal behavior in intercultural counseling. In P.B. Pedersen (Ed.), *Handbook of cross-cultural counseling and therapy.* Westport, CT: Greenwood Press.

Wyatt, G.E., & Parham, W.D. (1985). The inclusion of culturally sensitive course material in graduate school and training programs. *Psychotherapy, 22*, 461–468.

DUAL ROLE RELATIONSHIPS

Karen Strohm Kitchener and Susan Stefanowski Harding

Professionals consistently report that dual role relationships are one of the toughest ethical issues they face (APA Ethics Committee, 1988) despite the fact that the ethical codes of virtually every mental health profession prohibit or warn of the dangers of relationships involving conflicts of interest. For example, the *Ethical Standards* of the American Association for Counseling and Development (1988) explicitly prohibit any kind of sexual intimacy with clients and warn against entering into counseling relationships when members have other relationships (e.g., supervisory) with a potential client. Although such warnings exist, records indicate that dual role relationships represent the most frequent violations of ethical codes (APA Ethics Committee).

Several rationales have been offered for why professionals engage in dual relationships that are harmful if not debilitating to clients. Schoener and Gonsiorek (1988) suggested that some practitioners are simply uninformed or naive, not knowing the behavior is harmful, or deceive themselves into believing the relationships are benign. Other professionals are seriously disturbed. Although more drastic interventions should be used with therapists who have impulse control problems or character disorders (Schoener & Gonsiorek), education may cure the ignorance that leads some therapists to wander blindly into dangerous relationships. For example, one young therapist learned that even "informal lunches" with clients can cause unanticipated dynamics.

Can you be friends with patients? It is something I've always been taught was an absolute no-no, but I resisted the idea. It happened that one young woman I treated, well, we were on the same wave length. She asked me to have lunch with her. I did lots of soul searching and said that I would. Over the years I've done the same thing with two others. The truth is that it did set up some kind of dependency thing that continues to this day. It's never been an equal friendship and can't possibly be. (Quoted in Lakin, 1988, p. 26)

It should be noted, however, that not all dual role relationships can be avoided (Keith-Spiegel & Koocher, 1985; Kitchener, 1988) nor are they necessarily harmful. For example, the first author of this essay is both co-author and dissertation adviser of the second author. Such relationships are often considered

Karen Strohm Kitchener, PhD, is Associate Professor in the School of Education, University of Denver. Susan Stefanowski Harding is a school counselor, Rangeview High School, Aurora, Colorado. The authors wish to thank Jack Harding for reading and commenting on an earlier draft of this essay.

examples of mentoring and good opportunities for learning. Thus, the purposes of this essay are (1) to identify dual role relationships that have a high potential for being problematic and unethical and (2) to help counselors and student development specialists recognize those that may be ethically acceptable if they are handled with caution. By providing this information the authors hope to help practitioners avoid becoming involved in damaging relationships.

Identifying Problematic Dual Role Relationships

In a dual role relationship one person simultaneously or sequentially plays two or more roles with another person (Kitchener, 1988). Kitchener identified three potential factors in a dual role relationship that may result in a professional's causing harm to a consumer. They are: (1) incompatibility of expectations between roles, (2) divergence of the obligations associated with the roles, and (3) the power and prestige of the professional. Incompatibility of expectations and divergence of obligations may cause the professional to lose objectivity, divide loyalties, and neglect the well-being of the client. The power and prestige of the professional contains the potential for exploitation. Kitchener argued that as each of these increases so does the possibility of harming the consumer.

Keeping these factors in mind, it should be noted that people almost always occupy more than one role category such as teacher, administrator, supervisor, friend, and frequently these roles overlap with the same person. School counselors, for example, are often also coaches, sometimes working in both roles with the same students.

However, regarding the first factor in Kitchener's model, social psychologists (Deutsch & Krauss, 1965; Getzels & Guba, 1954; Secord & Backman, 1974) pointed out that conflicts between roles often occur when the expectations and responsibilities of one role conflict with those of another. For example, the expectations and responsibilities of a supervisor and therapist differ. A supervisor has responsibilities toward the supervisee, to the agency in which the supervisee is working, and to the client whom the supervisee is seeing. Confidentiality may or may not extend to what the supervisee tells the supervisor. By contrast, a counselor has a primary obligation to a client and confidentiality is assumed, except in narrowly defined instances such as child abuse. If a professional is acting as both therapist and supervisor for the same person, the client/supervisee may become frustrated and confused when the supervisory role requires behavior from the supervisor/therapist that conflicts with the therapy role. In fact, role theory indicates that the possibility of role conflict and the attendant frustration, confusion, and anger increase as the incompatibility of expectations associated with the roles increases (Getzels & Guba, 1954). Roles in which the compatibility of expectations is high are less likely to cause problems.

Regarding the second factor, when the obligations associated with two roles differ, the potential for conflicts of interest between the two roles increases. For example, AACD members' primary obligation is to promote the welfare of the consumer. The preamble of the *Ethical Standards* (AACD, 1988) states that members are "dedicated to the enhancement of the worth, dignity, potential, and uniqueness of each individual . . . ." Furthermore, the section on counseling relationships states

147

that a "member's primary obligation is to respect the integrity and promote the welfare of the client(s)." When this obligation to the consumer conflicts with the professional's self-interest arising from personal, political, or business relationships, the consumer's best interest may be compromised. For example, it would be difficult for a counselor to remain objective about a client's decision making after the counselor invested in a losing real estate transaction promoted by the client.

Finally, regarding the third factor, professionals by definition have influential positions. Influence presumes power and prestige. Consumers, whether students, clients, or research participants, usually come to the professional for some kind of help, such as financial aid from a college administrator or college references from a school counselor. By virtue of their need for help, consumers are in a dependent position and thus less powerful. Often because of emotional turmoil they are also particularly vulnerable to the influence of the professional. Because such relationships are asymmetrical, consumers may not be in a position to protect their interests or to evaluate the professional's advice. Furthermore, professionals who neglect their obligation to promote the welfare of the consumer because of their own pathology may use the power or authority associated with their role to manipulate consumers in harmful ways (Kitchener, 1988; Pope, 1988b; Schoener & Gonsiorek, 1988).

Thus, dual role relationships lie in a continuum from those that are potentially very harmful because all three factors are involved to those in which there is little potential for harm. On the other hand, as noted, AACD members have a special obligation to promote the welfare of individuals and society. As a result, even in relationships in which there is a low risk of harm, they have a special obligation to evaluate the risk and act responsibly. This includes being sensitive to potential role conflicts and power differentials and minimizing their impact if they occur. As Pope (1988a) argued, it is always the professional's responsibility to ensure, to the extent possible, that the consumer is not harmed by those who have the responsibility to be helpful. Acting responsibly would include not engaging in relationships in which there is even a low risk of harm unless there are offsetting benefits for the consumer.

For example, when faculty engage students in co-authorship ventures, there is a potential for exploitation because of the power differential. Students may have little recourse if their efforts are not fully acknowledged or if unreasonable demands are placed on them. On the other hand, if instructors accept the role of mentor, by definition they act as trusted guides for students' professional development. In such roles they are obligated to facilitate the learning of students and exercise caution in order not to exploit them. In addition, these experiences are often highly beneficial for students in terms of learning a professional skill and facilitating career advancement. In other words, the potential benefits to students are great and the risks of harm are low. However, faculty who fail to uphold role boundaries can take advantage of the trust and intimacy that often accompany mentoring relationships.

Sexual Relationships

Although all dual role relationships create dilemmas, sexual relationships between counselors and clients wreak particular havoc. Clients entrust their vulnerabilities, pain, inner thoughts, feelings, and hopes to a presumably wise and healing counselor or therapist. The therapeutic relationship is one of support, warmth, and trust. It creates a natural intimacy that may evolve into sexual feelings. In fact, 87% of psychotherapists Pope, Keith-Spiegel, and Tabachnick (1986) interviewed reported experiencing attraction to one or more of their clients. As Vasquez and Kitchener (1988) noted, however, compassion and passion are not synonymous. Passion precludes the objectivity and clarity of purpose that are essential to a counseling relationship. Furthermore, when clients enter into a counseling relationship they expect their well-being to be paramount. When a counselor enters into a sexual relationship with a client, that expectation is violated. The power differential is great and clients often feel helpless to object or are fearful that they will lose the counselor on whom they are dependent.

Even though sexual activity with clients is explicitly prohibited by every major mental health organization and is illegal in many states (Vasquez & Kitchener, 1988), complaints about sexual involvement are common. Pope and Bouhoutsos (1986) analyzed eight prevalence studies of sexual involvement with clients on a variety of mental health professionals published between 1973 and 1987. Incidence ranged from 3.6% to 12.1% for male therapists with an aggregate average of 8.3%, and from 0% to 3.1% for female therapists with an average of 1.7%. A 1987 study indicated an apparent decline among psychologists, with 3.6% for men and 1.5% for women, although Pope (1988b) pointed out that stricter sanctions on sexual activity may have led to less willingness to report sexual intimacy.

Although school counselors may think that such data have little relevance for them, recent research (Bajit & Pope, in press) suggests that adolescents also are exploited sexually by mental health professionals. Data on frequency of occurrence are not available, but reports indicate that 56% of the victims are girls ranging from ages 3 to 17, and 44% are boys ranging from ages 7 to 16.

Pope and Bouhoutsos (1986) described 10 scenarios that may lead to sexual intimacy, noting that awareness may help counselors avoid the traps into which their less thoughtful colleagues fall. They described situations ranging from outright rape and intimidation to less malevolent circumstances such as allowing the intimacy that develops in the therapeutic relationship to get out of control. Pope asserted that knowing the paths to sexual intimacy may act as a deterrent to sexual exploitation.

Little empirical evidence exists regarding characteristics of typical perpetrators, although Schoener and Gonsiorek (1988) categorized perpetrators based on clinical observations of more than 1,000 cases. The six categories are: (1) uniformed/naive, or those who do not have judgment or training regarding ethical boundaries; (2) healthy or mildly neurotic individuals whose sexual contact is limited and whose reaction is remorse; (3) severely neurotic or socially isolated individuals with serious emotional problems who deny, distort, or rationalize the appropriateness of the sexual contact; (4) those with character disorders that include impulse control problems, whose history of impulse control behavior may include legal problems; (5) individuals with sociopathic or narcissistic character disorders, whose long history of manipulation and detachment contributes to the appearance of a healthy and remorseful therapist; and (6) those with psychotic or borderline personality disorders who possess poor judgment, impaired reality testing, and possible thought disorders.

Motives and characteristics of perpetrators may be unclear, but the harm to clients is not. Like a snow scene paperweight that never quite settles, the clients' emotions remain in turmoil long after such encounters. In a study of mental health professionals treating clients who had been sexually intimate with prior therapists, Bouhoutsos, Holroyd, Lerman, Forer, and Greenberg (1983) found that therapists reported that 90% of the clients had been damaged. Harmful effects included "inability to trust, hesitation about seeking further help from professionals, severe depression, hospitalization, and suicide" (Pope, 1988b). Bouhoutsos et al. hypothesized that the remaining 10% of the clients may have also been damaged but experienced delayed reactions. They also suggested that the reports on this 10% may have been inaccurate because the therapists completing them may themselves have been sexually exploiting their clients and, therefore, denying the negative impact of such behavior.

Pope (1988b) identified consequences for sexually exploited clients in a therapist-patient sex syndrome. Similar to responses to rape, battering, incest, child abuse, and post-traumatic stress disorder, the therapist-patient sex syndrome includes 10 aspects. They are: ambivalence, including both rage and fear of separation; pervasive and persistent feelings of guilt; a sense of emptiness and isolation; sexual confusion that affects the client's sense of identity; identity, boundary, and role confusion; emotional liability; suppressed rage caused by the forceful influence of the therapist; impaired ability to trust; an increase in suicidal risk and self-destructive behavior; and cognitive dysfunction, particularly in the ability to concentrate. These outcomes suggest that sexual intimacy between counselors and clients violates the most fundamental ethical responsibilities of mental health professionals, particularly the obligation not to harm those whom they have agreed to help (Vasquez & Kitchener, 1988).

Recently some have argued that because of ongoing transference issues, it is equally harmful for counselors to engage in sexual relationships with former clients (APA Ethics Committee, 1988). Those who remain unconvinced by these arguments should be aware that such relationships are illegal in some states, and psychology licensing boards have often found violations of the current code when the accused claimed that the relationship began after termination (Sell, Gottlieb, & Schoenfeld, 1986).

Hotelling (1988) argued that counselors should be aware of the avenues of redress available to sexually exploited clients because filing a complaint can empower the client and counteract the feelings of exploitation and victimization that are the usual consequences of such encounters (Pope 1988b). She described the ethical, administrative, and legal options available, the possible consequences to the counselor or therapist, and the advantages and disadvantages of each approach. The client who has been a victim may choose to file an ethical complaint through a professional organization with which the perpetrator is affiliated. The professional organization may choose action ranging from education to expulsion. If the counselor or therapist is licensed, certified, or registered, the client may file a complaint with the appropriate board. As a result, the professional's license could be revoked to protect future clients, the therapist may be required to pay a fine, or employment might be terminated. The client may also file a complaint directly with a therapist's employer. If a written policy exists regarding sexual conduct, the perpetrator could be dismissed or reprimanded. Legal redress in the form of civil or criminal suits is another possibility if statutes of limitations do not prevent the suit.

Other Potentially Damaging Dual Relationships

As noted, most attention in the mental health fields has focused on the potentially damaging effects when counselors are sexually intimate with clients. However, other kinds of dual relationships between counselors and clients, as well as between professors or teachers and students, or administrators and those they supervise, can also be harmful and ethically problematic. In fact, ethical codes of some mental health professional associations, such as the American Psychological Association (1981), and the American College Personnel Association (1980), make statements about the potential hazards of relationships with research subjects, students, and employees, suggesting that any relationship in which there are conflicts of interest may be unethical.

For example, the AACD standards specifically warn against developing a counseling relationship with those for whom one has evaluative responsibilities. However, Roberts, Murrell, Thomas, and Claxton (1982) reported that 35% of the counselor educators they surveyed did not consider it unethical to counsel students even if they were in their classes. As Stadler (1986) noted, teachers sometimes enter into such relationships in an attempt to be altruistic; however, the unintended negative consequences often leave both parties dissatisfied because the roles of teacher and counselor have different expectations and obligations in regard to confidentiality and evaluation. Such special relationships between a faculty member and student can also lead to envy and claims of favoritism by other students and faculty.

Similar problems can arise when faculty members or supervisors enter into sexual relationships or close friendships with students. Sexual relationships are often problematic because the obligations of being a teacher and lover are so different. As a teacher, the primary concern is for the welfare of the student. As lovers, both parties cannot help being, at least to some extent, self-interested. Teaching and supervising assume that faculty members or supervisors can objectively evaluate the person for whom they are responsible. Little objectivity is possible when the person is also a lover. The power differential between students and educators is so great that issues of coercion and abuse of power can also be involved. In fact, Glaser and Thorpe (1986), in a survey of female clinical psychologists, found that 95% believed that sexual contact between graduate students and educators was ethically inappropriate and would have a harmful effect on working relationships. Similarly, even close friendships, although less volatile than sexual relationships, can lead to loss of objectivity and confusion when the supervisor or teacher must evaluate the supervisee or student.

Counseling friends or even relatives of friends also may involve "faulty expectations, mixed allegiances, and misinterpretation of motives leading to disappointment, anger, and sometimes a total collapse of relationships" (Keith-Spiegel & Koocher, 1985, p. 269). As Keith-Spiegel and Koocher noted, both kinds of relationships are complex and intimate but they differ in function and purpose. These differences in expectations, as with any relationships involving role conflict, often lead to frustration and confusion.

Although bartering goods or services in exchange for therapy or counseling is often initially motivated by an altruistic concern for the welfare of those who cannot afford to pay for services, it too is fraught with potential traps. Bartering services for therapy is considered unethical by the American Psychological Association (APA Ethics Committee, 1988). Part of the difficulty arises from an inequality in power between the client and counselor. Usually, the services the client is bartering, such as typing, are not considered as valuable monetarily as are the services of the counselor. Ultimately the client can become a kind of indentured servant to the counselor as he or she falls further and further behind in the amount owed (Keith-Spiegel & Koocher, 1985).

When counselors agree to accept services for therapy, they become the client's employer. In fact, counseling an employee involves all three of the factors characteristic of potentially harmful relationships. The roles of employer and therapist have different obligations and expectations. An employer is concerned about the quality of services or goods received and may become angry or upset when the quality does not meet expectations. These emotions can interfere with therapeutic obligations to be accepting and understanding of clients. An employer is implicitly obligated to give employees feedback about their performance, an act which may not be therapeutic. Last, there is a power differential favoring the employer/therapist, which leaves the less powerful client open to exploitation.

Similar objections can be raised about entering into business relationships with clients or students (Pope, 1988b). Business relationships seek the financial gain of both parties. Although counselors and teachers are motivated by financial gain, their primary ethical obligation is the welfare of the consumer. The conflicting motives and emotions that business relationships arouse can interfere with the counseling relationship or with fair evaluations of students.

Conclusions

Counselors and others concerned with human development cannot afford to stumble blindly into dual relationships because of naiveté or because they do not consider the long-term consequences of their actions. State licensing boards and legislatures or university governing boards will mandate appropriate behavior unless mental health professions hold their own members accountable.

Furthermore, dual role relationships that cause pain and distress for consumers reduce the credibility of the profession and undermine its ability to be helpful. They destroy the faith of consumers in the possibility of having healthy relationships and often leave long-lasting scars.

Professionals, whatever their job titles, need to be aware of the potential conflicts of interest that may occur when they engage in more than one role with the same person. In particular, they must be sensitive to emotional over-involvement that limits their ability to be appropriately objective or leads to the misuse of power. They must assess the potential for relationships to deteriorate, for actions to be misinterpreted, and for conflicts to occur. Only after concluding that the risks of harm are small should they engage in relationships that have dual expectations. They should never enter such relationships when the potential for harm is high unless there are strong offsetting, ethical benefits for the consumer and the risks are clearly discussed. It should be noted that there are no offsetting benefits for entering into a sexual relationship with a client. Finally, professionals must take responsibility for clarifying expectations and redressing problems should they occur even when the potential for harm is low.

Despite the extent of damage that dual role relationships can cause, there is hope for the consumer and for the profession. Hope to educate the uninformed or naive potential perpetrator comes in the form of an increase in the number of classes on ethics in graduate programs or in postgraduate training and reading. For more seriously disturbed perpetrators, hope for the consumer comes in stricter codes of ethics that address dual role relationships, in laws that prohibit sexual relationships, and in harsher sanctions for breaking laws or codes. These may serve as necessary external deterrents for such individuals.

References

American Association for Counseling and Development. (1988). *Ethical standards.* Alexandria, VA: Author.

American College Personnel Association. (1989). *Statement of ethical and professional standards.* Alexandria, VA: American Association for Counseling and Development.

American Psychological Association. (1981). Ethical principles of psychologists. *American Psychologist, 36,* 631–638.

American Psychological Association. Ethics Committee. (1988). Trends in ethics cases, common pitfalls, and published resources. *American Psychologist, 43,* 564–572.

Bajit, T.R., & Pope, K.S. (in press). Therapist-patient sexual intimacy involving children and adolescents. *American Psychologist.*

Bouhoutsos, J., Holroyd, J., Lerman, H., Forer, B., & Greenberg, M. (1983). Sexual intimacy between psychologists and patients. *Professional Psychology, 14,* 185–196.

Deutsch, M., & Krauss, R.M. (1965). *Theories in social psychology,* New York: Basic Books.

Getzels, J.W., & Guba, E.G. (1954). Role, role conflict, effectiveness. *American Sociological Review, 19,* 164–175.

Glaser, R.D., & Thorpe, J.S. (1986). Unethical intimacy: A survey of sexual contact and advances between psychology educators and female graduate students. *American Psychologist, 41,* 43–51.

Hotelling, K. (1988). Ethical, legal, and administrative options to address sexual relationships between counselor and client. *Journal of Counseling and Development, 67,* 233–237.

Keith-Spiegel, P., & Koocher, G.P. (1985). *Ethics in psychology.* Hillsdale, NJ: Erlbaum.

Kitchener, K.S. (1988). Dual role relationships: What makes them so problematic? *Journal of Counseling and Development, 67,* 217–221.

Lakin, M. (1988). *Ethical issues in psychotherapies.* Oxford: Oxford University Press.

Pope, K.S. (1988a). Dual relationships: A source of ethical, legal and clinical problems. *The Independent Practitioner, 8,* 17–25.

Pope, K.S. (1988b). How clients are harmed by sexual contact with mental health professionals: The syndrome and its prevalence. *Journal of Counseling and Development, 67,* 222–226.

Pope, K.S., & Bouhoutsos, J.C. (1986). *Sexual intimacy between therapists and patients.* New York: Praeger.

Pope, K.S., Keith-Spiegel, P., & Tabachnick, B.C. (1986). Sexual attraction to clients: The human therapist and the (sometimes) inhuman training system. *American Psychologist, 41,* 147–158.

Roberts, G.T., Murrell, P.H., Thomas, R.E., & Claxton, C.S. (1982). Ethical concerns for counselor educators. *Counselor Education and Supervision, 22,* 8–14.

Schoener, G.R., & Gonsiorek, J. (1988). Assessment and development of rehabilitation plans for counselors who have sexually exploited their clients. *Journal of Counseling and Development, 67,* 227–232.

Secord, P.F., & Backman, C.W. (1974). *Social psychology.* New York: McGraw-Hill.

Sell, J.M., Gottlieb, M.C., & Schoenfeld, R. (1986). Ethical considerations of social/romantic relationships with present and former clients. *Professional Psychology: Research and Practice, 17,* 504–508.

Stadler, H.A. (1986). To counsel or not to counsel: The ethical dilemma of dual relationships. *Journal of Counseling and Human Service Professions, 1*(1), 134–140.

Vasquez, M.J., & Kitchener, K.S. (1988). Introduction to special feature. *Journal of Counseling and Development, 67,* 214–215.

ETHICAL CONFLICTS IN CASES OF SUSPECTED CHILD ABUSE

J. Jeffries McWhirter and Jeffrey L. Okey

A Review of the Problem

The increasing incidence of reported child abuse and neglect is well documented in both the popular press (Goldberg, 1987; Harrell, 1987) and the professional literature (Crabbs & Crabbs, 1988). In fact, some authors argue that the plethora of literature on the subject has created a "child abuse hysteria syndrome" characterized by overzealousness in the pursuit and reporting of suspected child abuse and neglect (Spiegel, 1988). Recent legislation reflects this increasing awareness of the problem. All 50 states have now enacted dual-faceted laws that (a) mandate that certain professionals must report suspected child abuse and (b) create an organization—such as Children's Protective Services (CPS)—whose job it is to investigate such reports and intervene where necessary (Sandberg, Crabbs, & Crabbs, 1988). Though the specific reporting requirements (who must report, in what time frame a report must be made, what constitutes "abuse," etc.) vary slightly from state to state, the counselor's legal obligations have been clarified as a result of such legislation. The counselor must be familiar with the most recent local statutes, and then report as mandated.

All professional counselors will recognize, however, that their responsibilities in regard to child abuse do not end with an obligatory report to the appropriate agency. Quite the contrary, mandatory reporting laws have increased the number and scope of the ethical and moral dilemmas that counselors who work with children face. This essay will identify the conflicts that a counselor dealing with a suspected abuse situation confronts, cite the *Ethical Standards* (AACD, 1988) deemed most germane to these situations (specifically, standards A.3, A.6, B.1, B.2, B.4, and B.18), and make recommendations for the responsible handling of such cases. In order to facilitate this explication, a fictional case study laden with ethical conflicts will be presented first, then referred to throughout the remainder of the text. In conclusion, responsible handling of suspected child

J. Jeffries McWhirter, PhD, is Professor in the Division of Psychology in Education, Arizona State University. Jeffrey L. Okey, MA, is Graduate Assistant in the Division of Psychology in Education, Arizona State University.

abuse cases will be shown to be a natural outgrowth of the professional counselor's overall ethical functioning.

Case Study

John Turner is an elementary school counselor for a large, urban school district in the Midwest. Though his district has made a stronger commitment to elementary school counseling than several other nearby districts, he is still assigned to two different schools with student populations of approximately 400 each. At 7:45 a.m. one Friday morning, while confirming the day's schedule, John is approached by Ms. Finch, one of the third-grade teachers. Ms. Finch reports that Mandy, a new student, just got off the bus and is clearly distraught—she is crying, disheveled, and mumbling something about being in a fight with her parents. Ms. Finch asks if John would talk to her. John agrees, reschedules his early appointments, and sets off to find Mandy and escort her to his office.

Upon first hearing Ms. Finch's report of Mandy's behavior, John is alerted to the possibility that some type of abuse is involved. At this point, there is minimal suspicion of abuse—Mandy may simply be upset about appropriate parental discipline. However, her emotional state warrants some attention and exploration.

When John first meets Mandy, he is struck by the redness of her face, a redness all the more apparent due to its proximity to her orange-red hair. He introduces himself and asks her to come to talk with him in his office. She readily agrees. Now sitting across from her in his office, John notices that Mandy's face is quite puffy. The puffiness could be from crying, he thinks to himself, but notes that it seems excessive.

John begins, "Can you tell me what's bothering you?" Mandy is eager to respond. She reports that her mother threw one of her brother's toy trucks at her and hit her in the face. When asked why, Mandy responds that she was in trouble because she didn't wake her dad up in time for work. John asks her to point out where she was hit. Mandy points to her upper left cheek, an area that is clearly more swollen than the rest of her face, although no abrasion or discoloration is present. John asks if anything like this has happened before. Mandy responds, "Yes, all the time. Mom is always throwing things at me." When asked if she has been hurt in any other way at home, she says, "Yes, sometimes Mom throws me on the ground and kicks me all over." No other bruises are apparent, and Mandy reports having no other bruises at this time. Finally, when asked how she would feel going home today, she says that she is afraid and doesn't want to go home. She then begins crying vehemently. John lets her cry for a bit and then lets her know he will try to make sure she is safe. He then returns her to class saying that he will talk with her later.

Following this preliminary interview, John had reason to believe that Mandy was the victim of ongoing physical abuse in her family. As a school counselor, his legal obligations were immediately clear: The law in his state mandates that he make an oral report of suspected child abuse within 24 hours, to be followed by a written report within 48 hours. Still, John was not sure how to respond. He knew from previous experience that a CPS caseworker would come immediately to the school only in the event of (a) sexual abuse, (b) traumatic physical injury (cuts, burns, breaks, severe bruises), or (c) expected future harm. In a case such as Mandy's, a caseworker would typically call the home that day and set an appointment for a future interview, usually within the week. John's concern was that if the mother was as volatile as reported, she might retaliate physically against the girl for "telling on her." And, this being a Friday, he could possibly be putting Mandy at risk for a more traumatic injury with no chance to check on her until the following Monday. John decided to get more background information and to consult with his principal.

John found that neither the teacher nor the principal had met Mandy's parents. The school secretary hadn't either, and reported that Mandy's older brother had picked up and returned the enrollment papers for her. John also learned that Mandy's behavior today was atypical. She had seemed bright and cheerful earlier in this, her first week at the school. John's discussion with the principal centered around the theme of *how*, not whether, to make the report. The principal shared John's concerns about "setting up" Mandy for retaliation, especially given the lack of knowledge of her family and Mandy's expressed fear of going home. Together, they decided that because a report must be filed, perhaps a special request could be made to CPS to interview Mandy in school today and assess the family situation prior to sending her home.

John decided to call in the report to CPS and make a plea for immediate action due to the special circumstances. The CPS intake worker concurred and dispatched a caseworker. In the meantime, John oriented Mandy to the interview process that was about to take place and assured her that he would be with her throughout the entire process. The caseworker arrived to interview Mandy. He received substantially the same information as was reported and decided to take Mandy into protective custody. The caseworker called a city police officer to authorize, and provide transportation to, the temporary foster placement. John continued to orient Mandy to these events and provided support throughout the process. Mandy was taken into protective custody and the caseworker contacted the family. John was later informed by the CPS caseworker that investigation resulted in Mandy's long-term foster placement and the possible permanent removal of parental rights. John was not, however, privy to further specifics of the abusive situation. Mandy's foster placement was in another district and thus precluded John's ability to provide ongoing counseling. He was assured, however, that the CPS caseworker had alerted the counselor at the new school of Mandy's situation. John concluded his work on this case by informing Mandy's former teacher that a CPS report was made, that she was taken into protective custody, and that she would be withdrawn from school. Any other information was either confidential or unavailable.

Implications for Counselors

The preceding case study is not necessarily intended to be an ideal model of counselor behavior; rather, it is intended to illustrate the legal, ethical, and moral conflicts inherent in a typical case of suspected abuse. Here, the legal conflict is minimal. Grounds for *suspicion* of child abuse clearly exist and this must be reported.

The ethical conflicts are more complex. Questions that may come immediately to the counselor's mind include: What intervention(s) will be in the student's best interests? What are my responsibilities in regard to confidentiality? Does my institution's (school district's) procedure in such cases conflict with that of my professional organization (AACD)? Moral conflicts may or may not be present, depending on the individual counselor's belief system. For example, the counselor in the above case study may, based on prior experience, distrust the CPS parental contact procedures and believe the potential for harm to the student is too great in a Friday report with no chance for immediate follow-up. In this case, the counselor may debate the relative merits of breaking the 24-hour reporting law and postpone the reporting until the following Monday. This behavior would be indefensible legally, but the individual counselor may still choose to follow his conscience and accept the consequences of this act of civil disobedience. Fortunately, most counselors can avoid such moral dilemmas by systematic application, both proactive and reactive, of the following AACD ethical standards selected specifically for their relevance to cases of suspected child abuse.

Standard A.3

"Ethical behavior among professional associates . . . must be expected at all times. When information is possessed that raises doubt as to the ethical behavior of professional colleagues . . . the member must take action to attempt to rectify such a condition. Such action shall use the institution's channels first and then use procedures established by the Association."

Standard A.3 states that counselors must be the guardians of ethical behavior. This standard clearly is crucial to the responsible handling of abuse cases because so many different professionals can be involved in one case of suspected abuse. In the case study, for example, John's ethical handling of the case was dependent on the ethical behavior of five different professionals—the teacher, the principal, the CPS intake worker, the CPS caseworker, and the city police officer. Without proper intervention on the part of the counselor, any one of these individuals may have been insensitive to the needs of the student or to ethical issues.

Adherence to this standard requires both proactive and reactive intervention on the part of the counselor. Proactively, the effective counselor would conduct inservice training about child abuse with school faculty. Reactively, were an ethical standard to be broken by one of the professionals involved, the counselor would have to intervene. Specifically, the counselor would first raise the concern directly with the individual. If this brought no resolution, the counselor would appeal through the individual's institutional channels. If still no resolution were forthcoming, the counselor would appeal to the professional association for assistance. In short, this standard asserts that counselors are the ethical leaders of their respective multidisciplinary teams and holds them accountable for the teams' behavior.

Standard A.6

"When members provide information to the public or to subordinates, peers, or supervisors, they have a responsibility to ensure that the content is general, unidentified client information that is accurate, unbiased, and consists of objective, factual data."

Standard A.6, when viewed in light of suspected abuse cases, calls for the protection of student/family confidentiality when distributing data on such cases. Because numerous agencies and individuals are in need of these data—legislators, school board members, school faculty, school administrators, CPS agencies, researchers, and parent groups, to name a few—this standard is often called into play. Vigilance is required on the part of the counselor to ensure its consistent application. For example, were John to conduct faculty inservice on child abuse, he would no doubt want to include data on the type and prevalence of abuse among his school's student population. However, if these data could not be adequately stripped of information identifying individual students, John would have to resort to reporting only state or national data in order to uphold this standard.

Standard B.1

"The member's primary obligation is to respect the integrity and promote the welfare of the client(s), whether the client(s) is (are) assisted individually or in a group relationship."

Simply put, the counselor's primary obligation is to intervene in such a way as to promote the overall welfare of the child. The ethical counselor must ask: "What is in this child's best interest?" In essence, this is the premise all parties involved in the case study use. John knew he had to report his suspicion of abuse, but he also knew that early investigation was crucial to Mandy's well-being. Therefore, he encouraged early CPS intervention.

The application of this standard leads to the often-heard reporting cliché: "When in doubt (whether to report or not), err on the side of the child" (Sandberg et al., 1988). Thus, the counselor must weigh the requirement to report versus the potential harm to the child. The welfare of the child is promoted by attending to his or her needs; a timely report may not be enough.

Standard B.1 also contains implications for follow-up work with abused students as well. If Mandy were to have returned to his school, John would have needed to attend carefully to her inclusion in group experiences and continue follow-up counseling with her.

Standard B.2

"Members make provisions for maintaining confidentiality in the storage and disposal of records and follow an established record retention and disposition policy. The counseling relationship and information resulting therefrom must be kept confidential . . ."

Though standard B.2 is ingrained in the minds of ethical counselors, it is perhaps the easiest standard to violate—particularly in suspected abuse cases. Because cases of suspected abuse require the counselor to divulge personal client information to various authorities, it is relatively easy to temporarily forsake confidentiality for the sake of facilitating the process. When handling the reporting process ethically, the counselor must continually ask *who* requires *what*

159

information, then provide only that. For example, when John reported back to the teacher in the case study, he evidenced his practice of this standard by informing her only of the obvious actions taken (a report was made and the child was withdrawn from school), not the specific details (the type or extent of abuse).

The proactive component of ethical counselor behavior is also emphasized in standard B.2 in that the counselor should develop a system for handling client information in a confidential manner prior to the need for its use.

Standard B.4

"When the client's condition indicates that there is clear and imminent danger to the client or others, the member must take reasonable personal action or inform responsible authorities. Consultation with other professionals must be used where possible. The assumption of responsibility for the client's (s') behavior must be taken only after careful deliberation. The client must be involved in the resumption of responsibility as quickly as possible."

Standard B.4 can be seen, in part, as an ethical reinforcement of the mandatory reporting laws for cases of suspected child abuse. This standard further mandates the counselor to consult with other professionals whenever possible when faced with such a situation. Implicit in this mandate is yet another proactive responsibility. Specifically, the counselor should have in place a crisis/consultation team to determine appropriate action on suspected abuse cases as they arise.

John, the counselor in the case study, evidenced good intent in this regard by consulting with his principal, but he did not have ready access to a team of peers with whom he could consult. To ensure adherence to this standard, John should devise a plan whereby a consultation team could be quickly assembled— even if only by phone—to provide assistance in the event of future abuse cases.

In suspected child abuse cases, "assumption of responsibility for the client" should occur only when it is in the child's best interests to do so, that is, when it is suspected that parents are *not* assuming this responsibility.

Standard B.18

"Should the member be engaged in a work setting that calls for any variation from the above statements, the member is obligated to consult with other professionals whenever possible to consider justifiable alternatives."

Standard B.18 once again recognizes the professional counselor as an ethical leader in the workplace, whether that workplace be a school, agency, or private practice setting. This standard also recognizes that practices in various work settings may conflict with the AACD *Ethical Standards*. In such cases, the counselor attempts to resolve conflicts to the satisfaction of both sides. For example, if it were the policy of the school district in the case study to deny CPS caseworkers access to students on school grounds, this would conflict with standard B.1, which obliges the counselor to "promote the welfare of the client" above all else. John would then implement standard B.18 by consulting with a team of professionals in an attempt to resolve this conflict.

Conclusion

The legal, ethical, and moral dilemmas addressed in this essay represent, but do not exhaust, conflicts counselors often face in cases of suspected child abuse. Likewise, the ethical standards chosen as particularly germane to suspected child abuse cases are intended to represent, but not exhaust, the themes of the AACD *Ethical Standards* (1988). In short, specific analysis of all possible dilemmas in light of each ethical standard is a task beyond the scope of this essay.

What has been attempted is to extract the major themes from the AACD *Ethical Standards* (1988) and to apply them to a representative case of child abuse. In so doing, two major themes emerge that can be applied directly to any number of conflicts: (a) vigilant proactivity, and (b) consultative reactivity. "Vigilant proactivity" refers to the theme in nearly all the ethical standards that the ethical counselor must take action *prior* to the development of an ethical conflict. This action may take the form of continued education, establishment of record-keeping procedures, data collection, philosophical development, and team building. In regard to cases of suspected child abuse, the ethical counselor must be vigilant in the development of adequate systems and procedures to handle such occurrences.

"Consultative reactivity" refers to the theme in nearly all the ethical standards that the ethical counselor will resolve ethical conflicts as they arise by means of consultation with other qualified professionals. This consultation may occur as part of an established, ongoing process, or it may occur on the spur of the moment as an issue develops. In regard to cases of suspected child abuse, the ethical counselor will seek out other professionals with whom to discuss the relative merits of the numerous interventions that might be implemented.

Finally, it should be noted that these two themes are central to ethical and common-sense functioning in all counseling pursuits. The counselor who consistently practices "vigilant proactivity" (diligent preparation) and "consultative reactivity" (asking for assistance) should be able to resolve successfully not only conflicts surrounding suspected child abuse and other ethical issues, but also conflicts surrounding other proposed counseling interventions.

References

American Association for Counseling and Development. (1988). *Ethical standards.* Alexandria, VA: Author.

Crabbs, M.A., & Crabbs, S.K. (1988). Editorial. *Elementary School Guidance & Counseling, 22,* 259–260.

Goldberg, B. (1987). *The CBS Evening News With Dan Rather* (Television Program). New York: Columbia Broadcasting Systems.

Harrell, J. (Producer). (1987). *The Phil Donahue Show* (Television Program). New York: National Broadcasting Company.

Sandberg, D.N., Crabbs, S., & Crabbs, M.A. (1988). Legal issues in child abuse: Questions and answers for counselors. *Elementary School Guidance & Counseling, 22,* 268–274.

Spiegel, L.D. (1988). Child abuse hysteria and the elementary school counselor. *Elementary School Guidance & Counseling, 22,* 275–283.

COUNSELING RECORDS: LEGAL AND ETHICAL ISSUES

Theodore P. Remley, Jr.

The Problem

Counselors understand that they have a legal and ethical obligation to protect the privacy of their clients. Confusion begins, however, as counselors begin to realize that there are exceptions to their duty to clients to keep information confidential, and that in some cases, failing to disclose personal or private information could be a violation of counselors' legal or ethical responsibilities. In addition, some counselors may not understand that the confidentiality surrounding their interactions with clients is meant to protect the privacy of the clients and that the counselors themselves do not have a right to keep interactions secret for their own purposes.

This general confusion regarding confidentiality in counseling relationships is the foundation for misunderstandings regarding counseling records. Written counseling records are a special area of concern for counselors, and the following legal and ethical principles need to be reviewed.

- Is there a legal or ethical obligation to keep counseling records?
- If so, what should the records contain?
- Under what circumstances might counselors have a legal or ethical obligation to disclose their counseling records to clients or to third parties?
- What procedures should be followed in maintaining, transferring, and discarding counseling records?
- What responsibilities do counselors have as the custodians of educational records?

AACD Ethical Standards

The *Ethical Standards* of the American Association for Counseling and Development (1988) contain some provisions that give direction for the use of counseling records. Counselors must understand, however, that the *Ethical Standards* do not answer all ethical or legal questions that may arise in practice.

Standard A.6 states that counselors must be sure that specific identifiable information about clients is not released when they provide to others general information about their practice. Several provisions address the issue of coun-

---

Theodore P. Remley, Jr., JD, PhD, is an Associate Professor and Head of the Department of Counselor Education, Mississippi State University.

seling records in Section B: Counseling Relationship. Standard B.2 requires that counselors establish a record retention and disposition policy and then follow the policy that has been developed.

Standard B.4 provides an exception to the confidentiality requirement of counselors. It states that counselors must take some action or inform responsible authorities when a client seems to be a danger to self or others. Consultation with other professionals is required whenever possible. Records might need to be disclosed to a third party in emergency circumstances.

Standard B.5 indicates that counseling records are not to be considered a part of the records of institutions or agencies in which counselors are employed unless specified by state statute or regulation. Instead counseling records are to be considered "professional information for use in counseling." Despite this standard, courts would be able to subpoena counseling records as records of an institution or agency. In addition, if an employer demanded access to counseling records, counselors most likely would be considered insubordinate if they refused to comply with their supervisor's request. (Note: Counselors are advised in standard A.2 to "seriously consider" resigning their employment if their employer requires them to compromise their ethical standards.)

Standard B.6 requires that records stored on a computer be limited to necessary information, be destroyed when no longer of use, and be restricted in access to appropriate persons. Case studies used in counselor training or research must be disguised to ensure client privacy, according to standard B.7. Standard B.11 allows counselors to consult with other professionals about a client. Consultation could include the disclosure of client records to the consultant. Standard G.10 requires, however, that counselors inform clients that they will be disclosing information to supervisors regarding the client's case when counselors intend to receive supervision of their work. Counselors must ensure that clients know in advance who will receive the results of tests that are administered, according to standard C.9. Standard D.10 requires that counselors take care to disguise the identity of subjects when research data are supplied to others.

Implications for Counselors

For the purposes of this discussion, attention will be focused on written or taped records counselors create to assist them in their counseling responsibilities. All counselors should maintain important business records related to dates of sessions, payment of fees, or health insurance reimbursement. A separate section is included for counselors who are responsible for educational records that schools, colleges, and universities keep.

Are Counseling Records Required?

The general response to this question is that counselors are not required to keep clinical case notes, although business records are essential. If counselors believe they need to create and maintain case notes in order to practice effectively, they should do so. On the other hand, if counselors believe such records are not necessary, generally there is no legal or ethical obligation to keep them.

Counselors should be aware that some of their peers might feel they are unprofessional if they do not maintain some type of clinical notes. There are no specific general legal or ethical principles that require counselors in all settings to keep clinical records. However, a court of law could determine that a counselor breached professional responsibilities to clients if the lack of clinical records were found to harm a client in some way *and* if the court determined that the standard practice of counselors in the community was to maintain clinical records. Because counselors have a duty to adhere to standard practices in the community, they are advised to maintain some type of clinical records.

Clinical counseling records are required in some circumstances. Agencies regulated by governmental (state and federal) entities, governmental agencies themselves, and some agencies receiving governmental funding must maintain clinical records that are mandated by governmental regulations. Counselors have the responsibility of informing themselves of all governmental rules and regulations that apply to their work environments. Private (nongovernmental) accrediting agencies and funding sources may also impose certain clinical recordkeeping requirements on counselors.

Counselors keep counseling records for a variety of reasons. Many counselors need to maintain notes from previous sessions to refresh their memory and to help plan future directions. Occasionally counselors keep records to document their actions or treatment plans in the event they are questioned at some later point regarding their interactions with a particular client. Although it may be appropriate in unusual circumstances for counselors to "cover" themselves by including data in the records of their clients, such situations are unusual and self-protection should not be the primary motivation for keeping routine counseling records.

What Should Be Included in Counseling Records?

The guidelines for the content of counseling records presented below are designed to assist counselors who keep counseling records to fulfill their legal and ethical obligations.

1. Separate factual from speculative information. Notes from sessions should, at a minimum, contain two separate sections. In an objective section, factual observations made by the counselor and actual exchanges that took place should be recorded. In a subjective section, the counselor may record clinical diagnoses, speculate on material from the session, offer hypotheses, and plan future strategies. The reason for including both objective and subjective sections is to allow counselors to determine at some date in the future, either for themselves or third parties, what actually occurred during a session and what speculations the counselor made as a result. Clinical record keeping guidelines for related health professions are much more elaborate than the simple scheme suggested above. However, separating notes into objective and subjective sections should be sufficient.

2. Notes should be written as if they might at some point become public information. All entries should be professional and accurate. Although counselors have a responsibility to keep records confidential, many exceptions exist,

and counselors should create counseling records with the understanding that they might eventually be disclosed either to the client or to third parties.

3. Counselors should document in their counseling records some events that take place. If suggestions or directions are given to clients in sessions and it would be harmful to the clients if they did not follow these directions, the fact that counselors gave such suggestions or directions should be recorded in the counseling records. Any emergency actions taken should be entered in the record as well. If counselors believe clients are prone to distort facts, accurate and factual notes summarizing sessions should be kept in a precise manner. Whenever the possibility of future litigation exists, care should be taken to document interactions extensively.

4. Counselors must understand that all records they keep are subject to access by their clients or, unless protected by a privileged communication statute, to court subpoenas. Even where privileged communication statutes exist, clients involved in litigation may subpoena their own records. Many counselors keep "official" client counseling records in a file in their offices and "unofficial" notes regarding their clients in their desks or in other secret places. Most subpoenas for counseling records will demand all records related to the client that have been recorded and kept under any circumstances and located in any place. Counselors who fail to produce "unofficial" records when a court has ordered them to produce all of their records could be held in contempt for not responding to a court order and either fined or imprisoned. Counselors who have received a subpoena can be put under oath and asked whether they have any additional records. If they do not admit they are keeping "unofficial" records when asked, they could be guilty of perjury, which is a criminal offense.

When Must Records Be Disclosed?

Many circumstances exist in which counselors might be required to disclose counseling records. Even when the relationship between counselors and clients is privileged by state statute, counseling records may still be seen at some point by clients or third parties. The following are examples of circumstances in which counselors could be required to disclose counseling records they have created: (1) when clients request their records or request that their records be sent to a third party; (2) when records are subpoenaed or a counselor is asked to produce records in a court proceeding and no privileged communication statute exists or the privilege is not asserted by the client; (3) when the counselor is accused of some wrongdoing by a client and the charge is being investigated by a court or licensing or certifying board or (4) when the records of a deceased client are subpoenaed.

There are three general exceptions to the legal and ethical requirement that counselors keep confidential information related by clients. These exceptions apply to counseling records as well.

Exception one: Clients are a danger to themselves or others. Circumstances may arise in which counselors are obligated to tell third parties confidential information about clients who are in danger of harming themselves or others. In some instances, counselors might need to give their clients' counseling records

165

to someone else in order to serve the best interests of their clients. For example, it might be appropriate to give the counseling records to the treating mental health professional when a client has been involuntarily committed to a psychiatric hospital, particularly when the records are requested by the client's guardian or professionals associated with the facility treating the client. During hearings to determine whether a client should be involuntarily committed, the attorney assigned by a court to represent the client may demand that the counseling records be produced for review.

Exception two: Client requests records be released to self or third party. Although many counselors would refuse, clients generally have a legal right to inspect and obtain copies of records kept on their behalf by professionals. Similar to medical records, the law often interprets the records as the property of the client and the professional as the custodian of the client's property, even though the records were created by the counselor. In addition, clients may demand that counselors transfer copies of actual records or information from their records to third parties such as insurance companies, other mental health professionals, or potential employers.

Only in emergency situations or in compliance with a court order should a counselor release a client's records to a third party without the permission of the client. Permission does not have to be in writing. However, if counselors anticipate that certain clients may later deny they gave permission, counselors should demand that their clients grant the release of records in writing. Many agencies or institutions where counselors are employed require that requests for the release of records always be in writing, and in such cases, counselors must follow the policies of their employer. In addition, some state and federal regulations require counselors subject to these directives to obtain written permission before records are released.

Many counselors believe that if their relationship with their clients is privileged by statute in their state that their counseling records could never be subpoenaed. This is not true, however. For example, clients themselves may subpoena their counseling records if they are involved in litigation in which their counseling is a relevant factor. In addition, records of deceased clients may be subpoenaed.

Counselors should not automatically hand over a client's records to the client or to a third party at the client's request. If counselors feel the disclosure of the records may be harmful to the client in some way, they should try to convince the client that he or she should not demand the records. Clients do have a legal right to their records, however.

Exception three: Court orders counselor to make records available. Some counselors feel that they should defy a court order to release a client's records if they feel such a release would violate their ethical responsibility to a client to keep their relationship confidential. Although counselors certainly should protest such orders, refusing to comply will result in the counselor being held in contempt of court and either fined or imprisoned. Legally, the client should be the one protesting such orders, not the counselor.

Judges do not allow contrary ethical standards of a profession to interfere with provisions of the law. Our laws of discovery state that litigants should have access to all information relevant to a case being litigated. When a court order is issued in our society, it supersedes any professional rules to the contrary. When citizens believe laws are wrong, they should become involved in the legislative process to have them changed. Counselors do not have the option of defying laws when they do not agree with them.

How Must Counseling Records Be Maintained?

The AACD *Ethical Standards* require that a policy be developed and followed for maintaining and disposing of counseling records. Counselors should develop such policies in a manner that ensures client confidentiality.

Counseling records must be stored in a fashion that limits access to appropriate personnel. Counselors may allow employees to see the counseling records they keep but should be aware that they are responsible for any breaches of confidentiality staff members may cause. Counselors who allow access to staff members should train their staff in the purpose and requirements of confidentiality. Counselors should monitor their staff's ability to maintain confidential information and revoke access to any staff members who are not capable of acting in a professional manner. In addition, counselors may disclose client records to their supervisors. However, the *Ethical Standards* require that clients be informed if the counselor is receiving supervision.

No specific rules exist for the storage of records. Counselors should use reasonable means to ensure that access is limited. Locked file cabinets may be sufficient in some instances and not enough of a precaution in others, depending on the circumstances. Counselors must themselves determine what is necessary to ensure the confidentiality of their clients and then take appropriate steps.

A frequent counselor concern is determining how long counseling records should be kept. There are no legal guidelines regarding this issue. Although business records should be maintained for a period of years for tax purposes, there are no such legal requirements for clinical case notes and counseling records. AACD has not developed standards that set a minimum time that counseling records should be kept, although other mental health organizations have promulgated such guidelines.

A general rule is that counseling records should be maintained only as long as necessary to provide quality services to clients. Some counselors may feel it is necessary to keep records at least 3 years after clients have terminated so that if clients reappear, they will have the information needed to counsel their clients in a professional manner. Other counselors may feel that counseling records should be disposed of as soon as clients terminate because they do not feel a need to have notes from prior sessions in order to be effective in counseling returning clients.

It is strongly recommended that counselors establish some specific policy that is reasonable and easy to follow regarding the discarding of counseling records. A method that does not require a great deal of clerical time is to destroy all records of a certain category on a specified date each year. For example, a counselor might choose to destroy the counseling records of all clients who had terminated in that calendar year or in the previous calendar year on December 31. Counselors should consider maintaining indefinitely a brief summary of all their cases.

167

Counselors should never destroy a particular counseling record when they anticipate a court subpoena or a request from the client for the record. Establishing a policy for the systematic elimination of records and following it, however, keeps the counselor from being accused of purposefully obstructing justice when a record is not available.

Counselors must ensure that records are destroyed in a manner that precludes their accidentally falling into the hands of others. As a result, records should be shredded, burned, or destroyed in some other manner that accomplishes the same purpose. Counselors who carelessly discard counseling records could be held responsible if a client's privacy is compromised as a result.

What Are the Requirements for Educational Records?

Counselors who are responsible for maintaining educational records in schools, colleges, or universities that receive federal funds must follow recordkeeping guidelines established by the Family Educational and Privacy Rights Act (FERPA 20 U.S.C. 1232(g)), commonly known as the "Buckley Amendment." The Buckley Amendment was passed to protect the privacy of students. Essentially, the amendment requires that students (or their parents if the students are under the age of 18) have access to their educational records and that their records not be released to third parties without their written permission.

Counselors who have administrative responsibility for students' educational records should read the exact language of the act. The provisions are clearly written and provide enough detailed information to allow counselors to develop policies and procedures that conform to the specifications of the law. Institutions that violate the Buckley Amendment could lose their federal funding.

Generally, all records regarding students kept in an educational institution by any employee are considered educational records. Exceptions include records that are kept in the sole possession of the maker and records made by mental health professionals for adults in postsecondary institutions.

Parents of minor students or adult students must be allowed to inspect their educational records upon request. Institutions must have procedures that allow access to records within 45 days of the request. A procedure, including a hearing, must be established whereby the contents of educational records can be challenged. Certain "directory information" may be published by educational institutions if students or their parents do not object. Records may not be released without written permission. However, schools may transfer records to other schools if parents are notified.

Records may be released to the parents or guardians of dependent adult students. Dependent students are defined as children or stepchildren who receive over half of their support (excluding scholarships) from the parent or guardian. Unless there has been a court order issued terminating all parental rights or this specific parental right, noncustodial parents have the same rights under the Buckley Amendment as custodial parents.

Conclusion

Counselors who maintain counseling or educational records should adhere to the AACD *Ethical Standards* related to recordkeeping practices. In addition, it is essential that counselors follow state statutes, federal laws, and their employer's policies regarding records. Although counselors should sometimes use records to document actions taken, more often counseling records should be used in ways that assist counselors to provide quality services to their clients.

The privacy of clients should be a primary concern of counselors. However, in order to fulfill their obligations to society and sometimes to the clients themselves, counselors occasionally must release their clients' records to third parties without their clients' permission.

ETHICAL USE OF COMPUTER APPLICATIONS IN COUNSELING: PAST, PRESENT, AND FUTURE PERSPECTIVES

James P. Sampson, Jr.

Computer technology is now a common resource that counselors and clients use to collect, process, and disseminate information. Beginning in the early 1970s and continuing to the present, many concerned professionals have identified ethical issues related to the use of computer applications in counseling. As a result, a substantial body of literature delineating issues and standards has evolved. This essay is intended to identify recurring ethical issues and current professional standards, as well as to discuss current major concerns and potential future developments. Supporting references are provided, where available, to facilitate a more detailed review of specific concerns.

Evolution of Ethical Issues

The following ethical issues have been raised in the literature. *Confidentiality* concerns have focused on potential client harm resulting from individuals' gaining inappropriate access to computer-maintained information, and harm resulting from excessive data collection and maintenance of out-of-date information as a result of the extensive data storage capacities of the computer (Denkowski & Denkowski, 1982; Godwin & Bode, 1971; Engels, Caulum, & Sampson, 1984; French, 1986; Lister, 1970; Meier & Geiger, 1986; Patterson, 1985; Sampson & Pyle, 1983; Space, 1981; Super, 1973; Talbutt, 1988; Walker & Myrick, 1985).

Counselor intervention concerns have focused on the potential client harm resulting from inadequate client prescreening, introduction, and follow-up related to the use of computer applications (Engels et al., 1984; Goodyear & Sinnett, 1984; Herr & Best, 1984; Sampson, 1986a; Sampson & Pyle, 1983; Talbutt, 1988).

James P. Sampson, Jr. is Associate Professor in the Department of Human Services and Studies and Co-Director of the Center for the Study of Technology in Counseling and Career Development at Florida State University. Appreciation is expressed to Jane G. Lenz, Robert C. Reardon, and Sandra M. Sampson for their review of an initial draft of this manuscript.

Assessment concerns have focused on potential client harm from the inappropriate use of computer-based test interpretations (CBTI) by inadequately trained counselors, the use of invalid CBTI programs by competent counselors, counselor dependence on CBTI, and the use of invalid test administration and scoring programs (Burkhead & Sampson, 1985; Butcher, 1987; Eberly & Cech, 1986; Eyde & Kowal, 1987; Farrell, 1984; Fowler, 1987; Merrell, 1985; Most, 1987; Sampson, 1983, 1986a; Sampson & Pyle, 1983; Turkington, 1984; Walker & Myrick, 1985; Wood, 1984; Zachary & Pope, 1984).

The *quality of computer-based information* involves the concern that clients may be making life decisions based on invalid information that is perceived as inherently accurate because the data are computer-generated (Katz, 1984; McKinlay, 1984; Sampson & Pyle, 1983; Talbutt, 1988).

The *use of computer-assisted instruction* has raised concerns of client harm resulting from misleading advertising and the use of computers as an inappropriate substitute for needed professional intervention (Jacob, 1985; Sampson, 1986b).

Equality of access to computer applications deals with potential harm when clients from various special populations are denied equal access to the potential benefits of using computer applications (Elwork & Gutkin, 1985; Haring-Hidore, 1984; Hofer & Green, 1985; Ibrahim, 1985; Sampson, 1986b; Walz, 1984).

Finally, *counselor training* concerns have focused on the potential client harm resulting from counselors who lack the knowledge and skills to help clients make effective use of computer applications (Engels et al., 1984; Johnson & Sampson, 1985; Loesch, 1986; Meier & Geiger, 1986; Sampson & Loesch, 1985).

Evolution of Ethical Standards

Several professional associations have reacted to the growing concern over ethical issues related to computer use by establishing new or revised ethical standards. These standards tend to place an emphasis on assessment issues, reflecting the considerable concern in the literature over the abuse of computer-assisted assessment.

Assessment. Initial efforts toward establishing ethical standards resulted in the *Interim Standards for Automated Test Scoring and Interpretation Practices* (American Psychological Association, 1966). The development of ethical standards continued with the *Guidelines for the Use of Computerized Testing Services* (Colorado Psychological Association, 1982), the *Principles for Dealing With Ethics Cases Involving Computerized Assessment* (Ohio Psychological Association, 1983), *Note on the Computerization of Printed Psychological Tests and Questionnaires* (British Psychological Society. Standing Committee on Test Standards, 1984), and the *Standards for Educational and Psychological Testing* (American Educational Research Association, American Psychological Association, & National Council on Measurement in Education, 1985). The most comprehensive standards relating to assessment are the *Guidelines for Computer-Based Tests and Interpretations* (American Psychological Association, 1986).

Career guidance. In addition to assessment, ethical standards have been developed relating to computer-assisted career guidance in the form of the Association of Computer-Based Systems for Career Information *Guidelines for the Use of Computer-Based Career Information and Guidance Systems* (Caulum & Lambert, 1985) and the *Ethical Standards* of the National Career Development Association, 1988.

General statements. General concerns related to confidentiality, assessment, and counselor intervention are included in the *Code of Ethics* of the National Board for Certified Counselors, 1987. In an attempt to further increase the likelihood of ethical practice, preparation standards for counselors now require the attainment of knowledge and skills related to using computers in counseling as stated in the *Accreditation Procedures Manual* of the Council for the Accreditation of Counseling and Related Educational Programs, 1988.

The 1988 revision of the AACD Ethical Standards. Efforts began in 1982 to revise the ethical standards of the American Association for Counseling and Development to incorporate statements related to computer applications. The current version of the *Ethical Standards* (American Association for Counseling and Development, 1988) includes nine statements associated with the use of computer applications (Allen, Sampson, & Herlihy, 1988). The issues addressed in the revised code include: (1) broadening the concept of counseling records to include electronic data storage (B.5); (2) potential misuse of computer-maintained client data (B.6); (3) client misconceptions of the inherent validity of computer-generated data (B.9); (4) the need for counselor interventions related to client use of computer applications (B.16); (5) potential negative impact of computer applications on various minority groups (B.19); (6) the development of self-help/stand-alone computer software (B.20); (7) counselor training required for use of computer-based test interpretations (C.4); (8) accuracy of computer-assisted test scoring programs (C.5); and (9) the validity of computer-based test interpretations (C.13).

Current Major Concerns

Despite this attention given to the ethical use of computer applications within the counseling process, issues related to counselor awareness, attitude, and training await further attention.

Counselor awareness. Many counselors face substantial caseloads of clients who have increasingly complex problems, coupled with declining (or at best steady-state) funding for services. In an effort to provide better client services at reduced costs, counselors may be susceptible to computer software marketing that implies a capability to "solve" some of these problems. Evidence for this includes the large amount of relatively inexpensive software sold in the United States that fails to address the issues of confidentiality, validity of information, and suggestions for counselor intervention in professional manuals or other training materials. When asked to explain this situation, software developers have responded that they are providing what counselors are asking for, namely software that meets specific needs with simple manuals that describe how to operate the software. Many counselors are not using effectively the power of the "purchase order" to insist on valid software that can be used in a confidential manner within the context of ongoing counseling interventions. Counselors need

172

to be more active and visible in being advocates for computer software quality assurance, as suggested by Walz (1984) and Watts (1986).

Counselor attitude. Counselors tend to have diverse attitudes toward the use of computer applications, ranging along a continuum from uninformed rejection to uncritical acceptance (Herr & Best, 1984; Walz, 1970). Both extremes in attitude limit the ethical and effective use of computer technology in counseling. Uninformed rejection of the use of computer technology potentially may result in clients' not having full access to information and learning experiences that directly relate to their needs. Conversely, uncritical acceptance of computer applications may result in clients' using software of potentially questionable validity in a potentially inappropriate manner, such as without needed counselor intervention. A moderate "middle-ground" attitude of cautious optimism is needed that views computer applications as potentially useful when valid software is used in an appropriately supported manner. This relates to Walz's (1970) concept of "committed but questioning" (p. 179), a more informed, moderate, disciplined attitude than found in the extremes noted earlier.

Counselor training. The literature on computer applications in counseling provides numerous descriptions of the content of computer software and typical client use of the software. Relatively few books and articles deal with appropriate counselor behaviors to help clients make effective use of computer software within the counseling process. Most computer software manuals share a similar limitation, focusing foremost on operational procedures, with some description of system content, and minimal, if any, information on recommended counselor intervention strategies. It is difficult for counselors to make ethical use of computer applications that they do not understand. This situation can be improved in three ways. First, inservice and preservice counselor training can incorporate more fully the training recommendations provided by Herr and Best (1984), Johnson and Sampson (1985), Sampson and Loesch (1985), and Sampson and Pyle (1983). Second, counselors can use the power of the "purchase order" to select only software that includes counselor training materials. Third, research on the efficacy of various approaches to counselor intervention needs to continue.

The Future

Past experience with computer applications, current developments, and anticipated growth provide at least a partial indication of future ethical issues related to using computers in counseling. First, rapidly expanding computer storage capacities and continuing data security problems will probably result in continuing concern over the extent and accessibility of confidential client data that are maintained on large computer systems and networks. Second, the lack of clarity in research and practice regarding counselor interventions is likely to result in continuing confusion regarding the minimum level of counselor assistance needed to help clients with differing needs to make effective use of computer applications. Third, self-help/stand-alone computer software, especially video-enhanced materials, is likely to become widely available, with growing concern expressed over the quality of information provided and the validity of this software for individuals with varying educational and cultural backgrounds. Fourth, as increasing numbers of clients use computer applications of all types, increasing concern is likely to be expressed over the validity of information contained in these systems. Finally, computer-based test interpretations (CBTI) will continue evolving, especially as "expert system" and "artificial intelligence" elements are fully integrated, with growing concern expressed as CBTI "seems" to duplicate counselor judgment in interpreting test results and recommending counseling interventions. Misuse of CBTI may result in professionals' (both counselors and noncounselors) making erroneous conclusions about clients that further may lead to inappropriate counseling interventions. The continued misuse of CBTI also may result in counselor overdependence on computer technology to the detriment of both counselor and client goal attainment (Sampson, 1986a).

Computer hardware and software have evolved at an exceptionally rapid rate, with performance generally improving as costs have declined. This rapid evolution has resulted in the development of a wide variety of counseling applications and the availability of computer technology in settings where this resource has been generally unavailable. Ethical standards, however, have tended to evolve slowly as professionals develop a consensus regarding relevant issues and appropriate statements of responsible practice. Because it is unlikely that computer technology will change to a slower rate of evolution, it seems clear that ethical standards related to computer applications will need more frequent review in the future.

References

Allen, V.B., Sampson, J.P., Jr., & Herlihy, B. (1988). Details of the new 1988 AACD ethical standards. *Journal of Counseling and Development, 67*, 157–158.

American Association for Counseling and Development. (1988). *Ethical standards*. Alexandria, VA: Author.

American Educational Research Association, American Psychological Association, & National Council on Measurement in Education. (1985). *Standards for educational and psychological testing*. Washington, DC: American Psychological Association.

American Psychological Association. (1966). Interim standards for automated test scoring and interpretation practices. *American Psychologist, 21*, 1141.

American Psychological Association. (1986). *Guidelines for computer-based tests and interpretations*. Washington, DC: Author.

British Psychological Society. Standing Committee on Test Standards. (1984). Note on the computerization of printed psychological tests and questionnaires. *Bulletin of the British Psychological Society, 37*, 416–417.

Burkhead, E.J., & Sampson, J.P., Jr. (1985). Computer-assisted assessment in support of the rehabilitation process. *Rehabilitation Counseling Bulletin, 28*, 262–274.

Butcher, J.N. (1987). The use of computers in psychological assessment: An overview of practices and issues. In J.N. Butcher (Ed.), *Computerized psychological assessment: A practitioner's guide* (pp. 3–14). New York: Basic Books.

Caulum, D., & Lambert, R. (Eds.). (1985). *Guidelines for the use of computer-based career information and guidance systems*. Eugene, OR: Association of Computer-Based Systems for Career Information, ACSCI Clearinghouse, University of Oregon.

Colorado Psychological Association. (1982). *Guidelines for the use of computerized testing services*. Denver: Author.

Council for the Accreditation of Counseling and Related Educational Programs. (1988). *Accreditation procedures manual*. Alexandria, VA: Author.

Denkowski, K.M., & Denkowski, G.C. (1982). Client-counselor confidentiality: An update of rationale, legal status, and implications. *Personnel and Guidance Journal, 60*, 371–375.

Eberly, C.G., & Cech, E.J. (1986). Integrating computer-assisted testing and assessment into the counseling process. *Measurement and Evaluation in Counseling and Development, 19*, 18–26.

Elwork, A., & Gutkin, T.B. (1985). The behavioral sciences in the computer age. *Computers and Human Behavior, 1*, 3–18.

Engels, D.W., Caulum, D., & Sampson, D.E. (1984). Computers in counselor education: An ethical perspective. *Counselor Education and Supervision, 24*, 193–203.

Eyde, L.D., & Kowal, D.M. (1987). Computerized test interpretation services: Ethical and professional concerns regarding U.S. producers and users. *Applied Psychology: An International Review, 36*, 401–417.

Farrell, A.D. (1984). When is a computerized assessment system ready for distribution? Some standards for evaluation. In M.D. Schwartz (Ed.), *Using computers in clinical practice: Psychotherapy and mental health applications* (pp. 185–189). New York: Haworth Press.

Fowler, R.D. (1987). Developing a computer-based test interpretation system. In J.N. Butcher (Ed.), *Computerized psychological assessment: A practitioner's guide* (pp. 50–63). New York: Basic Books.

French, C.F. (1986). Microcomputers and psychometric assessment. *British Journal of Guidance and Counselling, 14*, 33–45.

Godwin, W.F., & Bode, K.A. (1971). Privacy and the new technology. *Personnel and Guidance Journal, 50*, 298–304.

Goodyear, R.K., & Sinnett, E.R. (1984). Current and emerging ethical issues for counseling psychologists. *The Counseling Psychologist, 12*(3), 87–98.

Haring-Hidore, M. (1984). In pursuit of students who do not use computers for career guidance. *Journal of Counseling and Development, 63*, 139–140.

Herr, E.L., & Best, P. (1984). Computer technology and counseling: The role of the profession. *Journal of Counseling and Development, 63*, 192–195.

Hofer, P.J., & Green, B.F. (1985). The challenge of competence and creativity in computerized psychological testing. *Journal of Consulting and Clinical Psychology, 53*, 826–838.

Ibrahim, F.A. (1985). Human rights and ethical issues in the use of advanced technology. *Journal of Counseling and Development, 64*, 134–135.

Jacob, S. (1985). *Computer applications in school psychology: Proposed guidelines for good practice*. Unpublished manuscript, Central Michigan University, Department of Psychology, Mt. Pleasant.

Johnson, C.S., & Sampson, J.P., Jr. (1985). Training counselors to use computers. *Journal of Career Development, 12*, 118–128.

Katz, M.R. (1984). Computer-assisted guidance: A walkthrough with running comments. *Journal of Counseling and Development, 63*, 153–157.

Lister, C. (1970). Privacy and large-scale personal data systems. *Personnel and Guidance Journal, 49*, 207–211.

Loesch, L.C. (1986). Computer-assisted assessment: A reaction to Meier and Geiger. *Measurement and Evaluation in Counseling and Development, 19*, 35–37.

McKinlay, B. (1984). Standards of quality in systems of career information. *Journal of Counseling and Development, 63*, 149–152.

Meier, S.T., & Geiger, S.M. (1986). Implications of computer-assisted testing and assessment for professional practice and training. *Measurement and Evaluation in Counseling and Development, 19,* 29–34.

Merrell, K.W. (1985). Computer use in psychometric assessment: Evaluating benefits and potential problems. *Computers in Human Services, 1*(3), 59–67.

Most, R. (1987). Levels of error in computerized psychological inventories. *Applied Psychology: An International Review, 36*(3/4), 375–383.

National Board for Certified Counselors. (1987). *Code of ethics.* Alexandria, VA: Author.

National Career Development Association. (1988). Ethical standards. In *The professional practice of career counseling and consultation: A resource document* (pp. 11–17). Alexandria, VA: Author.

Ohio Psychological Association. (1983). *Principles for dealing with ethics cases involving computerized assessment.* Columbus: Author.

Patterson, M.B. (1985). Developing a code of ethics for computer users. *Journal of College Student Personnel, 26,* 255–256.

Sampson, J.P., Jr. (1983). Computer-assisted testing and assessment: Current status and implications for the future. *Measurement and Evaluation in Guidance, 15*(4), 293–299.

Sampson, J.P., Jr. (1986a). Computer technology and counseling psychology: Regression toward the machine? *The Counseling Psychologist, 14*(4), 567–583.

Sampson, J.P., Jr. (1986b). The use of computer-assisted instruction in support of psychotherapeutic processes. *Computers in Human Behavior, 2,* 1–19.

Sampson, J.P., Jr., & Loesch, L.C. (1985). Computer preparation standards for counselors and human development specialists. *Journal of Counseling and Development, 64,* 31–33.

Sampson, J.P., Jr., & Pyle, K.R. (1983). Ethical issues involved with the use of computer-assisted counseling, testing and guidance systems. *Personnel and Guidance Journal, 61,* 283–287.

Space, L.G. (1981). The computer as psychometrician. *Behavior Research Methods & Instrumentation, 13,* 595–606.

Super, D.E. (1973). Computers in support of vocational development and counseling. In H. Borow (Ed.), *Career guidance for a new age* (pp. 285–315). Boston: Houghton Mifflin.

Talbutt, L.C. (1988). Ethics and computer usage: Hidden answers for school counselors. *The School Counselor, 35,* 199–203.

Turkington, C. (1984). The growing use, and abuse, of computer testing. *APA Monitor, 15*(1), 7, 26.

Walz, G.R. (1970). Technology in guidance: A conceptual overview. *Personnel and Guidance Journal, 49,* 175–182.

Walz, G.W. (1984). Role of the counselor with computers. *Journal of Counseling and Development, 63,* 135–138.

Walker, N.W., & Myrick, C.C. (1985). Ethical considerations in the use of computers in psychological testing and assessment. *Journal of School Psychology, 23,* 51–57.

Watts, A.G. (1986). The role of the computer in career guidance. *International Journal for the Advancement of Counseling, 9,* 145–158.

Wood, S. (1984). Computer use in testing and assessment. *Journal of Counseling and Development, 63,* 177–179.

Zachary, R.A., & Pope, K.S. (1984). Legal and ethical issues in the clinical use of computerized testing. In M.D. Schwartz (Ed.), *Using computers in clinical practice: Psychotherapy and mental health applications* (pp. 151–164). New York: Haworth Press.

COUNSELOR IMPAIRMENT

Holly A. Stadler

Manuel had just turned 45. The birthday celebration given by the staff of the Crisis Center made him feel even older. He had founded the center when he was their age, just out of school, full of enthusiasm and idealism. In the 20 years that had passed, he had listened to many client callers who felt like he did now. He guessed that his uncle may have felt the same way because he ended up killing himself. Manuel thought of the truth in the saying, "It's lonely at the top."

As the director of the center he had to keep his feelings to himself, not wanting the young staff to see how frustrated he had become. He finally stopped doing phone work because it seemed like the clients were hanging up sooner than ever. He doubted that he was helping them at all and could contribute little in supervision. His body ached from the injuries of a recent major car accident. At his age he should have known better than to drive after spending the evening drowning his sorrows. He could kill himself doing that.

Grace couldn't find solace in her work even though she was immersed in it more than ever. Things just weren't as important now that she was alone after 10 years of being half of a couple. The break-up was 6 months ago, but it seemed like yesterday. Crying inside, she felt like she had nothing more to give to the children in the three elementary schools she served. Running from building to building, she never had the time to make friends with any of the staff. The school district had been hit hard by the closing of the county's largest employer, and the children seemed to bear the brunt of their parents' frustrations. The teachers told her there were more referrals than she could handle, so they referred only the children in greatest need. Where was she to get the energy to keep going? Grace was frightened. She had her clients to consider. She used to be so effective with them, but in her current condition she had nothing to offer.

Three years' sobriety meant a lot to Rodney. Despite the absence of support from his parents, he had managed to clean up after wasting his college years. He chose a graduate program in counseling because he wanted to use his experience as a recovered alcoholic and child of alcoholic

---

Holly A. Stadler, PhD, is Associate Professor in the Division of Counseling Psychology and Counselor Education, University of Missouri-Kansas City.

parents to help others. So why did he think he could go to student parties and drink? He wasn't using drugs like some of them, he wouldn't go that far to fit in. But there was so much competition in graduate school, and the emphasis on understanding feelings and being genuine was too much for him. He needed some relief from the pressure, a way to escape from the feelings that were being unleashed. Missing classes, putting off assignments until the last minute, and piling up incompletes didn't help. How could he get out of taking those self-exploration classes? What would he do when he got into practicum? Any supervisor could recognize immediately that he just wasn't making it.

Unfortunately, scenarios such as these are not as unusual in the counseling profession as we might like to believe. A common thread runs through each story: Something has happened to the person of the counselor. It might be the recurrence of a long-standing problem, the stress of work or school, a critical event in a counselor's life, or a combination of these. Of significance to our discussion is the fact that in each scenario something has happened to the person of the counselor *and* it has impaired the counselor's ability to function clinically. These counselors are not just having a "bad day." Their bad days have turned into weeks and months.

It would be the rare counselor who never experienced a frustrating day, a difficult client, or an emotional overload. But counselors who are functioning well can put these experiences into perspective; their skills remain intact and their personalities remain stable. On the other hand, impaired counselors have lost the capacity to transcend stressful events. They no longer function as well as they once did. The therapeutic skills of impaired counselors have diminished or deteriorated. Something has made such a forceful impact that their person has been affected.

These developments are critical to the work of the counselor. The literature of counseling is replete with references to the significance of the person of the counselor. The person of the counselor has been called the instrument of therapeutic change.

Guy (1987) described the importance of the counselor as a person:

Regardless of technique utilized, it is the optimism, integrity and enthusiasm of the therapist that create the context within which successful therapy is conducted. Even more important, it is the emotional stability and maturity of the therapist that provide an essential foundation for the relationship and a point of reference for the treatment. (p. 197)

When the person of the counselor goes awry, clients may suffer. In a review of studies of therapist dysfunctions McConnaughy (1987) noted that therapists with the lowest levels of emotional disturbance on the MMPI were more effective in reducing client depression and defensiveness than were more disturbed therapists. Furthermore, he identified the association between therapist personality integration and client willingness to remain in treatment. A therapist whose inner conflicts are activated by client material may respond to clients in ways that maintain their own equilibrium instead of facilitating client growth. Mc-

178

Connaughy's work reinforced the conclusion that the counselor's personality characteristics are crucial to the development of a positive therapeutic alliance.

Because counselor wellness is so critical to the success of counseling, it would seem that concern about the absence of counselor wellness would be the subject of much professional activity. At this time in the counseling profession, the opposite is true. Although counselor burnout has been addressed through research and writing, we know very little about its impact on clients. We have been reluctant to investigate the troubled counselor or to acknowledge the need to look at this phenomenon within the profession. To be fair, it is only recently that other professions (e.g., medicine, nursing, law, and psychology) have broached the subject of impairment. However, there may be some specific reasons why counselors have avoided or denied the existence of professional impairment. Counseling work is valued within our society, so it may be difficult for counselors to express their dissatisfaction with it (Farber, 1983) or to acknowledge how debilitating it can be. It also may be hard to give up the myth that training and experience in a mental health profession offer immunity from emotional problems (Thoresen, Nathan, Skorina, & Kilburg, 1983; Guy, 1987). Counselors are not invulnerable to emotional impairment, as much as we might wish them to be. If the profession were to acknowledge impairment, fears may be evoked of endangering the significant advances counseling has made in professionalization and recognition, with a subsequent loss of stature among other professions. Thus, at the time this essay is being written, we have no data on counselor impairment, no organization-sponsored avenues to assist troubled counselors, and no forum for systematic discussion of these concerns.

This essay will build on initial inquiry into the topic of counselor and counseling student impairment (Stadler, Willing, Eberhage, & Ward, 1988; Willing, Corber, & Stadler, 1988; Stadler & Willing, 1988), underscoring ethical concerns. Strategies for prevention and early identification of impaired counselors will be highlighted. The literatures of medicine and psychology will form the backdrop for our discussion because these professions have already begun the study of impairment. Even these literatures are limited and at times unclear, however.

Problems in Studying Impairment

We have seen that professional avoidance and denial may thwart the study of impairment. There are other problems as well—starting with a clear definition of impairment. Nearly all definitions refer to inadequate professional functioning (Robertson, 1980; Lalotis & Grayson, 1985; Nathan, in Kilburg, Nathan, & Thoresen, 1986; Guy, 1987; Mawardi, in Farber, 1983). In some definitions, the clinical inadequacy could be due to certain conditions such as physical or mental disabilities, aging, loss of motor skill, or alcohol or drug abuse (Robertson, 1980; Nathan, in Kilburg et al., 1986). In other definitions, inadequate functioning may be signaled by certain behaviors (e.g., sexual misconduct) that some say are evidence of underlying emotional problems (Wood, Klein, Cross, Lammers, & Elliott, 1985; Guy, 1987). For the purposes of this essay, Guy's definition is the clearest. According to that author, impairment is the "diminution or deterioration of therapeutic skills and abilities due to factors which have sufficiently impacted the personality of the therapist to result in potential clinical incompetence" (p. 199).

The terms used in the impairment literature make studying the problem somewhat confusing. Some of the terms are: *Incompetent*—lacking ability (Guy, 1987); one who is poorly trained or who has failed to keep current (Bissell & Haberman, 1984). *Distressed*—the professional's subjective experience that something is wrong. He or she may or may not be impaired in any area of functioning, including professional (Nathan, in Kilburg et al., 1986). *Burned out*—"The feeling of personal or emotional depletion that ensues from the stress that seems to be inherent in many professional careers" (Surran & Sheridan, 1985, p. 743). Burnout is a more pervasive condition than impairment in that it affects one's personal as well as professional life.

In addition to definitional problems, the study of impairments to date relies on self-report survey methodology for gathering information. The weaknesses of this type of methodology are subject self-selection bias, validity problems, and under- and overreporting (Guy, 1987). No studies have systematically investigated cross-cultural differences in impairment, although Bell (1986) has identified the concerns of the impaired Black physician. In addition, even though some definitions of impairment have included deterioration of clinical abilities due to aging, only one study (Guy, Stark, Poelstra, & Souder, 1987) has addressed that issue.

A final limitation of the impairment literature is that it is so new that it lacks historical referents that might suggest patterns or areas that should be of particular concern to the professions. For instance, we do not know if there is more or less impairment now than previously.

Ethical Concerns

Ethics scholars point to a variety of reasons why we should be concerned about professional impairment. Like certain other professionals, counselors enter into a covenant with their clients (May, 1983; Pellegrino, 1985). This covenant, the bond of trust between counselor and client, is developed at a time when clients are likely to be vulnerable and exploitable. Society sanctions this covenant for the help it brings to troubled people. Yet the covenant must be founded in trust that the counselor will be competent and ethical. When impaired counselors are unable to fulfill these obligations, they not only violate the covenant but harm the very clients whose care has been entrusted to them. The harm can extend beyond the client to the client's family, as well as to the image of the profession. The AACD *Ethical Standards* highlight the importance of counselors' competence as well as the need to refrain from harming others.

Discussion of professional impairment has also focused on covering up for impaired colleagues and the confidentiality of professionals in treatment. Bok (1979) posed the question, "Is it ever right to cover up for colleagues who are exposing innocent persons to risk because they are unable to do their work properly?" Conflicts between loyalty to a colleague and professional responsibility to maintain public trust are at the heart of these dilemmas. Bok contended that confidentiality cannot be used to protect secrets professionals keep about themselves. By using confidentiality as a shield to deflect legitimate public attention, professionals undermine the respect for persons and relationships that confidentiality was originally meant to protect. Kaslow (in Kilburg et al., 1986) supported this notion, and, as a therapist, would report professionals who were practicing incompetently. Annas (1978) took an even stronger position when confronting impaired physicians. He favored a legal requirement mandating physicians who know of a colleague's dangerous practices to report this to a medical licensing board.

Bissell (1983) and Schreiber (1987), on the other hand, stated that privacy, confidentiality, and trust are essential to the treatment of impaired professionals. However, the context of their position refers to professionals who have put aside their clinical work to receive treatment, primarily inpatient care for alcohol or drug abuse. It is unclear what position they would take in regard to the confidentiality of practitioners in treatment who continue their clinical work while impaired.

No writers have addressed directly the ethical dilemmas posed when a professional learns of an impaired colleague through counseling a client harmed by that colleague. Here, we are concerned about the client's confidentiality, not that of the impaired colleague. Minnesota has developed a mandatory reporting law to cover situations in which a counselor learns of an impaired colleague's sexual misconduct with a client. Outside of this jurisdiction it seems that the ethical obligation to respect client decision making as well as the directives of the AACD *Ethical Standards* uphold confidentiality unless the client consents to disclose such information.

Mechanisms of Impairment

Because impairment poses ethical problems and is a waste of human resources, counselors should be able to identify some indicators of impairment. Recognizing impairment in ourselves and our colleagues is the first step in combating the problem.

To discuss the recognition of impairment in the counseling profession, I will continue to draw on the literatures of medicine and psychology. The first area of exploration will be the problems or conditions counselors bring with them into the profession. Such preexisting conditions may heighten counselor vulnerability to negative environmental influences. These influences—job stress and life circumstances—will be the second group of impairment mechanisms to be explored. Finally, we will learn how preexisting conditions and environmental influences interact to produce professional impairment.

Preexisting Conditions

Three areas of concern—psychological problems, alcohol or drug abuse, and suicide—are most frequently cited as relevant to a discussion of impairment. Frequently, individuals enter the counseling profession in order to work through their own unresolved problems. Some also cite a desire to help others overcome problems similar to their own as a primary motivation for choosing a career in the helping professions.

Freudenberger (in Kilburg et al., 1986) enumerated a variety of unhealthy motives for working in the helping professions. The most common is an expression of unconscious needs such as excessive needs to compete, to be perfect, and to avoid feeling inferior. Other unhealthy motives he cited are the hope to resolve early childhood conflicts, the fulfillment of childhood fantasies of omnipotence and grandiosity, and the attempt to attain personal identity.

Depression (Guy, 1987) is a common preexisting condition among mental health professionals. The connection between depression and other serious psychological problems and suicide is cause for concern. Characteristic of psychologists who have committed suicide is a basic personality structure described as "distant, aloof, detached, depressed, lonely, self-seeking, self-indulgent, impulsive, intolerant of frustration, prone to substance abuse and mood swings" (Guy, p. 205). Counselors with a history of suicidal ruminations and attempts, a successful suicide within the family, and suicidal parents can trace these conditions to a time before entry into a helping profession. Counselors with a prior history of substance abuse and with physical and genetic vulnerability to substance abuse (Guy) seem to be predisposed to problems after entering the profession. In addition to the heightened vulnerability of counselors with preexisting problems, certain environmental factors also may be identified with impairment.

Environmental Influences

Stresses within a counselor's personal life may on their own or in combination with preexisting problems lead to work impairment. Relationship, parenting, economic, and social problems can severely test a counselor's ability to cope. Rippere and Williams (1985) noted that depression among mental health workers is more likely to develop as a response to life events than to job-related stressors. The psychic or physical pain and suffering associated with troubling personal circumstances may lead some counselors to seek relief through substance abuse (Guy, 1987). Social pressures and financial insecurity also precipitate experimentation with alcohol and drugs (Thoresen et al., 1983). Black health professionals can find themselves removed from their support systems as their upward mobility isolates them (Bell, 1986).

The personal difficulties that led some to enter a career in counseling may be exacerbated by the practice of that profession (Wheelis, 1958). The practice of counseling, including contact with certain types of clients, can reactivate a counselor's early experiences, open old wounds, and reawaken unresolved needs (Guy, 1987; Farber, 1983).

Practicing psychotherapists have reported particularly stressful client behaviors. The research findings of Hellman, Morrison, and Abramowitz (1986), and Deutsch (1984) point to client suicide ideation as the single greatest source of stress for therapists. They also note that other stressors are client resistance, psychopathological symptoms, and emotionality. Hellman et al. identified another source of therapist stress to be the therapeutic relationship. Respondents in their survey found it stressful to offer painful interpretations to clients, to control their own emotional reactivity, to not allow personal feelings to interfere with work, and to internalize their clients' difficulties. Counseling is a dynamic tension between empathy and professional distance. The counselor gives a great deal in making a "loan of the self" to the therapeutic enterprise (Squyres, 1986) while receiving little in return and sometimes doubting the effectiveness of counseling (Hellman et al.). Furthermore, counselors can find it difficult to be the object of client transference and fantasy for protracted periods of time (Squyres).

Incidence and Warning Signs

Whether because of a preexisting condition, life or work problems, or the interaction of all these factors, impaired counselors may exhibit characteristic problems. Six to 10% may experience alcoholism (Thoresen et al., 1983). The death-by-suicide rate among female psychologists is four times that of White women in general (Roeske, in Scott & Hawk, 1986). Fifty-seven percent of the female psychologists responding to a survey (Deutsch, 1984) reported experiencing more than one episode of depression, 11% reported substance abuse problems, 2% reported suicide attempts, and 82% reported relationship difficulties. Prochaska & Norcross (1983) found that 83% of the psychotherapists they surveyed had experienced one or more episodes of psychic distress. Lalotis & Grayson (1985) estimated that 5% to 15% of physicians are impaired by substance abuse or major psychiatric illness. Kahill (1986) found that 6.3% of the Canadian psychologists he surveyed acknowledged being burned out. Apparently psychologists are concerned about the incidence of impairment among their colleagues. A majority of the respondents to a survey by Wood et al. (1985) thought that the impairment of practitioners is becoming a serious problem.

A variety of warning signs points to the occurrence of impairment. Colleagues with substance abuse problems may first evidence marital, financial, time management, and interpersonal concerns. They also may have short-term memory loss, manifest arrogance and rigidity, and seem confused with chronic anxiety (Thoresen et al., 1983). Depression, cynicism and callousness, absenteeism, irregular office hours, and irritability are other warning signs (Maslach, 1978; Freudenberger, 1974; Thoresen et al., 1983). Difficulty moving through transition points in training (Surran & Sheridan, 1985), social isolation, and sleep problems (McCue, 1982) may indicate impairment in counseling students. Impaired practitioners may distance themselves from clients, becoming hardened, nonfeeling, and nongiving (Maslach). This distancing can extend to family and social relationships (Farber, 1983; Cogan, 1977).

Clients whose therapists committed suicide were aware of therapist depression and agitation prior to the suicide. Likewise, clients of substance-abusing therapists recognized their therapists' impairment (Guy, 1987). What can be done to prevent these tragedies? What interventions can be implemented prior to the development of impairment?

Prevention

Because counselors use their own feelings and selves to a degree that is unique among professions (Wheelis, 1958), care needs to be taken so that counselors can function adequately. Measures to promote counselor functioning can be introduced in counseling graduate programs and in the field.

Prevention and Early Intervention in Training

Individuals with conditions that might predispose them to impairment should know of their vulnerability when considering a career in counseling. Program information sent to prospective students can describe the emotional rewards and hazards of the profession. Introductory coursework also may present these issues as well as information about counselor impairment. Program faculty who are caring, responsible role models and who confront student and colleague impairment may dispel student perceptions that faculty are more likely to deny or avoid the issue (Willing et al., 1988). Responsible gate-keeping (Knoff & Prout, 1985) may mean that faculty terminate impaired students from counseling programs or require evidence of improved functioning prior to program completion. Many programs encourage personal counseling for students, impaired or not, to promote understanding and self-care and to enhance students' ability to cope with stressful work and life events. Program faculty may need to examine the ways in which they may promote overemphasis on students' academic lives to the detriment of their personal lives. Learning to manage a balanced life-style is crucial to healthy development as a counselor (Surran & Sheridan, 1985). Graduate training can reduce the shock and disillusionment new professionals experience by preparing students for the realities of the profession (Kahill, 1986).

Prevention and Early Intervention in the Field

New professionals are especially vulnerable to pressures to prove themselves quickly and to be accepted by their colleagues. They may downplay the impact of the process of adjusting to a new setting. Caring and insightful supervision can ease the transition into the profession through careful monitoring of new employees. It is wise to delay assigning new counselors the most difficult tasks until after the first year of employment (Olson, Heppner, Downing, & Pinkney, 1986). New counselors need time and support to learn a new professional role and understand a new work setting. Overcommitment to work and unbalanced life-styles should be discouraged so that counselors can take advantage of a full private life and supportive social networks (Kahill, 1986).

Specific aspects of the work environment can be arranged to reduce the likelihood of job stress that precipitates counselor impairment. Pines (in Scott & Hawk, 1986) offered a number of suggestions, including involvement in varied tasks without overload to stimulate counselor interest and sense of control. She strongly discouraged isolated practice because sharing, supportive co-workers can diffuse an overwhelming sense of responsibility and reduce stress.

Respecting a counselor's time off and limiting the number of client contacts and difficult cases contribute to counselor wellness (Freudenberger, 1974). Although counselors may spend their leisure time volunteering in other human service agencies and attending workshops that focus on emotional encounters, Freudenberger believes these experiences contribute to counselor stress. Relaxing, nonpsychologically oriented, nonstressful vacations are also important preventive measures.

Even the most experienced counselors can benefit from high-quality supervision and access to consultation. Ongoing supervision should be a normal occurrence in the professional lives of counselors. Counselors who are not properly trained or supervised may break under the weight of demands placed on them to work beyond their abilities. Employing counselors whose training prepares them for their work tasks is the clear response to this dilemma.

Too many counselors, especially those approaching retirement (Guy et al., 1987), rely on their own assessments or those of their clients to determine their clinical competence. It is appropriate that counselors be encouraged to monitor themselves because self-referrals are the most frequent points of entry into treatment programs for impaired professionals. Monitoring does not necessarily lead to help-seeking, however, because professionals with serious emotional problems underutilize treatment services (Guy, 1987). Colleague intervention may be necessary. Colleagues of impaired counselors can receive guidance from the work of Thoresen, Budd, and Krauskopf (1986) and Skorina (1988) to encourage entry into treatment. Reducing the stigma associated with counselor emotional problems and increasing the visibility of counselor self-help efforts (Wood et al., 1985) may encourage counselor help-seeking. Although some writers support voluntary self-regulatory efforts, others (Guy, 1987) encourage competence-based licensing procedures and reevaluation at suitable intervals.

Much remains to be done if the counseling profession is to examine impairment in its members and provide options for counselor assistance. The first step in the process is to move past denial and avoidance and to acknowledge the problem. To preserve the ethical covenant between counselor and client and the societal support for that covenant, counselors need to be able to uphold their responsibility to provide competent, unimpaired service.

References

Annas, G. (1978). Whom to call when the doctor is sick. *Hastings Center Report, 8*, 18–20.
Bell, C. (1986). Impaired black health professionals: Vulnerabilities and treatment approaches. *Journal of the National Medical Association, 78*, 925–930.
Bissell, L. (1983). Alcoholism in physicians. *Postgraduate Medicine, 74*, 177–230.
Bissell, L., & Haberman, P. (1984). *Alcoholism in the professions.* New York: Oxford Press.
Bok, S. (1979). *Lying. Moral choice in public and private life.* New York: Random House.
Cogan, T. (1977). A study of friendships among psychotherapists. (Doctoral Dissertation, Illinois Institute of Technology). *Dissertation Abstracts International, 78*, 859.
Deutsch, C. (1984). Self-reported sources of stress among psychotherapists. *Professional Psychology: Research and Practice, 15*, 833–845.
Farber, B. (1983). *Stress and burnout in the human services profession.* New York: Pergamon Press.
Freudenberger, H. (1974). Staff burnout. *Journal of Social Issues, 30*, 159–165.
Guy, J. (1987). *The personal life of the psychotherapist.* New York: Wiley.
Guy, J., Stark, M., Poelstra, P., & Souder, J. (1987). Psychotherapist retirement and age-related impairment: Results of a national survey. *Psychotherapy, 24*, 816–820.
Hellman, I., Morrison, T., & Abramowitz, S. (1986). The stresses of psychotherapeutic work: A replication and extension. *Journal of Clinical Psychology, 42*, 197–205.

Kahill, S. (1986). Relationship of burnout among professional psychologists to professional expectations and social support. *Psychological Reports, 59,* 1043–1051.

Kilburg, R., Nathan, P., & Thoresen, R. (1986). *Professionals in distress: Issues, syndromes, and solutions in psychology.* Washington, DC: American Psychological Association.

Knoff, H., & Prout, H. (1985). Terminating students from professional psychology programs: Criteria, procedures, and legal issues. *Professional Psychology: Research and Practice, 16,* 789–797.

Lalotis, D., & Grayson, J. (1985). Psychologist heal thyself: What is available for the impaired psychologist? *American Psychologist, 40,* 84–89.

Maslach, C. (1978). The client role in staff burnout. *Journal of Social Issues, 34,* 111–124.

May, W. (1983). *The physicians' covenant. Images of the healer in medical ethics.* Philadelphia: Westminster Press.

McConnaughy, E. (1987). The person of the therapist in psychotherapeutic practice. *Psychotherapy, 24,* 303–314.

McCue, J. (1982). The effects of stress on physicians and their practice. *New England Journal of Medicine, 306,* 458–463.

Olson, S., Heppner, P., Downing, N., & Pinkney, J. (1986). Is there life after graduate school? Coping with the transition to postdoctoral employment. *Professional Psychology: Research and Practice, 17,* 415–419.

Pellegrino, E. (1985). Professions as the conscience of society. *Journal of Medical Ethics, 11,* 117–122.

Prochaska, J., & Norcross, J. (1983). Psychotherapists' perspectives on treating themselves and their clients for psychic distress. *Professional Psychology: Research and Practice, 14,* 642–655.

Rippere,V., & Williams, R. (1985). *Wounded healers. Mental health workers' experiences of depression.* New York: Wiley.

Robertson, J. (Ed.). (1980). Legal aspects of impairment. In Proceedings of the Fourth AMA Conference on the Impaired Physician: Building Wellbeing (pp. 45–48). Chicago: American Medical Association.

Schreiber, S. (1987, November). Physicians at risk for suicide. *Medical Aspects of Human Sexuality,* 93–105.

Scott, C., & Hawk, J., Eds. (1986). *Heal thyself: The health of health care professionals.* New York: Brunner-Mazel.

Skorina, J. (1988). *Impaired psychologists.* Paper presented to Missouri Psychological Association, St. Louis.

Squyres, E. (1986). An alternative view of the spouse of the therapist. *Journal of Contemporary Psychotherapy, 16,* 97–106.

Stadler, H., & Willing, K. (1988). Impaired counselors. *Counseling and Human Development, 21,* 18.

Stadler, H., Willing, K., Eberhage, M., & Ward, W. (1988). Impairment: Implications for the counseling profession. *Journal of Counseling and Development, 66,* 258–260.

Surran, B., & Sheridan, E. (1985). Management of burnout: Training psychologists in professional life span perspectives. *Professional Psychology: Research and Practice, 16,* 741–752.

Thoresen, R., Budd, F., & Krauskopf, C. (1986). Perceptions of alcohol misuse and work behavior among professionals. *Professional Psychology: Research and Practice, 17,* 210–216.

Thoresen, R., Nathan, P., Skorina, J., & Kilburg, R. (1983). The alcoholic psychologist: Issues, problems, and implications for the profession. *Professional Psychology: Research and Practice, 14,* 670–684.

Wheelis, A. (1958). *The quest for identity*. New York: Norton.

Willing, K., Corber, J., & Stadler, H. (1988). *Incidence of impairment among counseling graduate students*. Unpublished manuscript. University of Missouri-Kansas City.

Wood, B., Klein, S., Cross, H., Lammers, C., & Elliott, J. (1985). Impaired practitioners: Psychologists' opinions about prevalence and proposals for intervention. *Professional Psychology: Research and Practice, 16*, 843–850.

APPENDICES
APPENDIX A

DIVISIONAL CODES OF ETHICS

AMERICAN COLLEGE PERSONNEL ASSOCIATION

Statement of Ethical Principles and Standards, 1989

Preamble

The American College Personnel Association (ACPA), a Division of the American Association for Counseling and Development (AACD), is an association whose members are dedicated to enhancing the worth, dignity, potential, and uniqueness of each individual within post-secondary educational institutions and thus to the service of society. ACPA members are committed to contributing to the comprehensive education of the student, protecting human rights, advancing knowledge of student growth and development, and promoting the effectiveness of institutional programs, services, and organizational units. As a means of supporting these commitments, members of ACPA subscribe to the following principles and standards of ethical conduct. Acceptance of membership in ACPA signifies that the member agrees to adhere to the provisions of this statement.

This statement is designed to complement the AACD *Ethical Standards* (1988) by addressing issues particularly relevant to college student affairs practice. Persons charged with duties in various functional areas of higher education are also encouraged to consult ethical standards specific to their professional responsibilities.

Use of This Statement

The principal purpose of this statement is to assist student affairs professionals in regulating their own behavior by sensitizing them to potential ethical problems and by providing standards useful in daily practice. Observance of ethical behavior also benefits fellow professionals and students due to the effects of modeling. Self-regulation is the most effective and preferred means of assuring ethical behavior. If, however, a professional observes conduct by a fellow professional that seems contrary to the provisions of this document, several courses of action are available.

Initiate a private conference. Because unethical conduct often is due to a lack of awareness or understanding of ethical standards, a private conference with the professional(s) about the conduct in question is an important initial line of action. This conference, if pursued in a spirit of collegiality and sincerity, often may resolve the ethical concern and promote future ethical conduct.

Pursue institutional remedies. If private consultation does not produce the desired results, institutional channels for resolving alleged ethical improprieties may be pursued. All student affairs divisions should have a widely-publicized process for addressing allegations of ethical misconduct.

Contact ACPA Ethics Committee. If the ACPA member is unsure about whether a particular activity or practice falls under the provisions of this statement, the Ethics Committee may be contacted in writing. The member should describe in reasonable detail (omitting data that would identify the person(s) as much as possible) the potentially unethical conduct or practices and the circumstances surrounding the situation. Members of the Committee or others in the Association will provide the member with a summary of opinions regarding the ethical appropriateness of the conduct or practice in question. Because these opinions are based on limited information, no specific situation or action will be judged "unethical." The responses rendered by the Committee are advisory only and are not an official statement on behalf of ACPA.

Request consultation from ACPA Ethics Committee. If the institution wants further assistance in resolving the controversy, an institutional representative may request on-campus consultation. Provided all parties to the controversy agree, a team of consultants selected by the Ethics Committee will visit the campus at the institution's expense to hear the allegations and to review the facts and circumstances. The team will advise institutional leadership on possible actions consistent with both the content and spirit of the *ACPA Statement of Ethical Principles and Standards*. Compliance with recommendations is voluntary. No sanctions will be imposed by ACPA. Institutional leaders remain responsible for assuring ethical conduct and practice. The consultation team will maintain confidentiality surrounding the process to the extent possible.

Submit complaint to AACD Ethics Committee. If the alleged misconduct may be a violation of the AACD *Ethical Standards*, the person charged is a member of AACD, and the institutional process is unavailable or produces unsatisfactory results, then proceedings against the individual(s) may be brought to the AACD Ethics Committee for review. Details regarding the procedures may be obtained by contacting AACD headquarters.

Ethical Principles

No statement of ethical standards can anticipate all situations that have ethical implications. When student affairs professionals are presented with dilemmas that are not explicitly addressed herein, five ethical principles may be used in conjunction with the four enumerated standards (Professional Responsibility and Competence, Student Learning and Development, Responsibility to the Institution, and Responsibility to Society) to assist in making decisions and determining appropriate courses of action.

Ethical principles should guide the behaviors of professionals in everyday practice. Principles, however, are not just guidelines for reaction when something goes wrong or when a complaint is raised. Adhering to ethical principles also calls for action. These principles include the following.

Act to benefit others. Service to humanity is the basic tenet underlying student affairs practice. Hence, student affairs professionals exist to (a) promote healthy social, physical, academic, moral, cognitive, career, and personality development of students; (b) bring a developmental perspective to the institution's total educational process and learning environment; (c) contribute to the effective functioning of the institution; and (d) provide programs and services consistent with this principle.

Promote justice. Student affairs professionals are committed to assuring fundamental fairness for all individuals within the academic community. In pursuit of this goal, the principles of impartiality, equity, and reciprocity (treating others as one would desire to be treated) are basic. When there are greater needs than resources available or when the interests of constituencies conflict, justice requires honest consideration of all claims and requests and equitable (not necessarily equal) distribution of goods and services. A crucial aspect of promoting justice is demonstrating an appreciation for human differences and opposing intolerance and bigotry concerning these differences. Important human differences include, but are not limited to, characteristics such as age, culture, ethnicity, gender, disabling condition, race, religion, or sexual/affectional orientation.

Respect autonomy. Student affairs professionals respect and promote individual autonomy and privacy. Students' freedom of choice and action are not restricted unless their actions significantly interfere with the welfare of others or the accomplishment of the institution's mission.

Be faithful. Student affairs professionals are truthful, honor agreements, and are trustworthy in the performance of their duties.

Do no harm. Student affairs professionals do not engage in activities that cause either physical or psychological damage to others. In addition to their personal actions, student affairs professionals are especially vigilant to assure that the institutional policies do not: (a) hinder students' opportunities to benefit from the learning experiences available in the environment; (b) threaten individuals' self-worth, dignity, or safety; or (c) discriminate unjustly or illegally.

Ethical Standards

Four ethical standards related to primary constituencies with whom student affairs professionals work—fellow professionals, students, educational institutions, and society—are specified.

1. *Professional Responsibility and Competence.* Student affairs professionals are responsible for promoting students' learning and development, enhancing the understanding of student life, and advancing the profession and its ideals. They possess the knowledge, skills, emotional stability, and maturity to discharge responsibilities as administrators, advisors, consultants, counselors, programmers, researchers, and teachers. High levels of professional competence are expected in the performance of their duties and responsibilities. They ultimately are responsible for the consequences of their actions or inaction.

As ACPA members, student affairs professionals will:

1.1 Adopt a professional lifestyle characterized by use of sound theoretical principles and a personal value system congruent with the basic tenets of the profession.

1.2 Contribute to the development of the profession (e.g., recruiting students to the profession, serving professional organizations, educating new professionals, improving professional practices, and conducting and reporting research).

1.3 Maintain and enhance professional effectiveness by improving skills and acquiring new knowledge.

1.4 Monitor their personal and professional functioning and effectiveness and seek assistance from appropriate professionals as needed.

1.5 Represent their professional credentials, competencies, and limitations accurately and correct any misrepresentations of these qualifications by others.

190

1.6 Establish fees for professional services after consideration of the ability of the recipient to pay. They will provide some services, including professional development activities for colleagues, for little or no remuneration.

1.7 Refrain from attitudes or actions that impinge on colleagues' dignity, moral code, privacy, worth, professional functioning, and/or personal growth.

1.8 Abstain from sexual harassment.

1.9 Abstain from sexual intimacies with colleagues or with staff for whom they have supervisory, evaluative, or instructional responsibility.

1.10 Refrain from using their positions to seek unjustified personal gains, sexual favors, unfair advantages, or unearned goods and services not normally accorded those in such positions.

1.11 Inform students of the nature and/or limits of confidentiality. They will share information about the students only in accordance with institutional policies and applicable laws, when given their permission, or when required to prevent personal harm to themselves or others.

1.12 Use records and electronically stored information only to accomplish legitimate, institutional purposes and to benefit students.

1.13 Define job responsibilities, decision-making procedures, mutual expectations, accountability procedures, and evaluation criteria with subordinates and supervisors.

1.14 Acknowledge contributions by others to program development, program implementation, evaluations, and reports.

1.15 Assure that participation by staff in planned activities that emphasize self-disclosure or other relatively intimate or personal involvement is voluntary and that the leader(s) of such activities do not have administrative, supervisory, or evaluative authority over participants.

1.16 Adhere to professional practices in securing positions: (a) represent education and experiences accurately; (b) respond to offers promptly; (c) accept only those positions they intend to assume; (d) advise current employer and all institutions at which applications are pending immediately when they sign a contract; and (e) inform their employers at least thirty days before leaving a position.

1.17 Gain approval of research plans involving human subjects from the institutional committee with oversight responsibility prior to initiation of the study. In the absence of such a committee, they will seek to create procedures to protect the rights and assure the safety of research participants.

1.18 Conduct and report research studies accurately. They will not engage in fraudulent research or will they distort or misrepresent their data or deliberately bias their results.

1.19 Cite previous works on a topic when writing or when speaking to professional audiences.

1.20 Acknowledge major contributions to research projects and professional writings through joint authorships with the principal contributor listed first. They will acknowledge minor technical or professional contributions in notes or introductory statements.

1.21 Not demand co-authorship of publications when their involvement was ancillary or unduly pressure others for joint authorship.

1.22 Share original research data with qualified others upon request.

1.23 Communicate the results of any research judged to be of value to other professionals and not withhold results reflecting unfavorably on specific institutions, programs, services, or prevailing opinion.

1.24 Submit manuscripts for consideration to only one journal at a time. They will not seek to publish previously published or accepted-for-publication materials in other media or publications without first informing all editors and/or publishers concerned. They will make appropriate references in the text and receive permission to use if copyrights are involved.

1.25 Support professional preparation program efforts by providing assistantships, practica, field placements, and consultation to students and faculty.

As ACPA members, preparation program faculty will:

1.26 Inform prospective graduate students of program expectations, predominant theoretical orientations, skills needed for successful completion, and employment of recent graduates.

1.27 Assure that required experiences involving self-disclosure are communicated to prospective graduate students. When the program offers experiences that emphasize self-disclosure or other relatively intimate or personal involvement (e.g., group or individual counseling or growth groups), professionals must not have current or anticipated administrative, supervisory, or evaluative authority over participants.

1.28 Provide graduate students with a broad knowledge base consisting of theory, research, and practice.

1.29 Inform graduate students of the ethical responsibilities and standards of the profession.

1.30 Assess all relevant competencies and interpersonal functioning of students throughout the program, communicate these assessments to students, and take appropriate corrective actions including dismissal when warranted.

1.31 Assure that field supervisors are qualified to provide supervision to graduate students and are informed of their ethical responsibilities in this role.

2. *Student Learning and Development.* Student development is an essential purpose of higher education, and the pursuit of this aim is a major responsibility of student affairs. Development is complex and includes cognitive, physical, moral, social, career, spiritual, personality, and educational dimensions. Professionals must be sensitive to the variety of backgrounds, cultures, and personal characteristics evident in the student population and use appropriate theoretical perspectives to identify learning opportunities and to reduce barriers that inhibit development.

As ACPA members, student affairs professionals will:

2.1 Treat students as individuals who possess dignity, worth, and the ability to be self-directed.

2.2 Avoid dual relationships with students (e.g., counselor/employer, supervisor/best friend, or faculty/sexual partner) that may involve incompatible roles and conflicting responsibilities.

2.3 Abstain from sexual harassment.

2.4 Abstain from sexual intimacies with clients or with students for whom they have supervisory, evaluative, or instructional responsibility.

2.5 Inform students of the conditions under which they may receive assistance and the limits of confidentiality when the counseling relationship is initiated.

2.6 Avoid entering or continuing helping relationships if benefits to students are unlikely. They will refer students to appropriate specialists and recognize that if the referral is declined, they are not obligated to continue the relationship.

2.7 Inform students about the purpose of assessment and make explicit the planned use of results prior to assessment.

2.8 Provide appropriate information to students prior to and following the use of any assessment procedure to place results in proper perspective with other relevant factors (e.g., socioeconomic, ethnic, cultural, and gender related experiences).

2.9 Confront students regarding issues, attitudes, and behaviors that have ethical implications.

3. *Responsibility to the Institution.* Institutions of higher education provide the context for student affairs practice. Institutional mission, policies, organizational structure, and culture, combined with individual judgment and professional standards, define and delimit the nature and extent of practice. Student affairs professionals share responsibility with other members of the academic community for fulfilling the institutional mission. Responsibility to promote the development of individual students and to support the institution's policies and interests require that professionals balance competing demands.

As ACPA members, student affairs professionals will:

3.1 Contribute to their institution by supporting its mission, goals, and policies.

3.2 Seek resolution when they and their institution encounter substantial disagreements concerning professional or personal values. Resolution may require sustained efforts to modify institutional policies and practices or result in voluntary termination of employment.

3.3 Recognize that conflicts among students, colleagues, or the institution should be resolved without diminishing appropriate obligations to any party involved.

3.4 Assure that information provided about the institution is factual and accurate.

3.5 Inform appropriate officials of conditions that may be disruptive or damaging to their institution.

3.6 Inform supervisors of conditions or practices that may restrict institutional or professional effectiveness.

3.7 Recognize their fiduciary responsibility to the institution. They will assure that funds for which they have oversight are expended following established procedures and in ways that optimize value, are accounted for properly, and contribute to the accomplishment of the institution's mission. They also will assure equipment, facilities, personnel, and other resources are used to promote the welfare of the institution and students.

3.8 Restrict their private interests, obligations, and transactions in ways to minimize conflicts of interest or the appearance of conflicts of interest. They will identify their personal views and actions as private citizens from those expressed or undertaken as institutional representatives.

3.9 Collaborate and share professional expertise with members of the academic community.

3.10 Evaluate programs, services, and organizational structures regularly and systematically to assure conformity to published standards and guidelines. Evaluations should be conducted using rigorous evaluation methods and principles, and the results should be made available to appropriate institutional personnel.

3.11 Evaluate job performance of subordinates regularly and recommend appropriate actions to enhance professional development and improve performance.

3.12 Provide fair and honest assessments of colleagues' job performance.

3.13 Seek evaluations of their job performance and/or services they provide.

3.14 Provide training to student affairs search and screening committee members who are unfamiliar with the profession.

3.15 Disseminate information that accurately describes the responsibilities of position vacancies, required qualifications, and the institution.

3.16 Follow a published interview and selection process that periodically notifies applicants of their status.

4. *Responsibility to Society.* Student affairs professionals, both as citizens and practitioners, have a responsibility to contribute to the improvement of the communities in which they live and work. They respect individuality and recognize that worth is not diminished by characteristics such as age, culture, ethnicity, gender, disabling condition, race, religion, or sexual/affectional orientation. Student affairs professionals work to protect human rights and promote an appreciation of human diversity in higher education.

As ACPA members, student affairs professionals will:

4.1 Assist students in becoming productive and responsible citizens.

4.2 Demonstrate concern for the welfare of all students and work for constructive change on behalf of students.

4.3 Not discriminate on the basis of age, culture, ethnicity, gender, disabling condition, race, religion, or sexual/affectional orientation. They will work to modify discriminatory practices.

4.4 Demonstrate regard for social codes and moral expectations of the communities in which they live and work. They will recognize that violations of accepted moral and legal standards may involve their clients, students or colleagues in damaging personal conflicts and may impugn the integrity of the profession, their own reputations, and that of the employing institution.

4.5 Report to the appropriate authority any condition that is likely to harm their clients and/or others.

Reference

American Association for Counseling and Development. (1988). *Ethical standards.* Alexandria, VA: Author.

As revised and approved by ACPA Executive Council, July 1989.

CODE OF ETHICS FOR MENTAL HEALTH COUNSELORS, 1987

(This code is an adaptation of the code of the Board of Licensed Professional Counselors in Virginia and APGA Code of Ethics.)

Preamble

Mental Health Counselors believe in the dignity and worth of the individual. They are committed to increasing knowledge of human behavior and understanding of themselves and others. While pursuing these endeavors, they make every reasonable effort to protect the welfare of those who seek their services or of any subject that may be the object of study. They use their skills only for purposes consistent with these values and do not knowingly permit their misuse by others. While demanding for themselves freedom of inquiry and community, mental health counselors accept the responsibility this freedom confers: competence, objectivity in the application of skills and concern for the best interests of clients, colleagues, and society in general. In the pursuit of these ideals, mental health counselors subscribe to the following principles:

Principle 1. Responsibility

In their commitment to the understanding of human behavior, mental health counselors value objectivity and integrity, and in providing services they maintain the highest standards. They accept responsibility for the consequences of their work and make every effort to insure that their services are used appropriately.

a. Mental health counselors accept ultimate responsibility for selecting appropriate areas for investigation and the methods relevant to minimize the possibility that their finding will be misleading. They provide thorough discussion of the limitations of their data and alternative hypotheses, especially where their work touches on social policy or might be misconstrued to the detriment of specific age, sex, ethnic, socioeconomic, or other social categories. In publishing reports of their work, they never discard observations that may modify the interpretation of results. Mental health counselors take credit only for the work they have actually done. In pursuing research, mental health counselors ascertain that their efforts will not lead to changes in individuals or organizations unless such changes are part of the agreement at the time of obtaining informed consent. Mental health counselors clarify in advance the expectations for sharing and utilizing research data. They avoid dual relationships which may limit objectivity, whether theoretical, political, or monetary, so that interference with data, subjects, and milieu is kept to a minimum.

b. As employees of an institution or agency, mental health counselors have the responsibility of remaining alert to institutional pressures which may distort reports of counseling findings or use them in ways counter to the promotion of human welfare.

c. When serving as members of governmental or other organizational bodies, mental health counselors remain accountable as individuals to the Code of Ethics of the American Mental Health Counselors Association (AMHCA).

d. As teachers, mental health counselors recognize their primary obligation to help others acquire knowledge and skill. They maintain high standards of scholarship and objectivity by presenting counseling information fully and accurately, and by giving appropriate recognition to alternative viewpoints.

e. As practitioners, mental health counselors know that they bear a heavy social responsibility because their recommendations and professional actions may alter the lives of others. They, therefore, remain fully cognizant of their impact and alert to personal, social, organizational, financial or political situations or pressures which might lead to misuse of their influence.

f. Mental health counselors provide reasonable and timely feedback to employees, trainees, supervisors, students, clients, and others whose work they may evaluate.

Principle 2. Competence

The maintenance of high standards of professional competence is a responsibility shared by all mental health counselors in the interest of the public and the profession as a whole. Mental health counselors recognize the boundaries of their competence and the limitations of their techniques and only provide services, use techniques, or offer opinions as professionals that meet recognized standards. Throughout their careers, mental health counselors maintain knowledge of professional information related to the services they render.

a. Mental health counselors accurately represent their competence, education, training and experience.

b. As teachers, mental health counselors perform their duties based on careful preparation so that their instruction is accurate, up-to-date and scholarly.

c. Mental health counselors recognize the need for continuing training to prepare themselves to serve persons of all ages and cultural backgrounds. They are open to new procedures and sensitive to differences between groups of people and changes in expectations and values over time.

d. Mental health counselors with the responsibility for decisions involving individuals or policies based on test results should know and understand literature relevant to the tests used and testing problems with which they deal.

e. Mental health counselors/practitioners recognize that their effectiveness depends in part upon their ability to maintain sound interpersonal relations, that temporary or more enduring aberrations on their part may interfere with their abilities or distort their appraisals of others. Therefore, they refrain from undertaking any activity in which their personal problems are likely to lead to inadequate professional services or harm to a client, or, if they are already engaged in such activity when they become aware of their personal problems, they would seek competent professional assistance to determine whether they should suspend or terminate services to one or all of their clients.

f. The mental health counselor has a responsibility both to the individual who is served and to the institution with which the service is performed to maintain high standards of professional conduct. The mental health counselor strives to maintain the highest levels of professional services offered to the individuals to be served. The mental health counselor also strives to assist the agency, organization or institution in providing the highest caliber of professional services. The acceptance of employment in an institution implies that the mental health counselor is in substantial agreement with the general policies and principles of the institution. If, despite concerted efforts, the member cannot reach agreement with the employer as to acceptable standards of conduct that allow for changes in institutional policy conducive to the positive growth and development of counselees, then terminating the affiliation should be seriously considered.

g. Ethical behavior among professional associates, mental health counselors and non-mental health counselors, is expected at all times. When information is possessed which raises serious doubt as to the ethical behavior of professional colleagues, whether Association members or not, the mental health counselor is obligated to take action to attempt to rectify such a condition. Such action shall utilize the institution's channels first and then utilize procedures established by the state, division, or Association.

h. The mental health counselor is aware of the intimacy of the counseling relationship and maintains a healthy respect for the personhood of the client and avoids engaging in activities that seek to meet the mental health counselor's personal needs at the expense of the client. Through awareness of the negative impact of both racial and sexual stereotyping and discrimination, the member strives to ensure the individual rights and personal dignity of the client in the counseling relationship.

Principle 3. Moral and Legal Standards

Mental health counselors moral, ethical and legal standards of behavior are a personal matter to the same degree as they are for any other citizen, except as these may compromise the fulfillment of their professional responsibilities, or reduce the trust in counseling or counselors held by the general public. Regarding their own behavior, mental health counselors should be aware of the prevailing community standards and of the possible impact upon the quality of professional services provided by their conformance to or deviation from these standards. Mental health counselors should also be aware of the possible impact of their public behavior upon the ability of colleagues to perform their professional duties.

a. To protect public confidence in the profession of counseling, mental health counselors will avoid public behavior that is clearly in violation of accepted moral and legal standards.

b. To protect students, mental health counselors/teachers will be aware of the diverse backgrounds of students and, when dealing with topics that may give offense, will see that the material is treated objectively, that it is clearly relevant to the course, and that it is treated in a manner for which the student is prepared.

c. Providers of counseling services conform to the statutes relating to such services as established by their state and its regulating professional board(s).

d. As employees, mental health counselors refuse to participate in employer's practices which are inconsistent with the moral and legal standards established by federal or state legislation regarding the treatment of employees or of the public. In particular and for example, mental health counselors will not condone practices which result in illegal or otherwise unjustifiable discrimination on the basis of race, sex, religion or national origin in hiring, promotion or training.

e. In providing counseling services to clients mental health counselors avoid any action that will violate or diminish the legal and civil rights of clients or of others who may be affected by the action.

f. Sexual conduct, not limited to sexual intercourse, between mental health counselors and clients is specifically in violation of this code of ethics. This does not, however, prohibit the use of explicit instructional aids including films and video tapes. Such use is within accepted practices of trained and competent sex therapists.

Principle 4. Public Statements

Mental health counselors in their professional roles may be expected or required to make public statements providing counseling information, professional opinions, or supply information about the availability of counseling products and services. In making such statements, mental health counselors take full account of the limits and uncertainties of present counseling knowledge and techniques. They represent, as objectively as possible, their professional qualifications, affiliations, and functions, as well as those of the institutions or organizations with which the statements may be associated. All public statements, announcements of services, and promotional activities should serve the purpose of providing sufficient information to aid the consumer public in making informed judgements and choices on matters that concern it.

a. When announcing professional counseling services, mental health counselors limit the information to: name, highest relevant degree conferred, certification or licensure, address, telephone number, office hours, cost of services, and a brief explanation of the other types of services offered but not evaluative as to their quality or uniqueness. They will not contain testimonials by implication. They will not claim uniqueness of skill or methods beyond those acceptable and public scientific evidence.

b. In announcing the availability of counseling services or products, mental health counselors will not display their affiliations with organizations or agencies in a manner that implies the sponsorship or certification of the organization or agency. They will not name their employer or professional associations unless the services are in fact to be provided by or under

195

the responsible, direct supervision and continuing control of such organizations or agencies.

c. Mental health counselors associated with the development or promotion of counseling device, books, or other products offered for commercial sale will make every effort to insure that announcements and advertisements are presented in a professional and factually informative manner without unsupported claims of superiority must be supported by scientifically acceptable evidence or by willingness to aid and encourage independent professional scrutiny or scientific test.

d. Mental health counselors engaged in radio, television or other public media activities will not participate in commercial announcements recommending to the general public the purchase or use of any proprietary or single-source product or service.

e. Mental health counselors who describe counseling or the services of professional counselors to the general public accept the obligation to present the material fairly and accurately, avoiding misrepresentation through sensationalism, exaggeration or superficiality. Mental health counselors will be guided by the primary obligation to aid the public in forming their own informed judgements, opinions and choices.

f. As teachers, mental health counselors ensure their statements in catalogs and course outlines are accurate, particularly in terms of subject matter to be covered, bases for grading, and nature of classroom experiences.

g. Mental health counselors accept the obligation to correct others who may represent their professional qualifications or associations with products or services in a manner incompatible with these guidelines.

h. Mental health counselors providing consultation, workshops, training, and other technical services may refer to previous satisfied clients in their advertising, provided there is no implication that such advertising refers to counseling services.

Principle 5. Confidentiality

Mental health counselors have a primary obligation to safeguard information about individuals obtained in the course of teaching, practice, or research. Personal information if communicated to others only with the person's written consent or in those circumstances where there is clear and imminent danger to the client, to others or to society. Disclosures of counseling information are restricted to what is necessary, relevant, and verifiable.

a. All materials in the official record shall be shared with the client who shall have the right to decide what information may be shared with anyone beyond the immediate provider of service and to be informed of the implications of the materials to be shared.

b. The anonymity of clients served in public and other agencies is preserved, if at all possible, by withholding names and personal identifying data. If external conditions require reporting such information, the client shall be so informed.

c. Information received in confidence by one agency or person shall not be forwarded to another person or agency without the client's written permission.

d. Service providers have a responsibility to insure the accuracy and to indicate the validity of data shared with their parties.

e. Case reports presented in classes, professional meetings, or in publications shall be so disguised that no identification is possible unless the client or responsible authority has read the report and agreed in writing to its presentation or publication.

f. Counseling reports and records are maintained under conditions of security and provisions are made for their destruction when they have outlived their usefulness. Mental health counselors insure that privacy and confidentiality are maintained by all persons in the employ or volunteers, and community aides.

g. Mental health counselors who ask that an individual reveal personal information in the course of interviewing, testing or evaluation, or who allow such information to be divulged, do so only after making certain that the person or authorized representative is fully aware of the purposes of the interview, testing or evaluation and of the ways in which the information will be used.

h. Sessions with clients are taped or otherwise recorded only with their written permission or the written permission of a responsible guardian. Even with guardian written consent one should not record a session against the expressed wishes of a client.

i. Where a child or adolescent is the primary client, the interests of the minor shall be paramount.

j. In work with families, the rights of each family member should be safeguarded. The provider of service also has the responsibility to discuss the contents of the record with the parent and/or child, as appropriate, and to keep separate those parts which should remain the property of each family member.

Principle 6. Welfare of the Consumer

Mental health counselors respect the integrity and protect the welfare of the people and groups with whom they work. When there is a conflict of interest between the client and the mental health counselor employing institution, the mental health counselors clarify the nature and direction of their loyalties and responsibilities and keep all parties informed of their commitments. Mental health counselors fully inform consumers as to the purpose and nature of any evaluative, treatment, educational or training procedure, and they freely acknowledge that clients, students, or subjects have freedom of choice with regard to participation.

a. Mental health counselors are continually cognizant both of their own needs and of their inherently powerful position "vis-a-vis" clients, in order to avoid exploiting the client's trust and dependency. Mental health counselors make every effort to avoid dual relationships with clients and/or relationships which might impair their professional judgement or increase the risk of client exploitation. Examples of such dual relationships include treating an employee or supervisor, treating a close friend or family relative and sexual relationships with clients.

b. Where mental health counselors work with members of an organization goes beyond reasonable conditions of employment, mental health counselors recognize possible conflicts of interest that may arise. When such conflicts occur, mental health counselors clarify the nature of the conflict and inform all parties of the nature and directions of the loyalties and responsibilities involved.

c. When acting as supervisors, trainers, or employers, mental health counselors accord recipients informed choice, confidentiality, and protection from physical and mental harm.

d. Financial arrangements in professional practice are in accord with professional standards that safeguard the best interests of the client and that are clearly understood by the client in advance of billing. This may best be done by the use of a contract. Mental health counselors are responsible for assisting clients in finding needed services in those instances where payment of the usual fee would be a hardship. No commission or rebate or other form of remuneration may be given or received for referral of clients for professional services, whether by an individual or by an agency.

e. Mental health counselors are responsible for making their services readily accessible to clients in a manner that facilitates the client's ability to make an informed choice when selecting a service provider. This responsibility includes a clear description of what the client may expect in the way of tests, reports, billing, therapeutic regime and schedules and the use of the mental health counselor's Statement of Professional Disclosure.

f. Mental health counselors who find that their services are not beneficial to the client have the responsibility to make this known to the responsible persons.

g. Mental health counselors are accountable to the parties who refer and support counseling services and to the general public and are cognizant of the indirect or long-range effects of their intervention.

h. The mental health counselor attempts to terminate a private service or consulting relationship when it is reasonably clear to the mental health counselor that the consumer is not benefitting from it. If a consumer is receiving services from another mental health professional, mental health counselors do not offer their services directly to the consumer without informing the professional persons already involved in order to avoid confusion and conflict for the consumer.

i. The mental health counselor has the responsibility to screen prospective group participants, especially when the emphasis is on self-understanding and growth through self-disclosure. The member should maintain an awareness of the group participants' compatibility throughout the life of the group.

j. The mental health counselor may choose to consult with any other professionally competent person about a client. In choosing a consultant, the mental health counselor should avoid placing the consultant in a conflict of interest situation that would preclude the consultant's being a proper party to the mental health counselor's efforts to help the clients.

k. If the mental health counselor is unable to be of professional assistance to the client, the mental health counselor should avoid initiating the counseling relationship or the mental health counselor terminates the relationship. In either event, the member is obligated to suggest appropriate alternatives. (It is incumbent upon the mental health counselor to be knowledgeable about referral resources so that a satisfactory referral can be initiated.) In the event the client declines the suggested referral, the mental health counselor is not obligated to continue the relationship.

l. When the mental health counselor has other relationships, particularly of an administrative, supervisor, and/or evaluative nature, with an individual seeking counseling services, the mental health counselor should not serve as the counselor but should refer the individual to another professional. Only in instances where such an alternative is unavailable and where the individual's situation definitely warrants counseling intervention should the mental health counselor enter into and/or maintain a counseling relationship. Dual relationships with clients which might impair the member's objectivity and professional judgement (such as with close friends or relatives, sexual intimacies with any client, etc.) must be avoided and/or the counseling relationship terminated through referral to another competent professional.

m. All experimental methods of treatment must be clearly indicated to prospective recipients, and safety precautions are to be adhered to by the mental health counselor instituting treatment.

n. When the member is engaged in short-term group treatment/training programs, e.g., marathons and other encounter-type or growth groups, the member ensures that there is professional assistance available during and following the group experience.

Principle 7. Professional Relationship

Mental health counselors act with due regard to the needs and feelings of their colleagues in counseling and other professions. Mental health counselors respect the prerogatives and obligations of the institutions or organizations with which they are associated.

a. Mental health counselors understand the areas of competence of related professions and make full use of other professional, technical, and administrative resources which best serve the interests of consumers. The absence of formal relationships with other professional workers does not relieve mental health counselors from the responsibility of securing for their clients the best possible professional service; indeed, this circumstance presents a challenge to the professional competence of mental health counselors, requiring special sensitivity to problems outside their areas of training, and foresight, diligence, and tact in obtaining the professional assistance needed by clients.

b. Mental health counselors know and take into account the traditions and practices of other professional groups with which they work and cooperate fully with members of such groups when research, services, and other functions are shared or in working for the benefit of public welfare.

c. Mental health counselors strive to provide positive conditions for those they employ and they spell out clearly the conditions of such employment. They encourage their employees to engage in activities that facilitate their further professional development.

d. Mental health counselors respect the viability, reputation, and the proprietary right of organizations which they serve. Mental health counselors show due regard for the interest of their present or prospective employers. In those instances where they are critical of policies, they attempt to effect change by constructive action within the organization.

e. In the pursuit of research, mental health counselors give sponsoring agencies, host institutions, and publication channels the same respect and opportunity for giving informed consent that they accord to individual research participants. They are aware of their obligation to future research workers and insure that host institutions are given feedback information and proper acknowledgment.

f. Credit is assigned to those who have contributed to a publication, in proportion to their contribution.

g. When a mental health counselor violates ethical standards, mental health counselors who know first-hand of such activities should, if possible, attempt to rectify the situation. Failing an informal solution, mental health counselors should bring such unethical activities to the attention of the appropriate state, and/or national committee on ethics and professional conduct. Only after all professional alternatives have been utilized will a mental health counselor begin legal action for resolution.

Principle 8. Utilization of Assessment Techniques

In the development, publication, and utilization of counseling assessment techniques, mental health counselors follow relevant standards. Individuals examined, or their legal guardians, have the right to know the results, the interpretations made, and where appropriate, the particulars on which final judgement was based. Test users should take precautions to protect test security but not at the expense of an individual's right to understand the basis for decisions that adversely affect that individual or that individual's dependents.

a. The client has the right to have and the provider has the responsibility to give explanations of test results in language the client can understand.

b. When a test is published or otherwise made available for operational use, it should be accompanied by a manual (or other published or readily available information) that makes every reasonable effort to describe fully the development of the test, the rationale, specifications followed in writing items analysis or other research. The test, the manual, the record forms and other accompanying material should help users make correct interpretations of the test results and should warn against common misuses. The test manual should state explicitly the purposes and applications for which the test is recommended and identify any special qualifications required to administer the test and to interpret it properly. Evidence of validity and reliability, along with other relevant research data, should be presented in support of any claims made.

c. Norms presented in test manuals should refer to defined and clearly described populations. These populations should be the groups with whom users of the test will ordinarily wish to compare the persons tested. Test users should consider the possibility of bias in tests or in test items. When indicated, there should be an investigation of possible differences in validity

198

for ethnic, sex, or other subsamples that can be identified when the test is given.

d. Mental health counselors who have the responsibility for decisions about individuals or policies that are based on test results should have a thorough understanding of counseling or educational measurement and of validation and other test research.

e. Mental health counselors should develop procedures for systematically eliminating from data files test score information that has, because of the lapse of time, become obsolete.

f. Any individual or organization offering test scoring and interpretation services must be able to demonstrate that their programs are based on appropriate research to establish the validity of the programs and procedures used in arriving at interpretations. The public offering of an automated test interpretation service will be considered as a professional-to-professional consultation. In this the formal responsibility of the consultant is to the consultee but his/her ultimate and overriding responsibility is to the client.

g. Counseling services for the purpose of diagnosis, treatment, or personalized advice are provided only in the context of a professional relationship, and are not given by means of public lectures or demonstrations, newspapers or magazine articles, radio or television programs, mail, or similar media. The preparation of personnel reports and recommendations based on test data secured solely by mail is unethical unless such appraisals are an integral part of a continuing client relationship with a company, as a result of which the consulting clinical mental health counselor has intimate knowledge of the client's personal situation and can be assured thereby that his written appraisals will be adequate to the purpose and will be properly interpreted by the client. These reports must not be embellished with such detailed analyses of the subject's personality traits as would be appropriate only for intensive interviews with the subjects.

Principle 9. Pursuit of Research Activities

The decision to undertake research should rest upon a considered judgment by the individual mental health counselor about how best to contribute to counseling and to human welfare. Mental health counselors carry out their investigations with respect for the people who participate and with concern for their dignity and welfare.

a. In planning a study the investigator has the personal responsibility to make a careful evaluation of its ethical acceptability, taking into account the following principles for research with human beings. To the extent that this ap-praisal, weighing scientific and humane values, suggests a deviation from any principle, the investigator incurs an increasingly serious obligation to seek ethical advice and to observe more stringent safeguards to protect the rights of the human research participants.

b. Mental health counselors know and take into account the traditions and practices of other professional groups with members of such groups when research, services, and other functions are shared or in working for the benefit of public welfare.

c. Ethical practice requires the investigator to inform the participant of all features of the research that reasonably might be expected to influence willingness to participate, and to explain all other aspects of the research about which the participant inquires. Failure to make full disclosure gives added emphasis to the investigators abiding responsibility to protect the welfare and dignity of the research participant.

d. Openness and honesty are essential characteristics of the relationship between investigator and research participant. When the methodological requirements of a study necessitate concealment or deception, the investigator is required to insure as soon as possible the participant's understanding of the reasons for this action and to restore the quality of the relationship with the investigator.

e. In the pursuit of research, mental health counselors give sponsoring agencies, host institutions, and publication channels the same respect and oppportunity for giving informed consent that they accord to individual research participants. They are aware of their obligation to future research workers and insure that host institutions are given feedback information and proper acknowledgment.

f. Credit is assigned to those who have contributed to a publication, in proportion to their contribution.

g. The ethical investigator protects participants from physical and mental discomfort, harm and danger. If the risk of such consequences exists, the investigator is required to inform the participant of that fact, secure consent before proceeding, and take all possible measures to minimize distress. A research procedure may not be used if it is likely to cause serious and lasting harm to participants.

h. After the data are collected, ethical practice requires the investigator to provide the participant with a full clarification of the nature of the study and to remove any misconceptions that may have arisen. Where scientific or humane values justify delaying or withholding information the investigator acquires a special responsibility to assure that there are no damaging consequences for the participants.

i. Where research procedures may result in undesirable consequences for the participant, the investigator has the responsibility to detect and remove or correct these consequences, including, where relevant, long-term aftereffects.

j. Information obtained about the research participants during the course of an investigation is confidential. When the possibility exists that others may obtain access to such information, ethical research practice requires that the possibility, together with the plans for protecting confidentiality be explained to the participants as a part of the procedure for obtaining informed consent.

Principle 10. Private Practice

a. A mental health counselor should assist where permitted by legislation or judicial decision the profession in fulfilling its duty to make counseling services available in private settings.

b. In advertising services as a private practitioner the mental health counselor should advertise the services in such a manner so as to accurately inform the public as to services, expertise, profession, techniques of counseling in a professional manner. A mental health counselor who assumes an executive leadership role in the organization shall not permit his/her name to be used in professional notices during periods when not actively engaged in the private practice of counseling.

The mental health counselor may list the following: Highest relevant degree, type and level of certification or license, type and/or description of services and other relevant information. Such information should not contain false, inaccurate, misleading, partial, out-of-context or deceptive material or statements.

c. The mental health counselor may join in partnership/corporation with other mental health counselors and/or other professionals provided that each mental health counselor of the partnership or corporation makes clear the separate specialities by name in compliance with the regulations of the locality.

d. A mental health counselor has an obligation to withdraw from a counseling relationship if it is believed that employment will result in the violation of the code of ethics, if their mental capacity or physical condition renders it difficult to carry out an effective professional relationship, or if the mental health counselor is discharged by the client because the counseling relationship is no longer productive for the client.

e. A mental health counselor should adhere to and support the regulations for private practice of the locality where the services are offered.

f. Mental health counselors are discouraged from deliberate attempts to utilize one's institutional affiliation to recruit clients for one's private practice. Mental health counselors are to refrain from offering their services in the private sector, when they are employed by an institution in which this is prohibited by stated policies reflecting conditions for employment.

g. In establishing fees for professional counseling services, mental health counselors should consider the financial status of clients and locality. In the event that the established fee structure is inappropriate for a client, assistance should be provided in finding services of acceptable cost.

Principle 11. Consulting

a. The mental health counselor acting as consultant must have a high degree of self-awareness of his/her own values, knowledge, skills and needs in entering a helping relationship which involves human and/or organizational change and that the focus of the relationship be on the issues to be resolved and not on the person(s) presenting the problem.

b. There should be understanding and agreement between the mental health counselor and client for the problem definition, change goals and predicted consequences of interventions selected.

c. The mental health counselor must be reasonably certain that she/he or the organization represented have the necessary competencies and resources for giving the kind of help which is needed now or may develop later and that appropriate referral resources are available to the consultant, if needed later.

d. The mental health counselor relationship must be one in which client adaptability and growth toward self-direction are encouraged and cultivated. The mental health counselor must maintain this role consistently and not become a decision maker or substitute for the client.

e. When announcing consultant availability for services, the mental health counselor conscientiously adheres to professional standards.

f. The mental health counselor is expected to refuse a private fee or other remuneration for consultation with persons who are entitled to these services through the member's employing institution or agency. The policies of a particular agency may make explicit provisions for private practice with agency counselees by members of its staff. In such instances, the counselees must be apprised of other options open to them should they seek private counseling services.

Principle 12. Client's Rights

The following apply to all consumers of mental health services, including both in- and outpatients in all state, county, local, and private

200

care mental health facilities, as well as patients/ clients of mental health practitioners in private practice.

The client has the right:

a. to be treated with consideration and respect;

b. to expect quality service provided by concerned, competent staff;

c. to a clear statement of the purposes, goals, techniques, rules of procedure, and limitations as well as potential dangers of the services to be performed and all other information related to or likely to affect the on-going counseling relationship;

d. to obtain information about their case record and to have this information explained clearly and directly;

e. to full, knowledgeable, and responsible participation in the on-going treatment plan, to the maximum feasible extent;

f. to expect complete confidentiality and that no information will be released without written consent;

g. to see and discuss their charges and payment records;

h. to refuse any recommended services and be advised of the consequences of this action.

CODE OF PROFESSIONAL ETHICS FOR REHABILITATION COUNSELORS, 1987

Adopted by:
American Rehabilitation Counseling Association, Commission on Rehabilitation Counselor Certification, and National Rehabilitation Counseling Association

Preamble

Rehabilitation Counselors are committed to facilitating the personal and socio-economic functioning of individuals with disabilities toward achieving maximum independence in living. In fulfilling this commitment, Rehabilitation Counselors work with people, programs, institutions, and other professional service delivery systems. Rehabilitation Counselors recognize that both action and inaction can be facilitating or debilitating. Rehabilitation Counselors may be called upon to provide counseling, vocational exploration, psychological and vocational assessment, evaluation of social, medical, vocational, and psychiatric information, job placement and job development services, and other rehabilitation services and do so in a manner that is consistent with their education and experience. Moreover, Rehabilitation Counselors must also demonstrate their adherence to certain ethical standards and ensure that such

standards are vigorously enforced. The Code of Professional Ethics, henceforth referred to as the Code, has been designed to accomplish these goals.

The basic objective of the Code is to serve the public interest by specifying and enforcing the minimum ethical conduct rightfully expected of Rehabilitation Counselors as professionals and by facilitating voluntary compliance with standards considerably higher than the required minimum. Accordingly, the Code consists of two kinds of standards, *CANONS AND RULES OF PROFESSIONAL CONDUCT.*

The Canons are general standards of an aspirational and inspirational nature reflecting the fundamental spirit of caring and respect which all true professionals share. They are maxims which on their merits serve as model standards of exemplary professional conduct. The Canons also express the general concepts and principles from which the more specific Rules are derived.

Unlike the Canons, the Rules are specific standards of a mandatory and enforceable nature. The Rules prescribe the absolute minimum level of ethical conduct required of every Rehabilitation Counselor, regardless of occupational position. Rehabilitation Counselors who violate the rules of the Code will be subject to disciplinary action. A rule violation will also be interpreted as a violation of the applicable Canon and the general principles embodied thereof. Since the use of the Certified Rehabilitation Counselor (CRC) designation is a privilege granted by the Commission on Rehabilitation Counselor Certification (CRCC), the CRCC reserves unto itself the power to suspend or to revoke the privilege or to approve other penalties for Rule violation. Disciplinary penalties will be imposed as warranted by the severity of the offense and its attendant circumstances. All disciplinary actions will be undertaken in accordance with published procedures and penalties designed to assure the proper enforcement of the rules within the framework of due process and equal protection of the laws.

When there is reason to question the ethical propriety of specific activities or types of conduct, persons are encouraged to refrain from engaging in such activities or types of conduct until the matter has been clarified. Individuals who need assistance in interpreting the Code may request an advisory opinion from CRCC.

Since the ultimate goal of the Code is to foster the highest ethical conduct, inquiries are strongly encouraged, and CRCC will respond as quickly as possible to answer reasonable questions about appropriate ethical conduct.

REHABILITATION COUNSELOR CODE OF ETHICS

Canon 1 — MORAL AND LEGAL STANDARDS

Rehabilitation Counselors shall behave in a legal, ethical, and moral manner in the conduct of their profession, maintaining the integrity of the Code and avoiding any conduct or activity which would cause harm to others.

Rules of Professional Conduct

R1.1 Rehabilitation Counselors will obey the laws and statutes in the legal jurisdiction in which they practice and are subject to disciplinary action for any violation, to the extent that such violation suggests the likelihood of professional misconduct.

R1.2 Rehabilitation Counselors will be thoroughly familiar with, will observe, and will discuss with their clients the legal limitations of their services, or benefits offered to clients so as to facilitate honest and open communication and realistic expectations.

R1.3 Rehabilitation Counselors will be alert to legal parameters relevant to their practices and to disparities between legally mandated ethical and professional standards and the rules of this Code. Where such disparities exist, Rehabilitation Counselors will follow the legal mandates and will formally communicate any disparities to the appropriate committee on professional ethics and conduct. In the absence of legal guidelines, the Code is ethically binding.

R1.4 Rehabilitation Counselors will not engage in any act or omission of a dishonest, deceitful, or fraudulent nature in the conduct of their professional activities. They will not allow the pursuit of financial gain or other personal benefit to interfere with the exercise of sound professional judgment and skills, nor will Rehabilitation Counselors abuse their relationships with clients to promote personal or financial gain or the financial gain of their employing agencies.

R1.5 Rehabilitation Counselors will understand and abide by all rules of professional conduct which are prescribed in the Code of Professional Ethics.

R1.6 Rehabilitation Counselors will not advocate, sanction, participate in, cause to be accomplished, otherwise carry out through another, or condone any act which Rehabili-

tation Counselors are prohibited from performing by the Rules of this Code.

R1.7 Rehabilitation Counselors' moral and ethical standards of behavior are a personal matter to the same degree as they are for any other citizen, except as these may compromise the fulfillment of their professional responsibilities or reduce the public trust in rehabilitation counselors. To protect public confidence, rehabilitation counselors will avoid public behavior that is clearly in violation of accepted moral and ethical standards.

R1.8 Rehabilitation Counselors will respect the rights and reputation of any institution, organization, or firm with which they may be associated when making oral or written statements. In those instances where they are critical of policies, they attempt to effect change by constructive action within the organization.

R1.9 Rehabilitation Counselors will refuse to participate in employers' practices which are inconsistent with the moral or legal standards regarding the treatment of employees or the public. Rehabilitation Counselors will not condone practices which result in illegal or otherwise unjustifiable discrimination on the basis of race, sex, religion, disability, or national origin in hiring, promotion or training.

Canon 2 — COUNSELOR-CLIENT RELATIONSHIP

Rehabilitation Counselors shall respect the integrity and protect the welfare of the people and groups with whom they work. Rehabilitation Counselors' primary obligation is to the person with the disability and Rehabilitation Counselors shall endeavor at all times to place that interest above their own.

Rules of Professional Conduct

R2.1 Rehabilitation Counselors will make clear the purposes, goals, and limitations that may affect the counseling relationship.

R2.2 Rehabilitation Counselors will not misrepresent their role or competency to clients. Rehabilitation Counselors will provide information on their credentials, if requested, and will refer clients to other specialists as the clients' needs dictate.

R2.3 Rehabilitation Counselors will be continually cognizant of their own needs, values, and of their potentially influential position, vis-a-vis clients, students, and subordinates. They avoid exploiting the trust and dependency of such persons. Rehabilitation Counselors make every effort to avoid dual relationships that could impair their professional judgment or increase the risk of exploitation. Examples of such dual relationships include, but are not limited to, research with and treatment of employees, students, supervisors, close friends, or relatives. Sexual intimacies with clients are unethical.

R2.4 Rehabilitation Counselors will clearly define for themselves the nature of their loyalties and responsibilities. It is the responsibility of Rehabilitation Counselors to clarify the nature of their relationships to all parties when services are provided at the request of a third party. Where the demands of an organization require Rehabilitation Counselors to violate these Ethical Principles, Rehabilitation Counselors will clarify the nature of the conflict between the demands and these principles. They will inform all parties of rehabilitation counselors' ethical responsibilities and take appropriate action.

R2.5 Rehabilitation Counselors will inform all parties of the nature of their loyalties and the ethical constraints thereof, if the primary obligation of Rehabilitation Counselors cannot be to persons with disabilities. When the Rehabilitation Counselor is involved in a conflict between two persons with disabilities, Rehabilitation Counselors' primary obligation is to the resolution of such conflicts in a manner consistent with the Code, the relevant facts, and applicable laws and statutes.

R2.6 Rehabilitation Counselors will honor clients' right to consent to participate in rehabilitation. Rehabilitation Counselors will inform clients or the clients' legal guardians of factors that may affect clients' decisions to participate in rehabilitation, and will obtain written consent after clients or their legal guardians are fully informed of such factors. Rehabilitation Counselors who work with minors or other persons who are unable to give voluntary, informed consent, will take special care to protect their clients' best interests.

R2.7 Rehabilitation Counselors will avoid initiating or continuing a consulting or counseling relationship if it is expected that the relationship can be of no benefit to clients, in which case Rehabilitation Counselors shall suggest to clients appropriate alternatives.

R2.8 Rehabilitation Counselors will recognize that families are usually an important factor in clients' rehabilitation and will strive to enlist the understanding and involvement of families as a positive resource in promoting the client's rehabilitation. The clients' permission will be secured prior to family involvement.

R2.9 Rehabilitation Counselors will counsel clients in devising an integrated, individualized rehabilitation plan which offers reasonable promise of success and is consistent with clients' abilities and circumstances. Rehabilitation Counselors will follow-up persistently on rehabilitation plans to ensure their continued viability and effectiveness.

R2.10 Rehabilitation Counselors will not participate in placing clients in positions that will result in damaging the interest and welfare of either clients or employers. Rehabilitation Counselors will recommend employment of clients in only jobs and circumstances that are consistent with the clients' overall abilities, vocational limitations, physical restrictions, general temperament, interest and aptitude patterns, social skills, education, general qualifications and other relevant characteristics and needs.

Canon 3 — CLIENT ADVOCACY

Rehabilitation counselors shall serve as advocates for persons with disabilities.

Rules of Professional Conduct

R3.1 Rehabilitation Counselors will at all times be obligated to promoting access for persons with disabilities to programs of service, facilities, transportation, and communication, so that clients will not be excluded from the opportunity to participate fully in rehabilitation, education, and society.

R3.2 Rehabilitation Counselors will assure, prior to referring clients to programs, facilities, or employment settings, that they are appropriately accessible.

R3.3 Rehabilitation Counselors will strive to understand the accessibility problems, of persons with cognitive, hearing, mobility, visual and/or other disabilities and demonstrate such understanding in the practice of their profession.

R3.4 Rehabilitation Counselors will strive to eliminate attitudinal barriers, including sterotyping and discrimination, toward persons with disabilities and shall enhance their own sensitivity and awareness toward persons with disabilities.

R3.5 Rehabilitation Counselors will keep themselves aware of the actions taken by cooperating agencies on behalf of their clients and will act as advocates of clients to ensure effective service delivery.

Canon 4 — PROFESSIONAL RELATIONSHIPS

Rehabilitation Counselors shall act with integrity in their relationships with colleagues, other organizations, agencies, institutions, referral sources, and other professions so as to facilitate the contribution of all specialists toward achieving maximum benefit for clients.

Rules of Professional Conduct

R4.1 Rehabilitation Counselors will ensure that there is fair mutual understanding on the part of all agencies cooperating in the rehabilitation of clients and that any rehabilitation plan is developed with such mutual understanding.

R4.2 Rehabilitation Counselors will abide by and help to implement "team" decisions in formulating rehabilitation plans and procedures, even when not personally agreeing with such decisions, unless these decisions breach ethical rules.

R4.3 Rehabilitation Counselors will refrain from committing receiving counselors to any prescribed courses of action in relation to clients, when transferring clients to other colleagues or agencies.

R4.4 Rehabilitation Counselors, as referring counselors, will promptly supply all information necessary for a cooperating agency or counselor to be effective in serving clients.

R4.5 Rehabilitation Counselors will not offer on-going professional counseling/case management services to clients receiving such services from other Rehabilitation Counselors without notifying the other counselor. File review and second opinion services are not included in the concept of professional counseling/case management services.

R4.6 Rehabilitation Counselors will secure from other specialists appropriate reports and evaluations, when such reports are essential for clients' rehabilitation.

R4.7 Rehabilitation Counselors will not discuss in a disparaging way with clients the competency of other counselors or agencies, or the judgments made, the methods used, or the quality of rehabilitation plans.

R4.8 Rehabilitation Counselors will not exploit their professional relationships with clients, supervisors, colleagues, students, or employees sexually or otherwise. Rehabilitation Counselors will not condone or engage in sexual harassment, defined as deliberate or repeated comments, gestures, or physical contacts of a sexual nature.

R4.9 Rehabilitation Counselors who know of an ethical violation by another Rehabilitation Counselor will informally attempt to resolve the issue with the counselor, when the misconduct is of a minor nature and/or appears to be due to lack of sensitivity, knowledge, or experience. If the violation does not seem amenable to an informal solution, or is of a more serious nature, Rehabilitation Counselors will bring it to the attention of the appropriate committee on professional ethics and conduct.

R4.10 Rehabilitation Counselors possessing information concerning an alleged violation of this Code, shall, upon request, reveal such information to the Commission on Rehabilitation Counselor Certification or other authority empowered to investigate or act upon the alleged violation unless the information is confidential or protected by law.

R4.11 Rehabilitation Counselors who employ or supervise other professionals or professionals in training will facilitate the further professional development of these individuals. They provide appropriate working conditions, timely evaluations, constructive consultation, and experience opportunities.

Canon 5 — PUBLIC STATEMENTS/ FEES

Rehabilitation Counselors shall adhere to professional standards in establishing fees and promoting their professional services.

Rules of Professional Conduct

R5.1 Rehabilitation Counselors will consider carefully the value of their services and the ability of clients to meet the financial burden. In establishing reasonable fees for professional services, Rehabilitation Counselors will be willing to contribute a portion of their services for which there may be little or no financial return.

R5.2 Rehabilitation Counselors will not accept for professional work a fee or any other form of remuneration from clients who are entitled to their services through an institution or agency or other benefits structure, unless clients have been fully informed of the availability of services from such other sources.

R5.3 Rehabilitation Counselors will neither give nor receive a commission or rebate or any other form of remuneration for referral of clients for professional services.

R5.4 Rehabilitation Counselors who describe rehabilitation counseling or the services of Rehabilitation Counselors to the general public will fairly and accurately present the material, avoiding misrepresentation through sensationalism, exaggeration, or superficiality.

Canon 6 — CONFIDENTIALITY

Rehabilitation Counselors shall respect the confidentiality of information obtained from clients in the course of their work.

Rules of Professional Conduct

R6.1 Rehabilitation Counselors will inform clients at the onset of the counseling relationship of the limits of confidentiality.

R6.2 Rehabilitation Counselors will take reasonable personal action, or inform responsible authorities, or inform those persons at risk, when clients' conditions or actions indicate that there is clear and imminent danger to clients or others after advising clients that this must be done. Consultation with other professionals may be used where appropriate. The assumption of responsibility for clients must be taken only after careful deliberation and clients must be involved in the resumption of responsibility as quickly as possible.

R6.3 Rehabilitation Counselors will not forward to another person, agency, or potential employer, any confidential information without the written permission of clients or the clients' legal guardian.

R6.4 Rehabilitation Counselors will ensure that there are defined policies and practices in other agencies cooperatively serving rehabilitation clients, which effectively protect information confidentiality and the general welfare of clients.

R6.5 Rehabilitation Counselors will safeguard the maintenance, storage and disposal of clients' records so that unauthorized persons shall not have access to the records. All non-professional persons who must have access to the client's records will be thoroughly briefed concerning the confidential standards to be observed.

R6.6 Rehabilitation Counselors, in the preparation of written and oral reports, will present only data germane to the purpose of the evaluation, rehabilitation progress, or rehabilitation plan, and will make every effort to avoid undue invasion of privacy.

R6.7 Rehabilitation Counselors will obtain written permission from clients or their legal guardians prior to taping or otherwise recording counseling sessions. Even with guardians' written consent, Rehabilitation Counselors shall not record a session against the expressed wishes of clients.

R6.8 Rehabilitation Counselors will persist in claiming the privileged status of confidential information obtained from clients, where communications are privileged by statute for Rehabilitation Counselors.

R6.9 Rehabilitation Counselors will provide prospective employers with only such information about clients as is necessary to identify suitability and shall secure the permission of clients or their legal guardians for the release of any information which might be considered confidential.

Canon 7 — ASSESSMENT

Rehabilitation Counselors shall promote the welfare of clients in the selection, utilization, and interpretation of assessment measures.

Rules of Professional Conduct

R7.1 Rehabilitation Counselors will recognize that different tests demand different levels of competence for administration, scoring, and interpretation, and will recognize the limits of their competence and perform only those functions for which they are trained.

R7.2 Rehabilitation Counselors will consider carefully the specific validity, reliability, and appropriateness of a test, when selecting such a test for use in a given situation or with particular clients. Rehabilitation Counselors will proceed with caution when attempting to

evaluate and interpret the performance of persons with disabilities, minority group members, or other persons who are not represented in the norm on which the instrument was standardized. Rehabilitation Counselors will recognize the effects of socioeconomic, ethnic, disability, and cultural factors on test scores.

R7.3 Rehabilitation Counselors will administer tests under the same conditions that were established in their standardization. When tests are not administered under standard conditions, as may be necessary to accommodate modifications for clients with disabilities or when unusual behavior or irregularities occur during the testing session, those conditions will be noted and taken into account in interpretation.

R7.4 Rehabilitation Counselors will ensure that instrument limitations are not exceeded and that periodic reassessments are made to prevent client stereotyping.

R7.5 Rehabilitation Counselors will make known the purpose of testing and the explicit use of the results to clients prior to testing. Recognizing the right of clients to have test results, Rehabilitation Counselors will give explanations of test results in language clients can understand.

R7.6 Rehabilitation Counselors will see that specific interpretation accompanies any release of individual data. The clients' welfare and explicit prior permission will be the criteria for determining the recipients of the test results. The interpretation of test data will be related to the particular goals of evaluation.

R7.7 Rehabilitation Counselors will attempt to ensure when utilizing computerized assessment services that such services are based on appropriate research to establish the validity of the programs and procedures used in arriving at interpretations. The public offering of an automated test interpretation service will be considered as a professional-to-professional consultation. In this the formal responsibility of the consultant is to the consultee, but the ultimate and overriding responsibility is to clients.

R7.8 Rehabilitation Counselors will not prepare treatment plans nor make recommendations based on test data secured solely by mail, unless such appraisals are an integral part of the continuing client relationship.

R7.9 Rehabilitation Counselors will recognize that assessment results may become obsolete. They make every effort to avoid and prevent the misuse of obsolete measures.

Canon 8 — RESEARCH ACTIVITIES

Rehabilitation Counselors shall assist in efforts to expand the knowledge needed to more effectively serve persons with disabilities.

Rules of Professional Conduct

R8.1 Rehabilitation Counselors will ensure that data for research meets rigid standards of validity, honesty, and protection of confidentiality.

R8.2 Rehabilitation Counselors will be aware of and responsive to all pertinent guidelines on research with human subjects. In planning any research activity dealing with human subjects, Rehabilitation Counselors will ensure that the research problems, design, and execution are in full compliance with such guidelines.

R8.3 Rehabilitation Counselors presenting case studies in classes, professional meetings, or publications will confine the content to that which can be disguised to ensure full protection of the identity of clients.

R8.4 Rehabilitation Counselors will assign credit to those who have contributed to publications in proportion to their contribution.

R8.5 Rehabilitation Counselors recognize that honesty and openness are essential characteristics of the relationship between Rehabilitation Counselors and research participants. When the methodological requirements of a study necessitate concealment or deception, Rehabilitation Counselors will ensure the participants' understanding of the reasons for this action.

Canon 9 — COMPETENCE

Rehabilitation Counselors shall establish and maintain their professional competencies at such a level that their clients receive the benefit of the highest quality of services the profession is capable of offering.

Rules of Professional Conduct

R9.1 Rehabilitation Counselors will function within the limits of their defined role, training, and technical competency and will accept only those positions for which they are professionally qualified.

R9.2 Rehabilitation Counselors will continuously strive through reading, attending professional meetings, and taking courses of instruction to keep abreast of new developments and concepts and practices that are essential to the provision of the highest quality of service to their clients.

R9.3 Rehabilitation Counselors, recognizing that personal problems and conflicts may interfere with their professional effectiveness, will refrain from undertaking any activity in which their personal problems are likely to lead to inadequate performance. If they are already engaged in such activity when they become aware of their personal problems, they will seek competent professional assistance to determine whether they should

suspend, terminate or limit the scope of their professional activities.

R9.4 Rehabilitation Counselors who are educators will perform their duties based on careful preparation so that their instruction is accurate, up-to-date and scholarly.

R9.5 Rehabilitation Counselors who are educators will ensure that statements in catalogs and course outlines are accurate, particularly in terms of subject matter covered, bases for grading, and nature of classroom experiences.

R9.6 Rehabilitation Counselors who are educators will maintain high standards of knowledge and skill by presenting rehabilitation counseling information fully and accurately, and by giving appropriate recognition to alternative viewpoints.

Canon 10 — CRC CREDENTIAL

Rehabilitation Counselors holding the Certified Rehabilitation Counselor (CRC) designation shall honor the integrity and respect the limitations placed upon its use.

Rules of Professional Conduct

R10.1 Certified Rehabilitation Counselors will use the Certified Rehabilitation Counselor (CRC) designation only in accordance with the relevant GUIDELINES promulgated by the Commission on Rehabilitation Counselor Certification.

R10.2 Certified Rehabilitation Counselors will not attribute to the mere possession of the designation depth or scope of knowledge, skill, and professional capabilities greater than those demonstrated by achievement of the CRC designation.

R10.3 Certified Rehabilitation Counselors will not make unfair comparisons between a person who holds the Certified Rehabilitation Counselor (CRC) designation and one who does not.

R10.4 Certified Rehabilitation Counselors will not write, speak, or act in such a way as to lead another to believe Certified Rehabilitation Counselors are officially representing the Commission on Rehabilitation Counselor Certification, unless such written permission has been granted by the said Commission.

R10.5 Certified Rehabilitation Counselors will make no claim to unique skills or devices not available to others in the profession unless the special efficacy of such unique skills or device has been demonstrated by scientifically accepted evidence.

R10.6 Certified Rehabilitation Counselors will not initiate or support candidacy for certification by the Commission on Rehabilitation Counselor Certification of any individual known to engage in professional practices which violate the ethical standards prescribed by this Code.

AMERICAN SCHOOL COUNSELOR ASSOCIATION

ETHICAL STANDARDS FOR SCHOOL COUNSELORS, 1972

Preamble

The American School Counselor Association is a professional organization whose members have a unique and distinctive preparation, grounded in the behavioral sciences, with training in clinical skills adapted to the school setting. School counselors subscribe to the following basic tenets of the counseling process from which professional responsibilities are derived:

1. Each person has the right to respect and dignity as a human being and to counseling services without prejudice as to person, character, belief or practice.

2. Each person has the right to self-direction and self-development.

3. Each person has the right of choice and the responsibility for decisions reached.

4. The counselor assists in the growth and development of each individual and uses his/her highly specialized skills to insure that the rights of the counselee are properly protected within the structure of the school program.

5. The counselor-client relationship is private and thereby requires compliance with all laws, policies and ethical standards pertaining to confidentiality.

In this document, the American School Counselor Association has identified the standards of conduct necessary to maintain and regulate the high standards of integrity and leadership among its members. The Association recognizes the basic commitment of its members to the Ethical Standards of its parent organization, the American Association for Counseling and Development, and nothing in this document shall be construed to supplant that code. The Ethical Standards for School Counselors was developed to complement the AACD standards by clarifying the nature of ethical responsibilities of counselors in the school setting. The purposes of this document are to:

1. Serve as a guide for the ethical practices of all school counselors regardless of level, area, or population served.

2. Provide benchmarks for both self-appraisal and peer evaluations regarding counselor responsibilities to pupils, parents, professional colleagues, school and community, self, and the counseling profession.

3. Inform those served by the school counselor of acceptable counselor practices and expected professional deportment.

A. Responsibilities to Pupils

The school counselor:

1. Has a primary obligation and loyalty to the pupil, who is to be treated with respect as a unique individual.

2. Is concerned with the total needs of the pupil (educational, vocational, personal and social) and encourages the maximum growth and development of each counselee.

3. Informs the counselee of the purposes, goals, techniques, and rules of procedure under which she/he may receive counseling assistance at or before the time when the counseling relationship is entered. Prior notice includes the possible necessity for consulting with other professionals, privileged communication, and legal or authoritative restraints.

4. Refrains from consciously encouraging the counselee's acceptance of values, lifestyles, plans, decisions, and beliefs that represent only the counselor's personal orientation.

5. Is responsible for keeping abreast of laws relating to pupils and ensures that the rights of pupils are adequately provided for and protected.

6. Makes appropriate referrals when professional assistance can no longer be adequately provided to the counselee. Appropriate referral necessitates knowledge about available resources.

7. Protects the confidentiality of pupil records and releases personal data only according to prescribed laws and school policies. The counselor shall provide an accurate, objective, and appropriately detailed interpretation of pupil information.

8. Protects the confidentiality of information received in the counseling process as specified by law and ethical standards.

9. Informs the appropriate authorities when the counselee's condition indicates a clear and imminent danger to the counselee or others. This is to be done after careful deliberation and, where possible, after consultation with other professionals.

10. Provides explanations of the nature, purposes, and results of tests in language that is understandable to the client(s).

11. Adheres to relevant standards regarding selection, administration, and interpretation of assessment techniques.

B. Responsibilities to Parents

The school counselor:

1. Respects the inherent rights and responsibilities of parents for their children and endeavors to establish a cooperative relationship

with parents to facilitate the maximum development of the counselee.

2. Informs parents of the counselor's role with emphasis on the confidential nature of the counseling relationship between the counselor and counselee.

3. Provides parents with accurate, comprehensive and relevant information in an objective and caring manner.

4. Treats information received from parents in a confidential and appropriate manner.

5. Shares information about a counselee only with those persons properly authorized to receive such information.

6. Follows local guidelines when assisting parents experiencing family difficulties which interfere with the counselee's effectiveness and welfare.

C. Responsibilities to Colleagues and Professional Associates

The school counselor:

1. Establishes and maintains a cooperative relationship with faculty, staff, and administration to facilitate the provision of optimum guidance and counseling services.

2. Promotes awareness and adherence to appropriate guidelines regarding confidentiality, the distinction between public and private information, and staff consultation.

3. Treats colleagues with respect, courtesy, fairness, and good faith. The qualifications, views, and findings of colleagues are represented accurately and fairly to enhance the image of competent professionals.

4. Provides professional personnel with accurate, objective, concise and meaningful data necessary to adequately evaluate, counsel, and assist the counselee.

5. Is aware of and fully utilizes related professions and organizations to whom the counselees may be referred.

D. Responsibilities to the School and Community

The school counselor:

1. Supports and protects the educational program against any infringement not in the best interest of pupils.

2. Informs appropriate officials of conditions that may be potentially disruptive or damaging to the schools' mission, personnel, and property.

3. Delineates and promotes the counselor's role and function in meeting the needs of those served. The counselor will notify appropriate school officials of conditions which may limit or curtail their effectiveness in providing services.

4. Assists in the development of (1) curricular and environmental conditions appropriate for the school and community, (2) educational procedures and programs to meet pupil needs, and (3) a systematic evaluation process for guidance and counseling programs, services, and personnel.

5. Works cooperatively with agencies, organizations, and individuals in the school and community in the best interest of counselees and without regard to personal reward or remuneration.

E. Responsibilities to Self

The school counselor:

1. Functions within the boundaries of individual professional competence and accepts responsibility for the consequences of his/her actions.

2. Is aware of the potential effects of personal characteristics on services to clients.

3. Monitors personal functioning and effectiveness and refrains from any activity likely to lead to inadequate professional services or harm to a client.

4. Strives through personal initiative to maintain professional competence and keep abreast of innovations and trends in the profession.

F. Responsibilities to the Profession

The school counselor:

1. Conducts herself/himself in such a manner as to bring credit to self and the profession.

2. Conducts appropriate research and reports findings in a manner consistent with acceptable educational and psychological research practices.

3. Actively participates in local, state, and national associations which foster the development and improvement of school counseling.

4. Adheres to ethical standards of the profession, other official policy statements pertaining to counseling, and relevant statutes established by federal, state, and local governments.

5. Clearly distinguishes between statements and actions made as a private individual and as a representative of the school counseling profession.

G. Maintenance of Standards

Ethical behavior among professional school counselors is expected at all times. When there exists serious doubt as to the ethical behavior of colleagues, or if counselors are forced to work in situations or abide by policies which do not reflect the standards as outlined in these *Ethical Standards for School Counselors* or the AACD *Ethical Standards*, the counselor is obligated to take appropriate action to rectify the condition. The following procedure may serve as a guide:

1. The counselor shall utilize the channels established within the school and/or system. This may include both informal and formal procedures.

2. If the matter remains unresolved, referral for review and appropriate action should be made to the Ethics Committee in the following sequence:

—local counselor association
—state counselor association
—national counselor association

H. References

School counselors are responsible for being aware of and acting in accord with the standards and positions of the counseling profession as represented in such official documents as those listed below. A more extensive bibliography is available from the ASCA Ethics Committee upon request.

Ethical Standards (1981). American Association for Counseling and Development. Alexandria, VA.

Ethical Guidelines for Group Leaders (1980). Association for Specialists in Group Work. Alexandria, VA.

Principles of Confidentiality (1974). ASCA Position Statement. American School Counselor Association. Alexandria, VA.

Standards for Educational and Psychological Tests and Manuals (1974). American Psychological Association. Washington, DC.

Ethical Principles in the Conduct of Research with Human Participants (1973). American Psychological Association. Washington, DC.

(*Ethical Standards for School Counselors* is an adaptation of the ASCA *Code of Ethics* (1972) and the California School Counselor Association *Code of Ethics* (revised, 1984). Adopted by the ASCA Delegate Assembly March 19, 1984.)

ETHICAL GUIDELINES FOR GROUP COUNSELORS, 1989

June 1, 1989 Final Draft
Approved by the Association for Specialists in Group Work (ASGW) Executive Board, June 1, 1989

Preamble

One characteristic of any professional group is the possession of a body of knowledge, skills, and voluntarily, self-professed standards for ethical practice. A Code of Ethics consists of those standards that have been formally and publicly

acknowledged by the members of a profession to serve as the guidelines for professional conduct, discharge of duties, and the resolution of moral dilemmas. By this document, the Association for Specialists in Group Work (ASGW) has identified the standards of conduct appropriate for ethical behavior among its members.

The Association for Specialists in Group Work recognizes the basic commitment of its members to the Ethical Standards of its parent organization, the American Association for Counseling and Development (AACD) and nothing in this document shall be construed to supplant that code. These standards are intended to complement the AACD standards in the area of group work by clarifying the nature of ethical responsibility of the counselor in the group setting and by stimulating a greater concern for competent group leadership.

The group counselor is expected to be a professional agent and to take the processes of ethical responsibility seriously. ASGW views "ethical process" as being integral to group work and views group counselors as "ethical agents." Group counselors, by their very nature in being responsible and responsive to their group members, necessarily embrace a certain potential for ethical vulnerability. It is incumbent upon group counselors to give considerable attention to the intent and context of their actions because the attempts of counselors to influence human behavior through group work always have ethical implications.

The following ethical guidelines have been developed to encourage ethical behavior of group counselors. These guidelines are written for students and practitioners, and are meant to stimulate reflection, self-examination, and discussion of issues and practices. They address the group counselor's responsibility for providing information about group work to clients and the group counselor's responsibility for providing group counseling services to clients. A final section discusses the group counselor's responsibility for safeguarding ethical practice and procedures for reporting unethical behavior. Group counselors are expected to make known these standards to group members.

Ethical Guidelines

1. *Orientation and Providing Information:* Group counselors adequately prepare prospective or new group members by providing as much information about the existing or proposed group as necessary.

- Minimally, information related to each of the following areas should be provided.

   (a) Entrance procedures, time parameters of the group experience, group participation expectations, methods of payment (where appropriate), and termination

209

procedures are explained by the group counselor as appropriate to the level of maturity of group members and the nature and purpose(s) of the group.

(b) Group counselors have available for distribution, a professional disclosure statement that includes information on the group counselor's qualifications and group services that can be provided, particularly as related to the nature and purpose(s) of the specific group.

(c) Group counselors communicate the role expectations, rights, and responsibilities of group members and group counselor(s).

(d) The group goals are stated as concisely as possible by the group counselor including "whose" goal it is (the group counselor's, the institution's, the parent's, the law's, society's, etc.) and the role of group members in influencing or determining the group's goal(s).

(e) Group counselors explore with group members the risks of potential life changes that may occur because of the group experience and help members explore their readiness to face these possibilities.

(f) Group members are informed by the group counselor of unusual or experimental procedures that might be expected in their group experience.

(g) Group counselors explain, as realistically as possible, what services can and cannot be provided within the particular group structure offered.

(h) Group counselors emphasize the need to promote full psychological functioning and presence among group members. They inquire from prospective group members whether they are using any kind of drug or medication that may affect functioning in the group. They do not permit any use of alcohol and/or illegal drugs during group sessions and they discourage the use of alcohol and/or drugs (legal or illegal) prior to group meetings which may affect the physical or emotional presence of the member or other group members.

(i) Group counselors inquire from prospective group members whether they have ever been a client in counseling or psychotherapy. If a prospective group member is already in a counseling relationship with another professional person, the group counselor advises the prospective group member to notify the other professional of their participation in the group.

(j) Group counselors clearly inform group members about the policies pertaining to the group counselor's willingness to consult with them between group sessions.

(k) In establishing fees for group counseling services, group counselors consider the financial status and the locality of prospective group members. Group members are not charged fees for group sessions where the group counselor is not present and the policy of charging for sessions missed by a group member is clearly communicated. Fees for participating as a group member are contracted between group counselor and group member for a specified period of time. Group counselors do not increase fees for group counseling services until the existing contracted fee structure has expired. In the event that the established fee structure is inappropriate for a prospective member, group counselors assist in finding comparable services of acceptable cost.

2. *Screening of Members:* The group counselor screens prospective group members (when appropriate to their theoretical orientation). Insofar as possible, the counselor selects group members whose needs and goals are compatible with the goals of the group, who will not impede the group process, and whose well-being will not be jeopardized by the group experience. An orientation to the group (i.e., ASGW Ethical Guideline #1), is included during the screening process.

• Screening may be accomplished in one or more ways, such as the following:

(a) Individual interview,
(b) Group interview of prospective group members,
(c) Interview as part of a team staffing, and
(d) Completion of a written questionnaire by prospective group members.

3. *Confidentiality:* Group counselors protect members by defining clearly what confidentiality means, why it is important, and the difficulties involved in enforcement.

(a) Group counselors take steps to protect members by defining confidentiality and the limits of confidentiality (i.e., when a group member's condition indicates that there is clear and imminent danger to the member, others, or physical property, the group counselor takes reasonable personal action and/or informs responsible authorities).

(b) Group counselors stress the importance of confidentiality and set a norm of confidentiality regarding all group participants' disclosures. The importance of maintaining confidentiality is emphasized before the group begins and at various times in the group. The fact that confidentiality cannot be guaranteed is clearly stated.

210

(c) Members are made aware of the difficulties involved in enforcing and ensuring confidentiality in a group setting. The counselor provides examples of how confidentiality can non-maliciously be broken to increase members' awareness, and helps to lessen the likelihood that this breach of confidence will occur. Group counselors inform group members about the potential consequences of intentionally breaching confidentiality.

(d) Group counselors can only ensure confidentiality on their part and not on the part of the members.

(e) Group counselors video or audio tape a group session only with the prior consent, and the members' knowledge of how the tape will be used.

(f) When working with minors, the group counselor specifies the limits of confidentiality.

(g) Participants in a mandatory group are made aware of any reporting procedures required of the group counselor.

(h) Group counselors store or dispose of group member records (written, audio, video, etc.) in ways that maintain confidentiality.

(i) Instructors of group counseling courses maintain the anonymity of group members whenever discussing group counseling cases.

4. *Voluntary/Involuntary Participation:* Group counselors inform members whether participation is voluntary or involuntary.

(a) Group counselors take steps to ensure informed consent procedures in both voluntary and involuntary groups.

(b) When working with minors in a group, counselors are expected to follow the procedures specified by the institution in which they are practicing.

(c) With involuntary groups, every attempt is made to enlist the cooperation of the members and their continuance in the group on a voluntary basis.

(d) Group counselors do not certify that group treatment has been received by members who merely attend sessions, but did not meet the defined group expectations. Group members are informed about the consequences for failing to participate in a group.

5. *Leaving a Group:* Provisions are made to assist a group member to terminate in an effective way.

(a) Procedures to be followed for a group member who chooses to exit a group prematurely are discussed by the counselor with all group members either before the group begins, during a pre-screening interview, or during the initial group session.

(b) In the case of legally mandated group counseling, group counselors inform members of the possible consequences for premature self termination.

(c) Ideally, both the group counselor and the member can work cooperatively to determine the degree to which a group experience is productive or counterproductive for that individual.

(d) Members ultimately have a right to discontinue membership in the group, at a designated time, if the predetermined trial period proves to be unsatisfactory.

(e) Members have the right to exit a group, but it is important that they be made aware of the importance of informing the counselor and the group members prior to deciding to leave. The counselor discusses the possible risks of leaving the group prematurely with a member who is considering this option.

(f) Before leaving a group, the group counselor encourages members (if appropriate) to discuss their reasons for wanting to discontinue membership in the group. Counselors intervene if other members use undue pressure to force a member to remain in the group.

6. *Coercion and Pressure:* Group counselors protect member rights against physical threats, intimidation, coercion, and undue peer pressure insofar as is reasonably possible.

(a) It is essential to differentiate between "therapeutic pressure" that is part of any group and "undue pressure," which is not therapeutic.

(b) The purpose of a group is to help participants find their own answer, not to pressure them into doing what the group thinks is appropriate.

(c) Counselors exert care not to coerce participants to change in directions which they clearly state they do not choose.

(d) Counselors have a responsibility to intervene when others use undue pressure or attempt to persuade members against their will.

(e) Counselors intervene when any member attempts to act out aggression in a physical way that might harm another member or themselves.

(f) Counselors intervene when a member is verbally abusive or inappropriately confrontive to another member.

7. *Imposing Counselor Values:* Group counselors develop an awareness of their own values and needs and the potential impact they have on the interventions likely to be made.

211

(a) Although group counselors take care to avoid imposing their values on members, it is appropriate that they expose their own beliefs, decisions, needs, and values, when concealing them would create problems for the members.

(b) There are values implicit in any group, and these are made clear to potential members before they join the group. (Examples of certain values include: expressing feelings, being direct and honest, sharing personal material with others, learning how to trust, improving interpersonal communication, and deciding for oneself.)

(c) Personal and professional needs of group counselors are not met at the members' expense.

(d) Group counselors avoid using the group for their own therapy.

(e) Group counselors are aware of their own values and assumptions and how these apply in a multicultural context.

(f) Group counselors take steps to increase their awareness of ways that their personal reactions to members might inhibit the group process and they monitor their countertransference. Through an awareness of the impact of sterotyping and discrimination (i.e., biases based on age, disability, ethnicity, gender, race, religion, or sexual preference), group counselors guard the individual rights and personal dignity of all group members.

88. *Equitable Treatment:* Group counselors make every reasonable effort to treat each member individually and equally.

(a) Group counselors recognize and respect differences (e.g., cultural, racial, religious, lifestyle, age, disability, gender) among group members.

(b) Group counselors maintain an awareness of their behvior toward individual group members and are alert to the potential detrimental effects of favoritism or partiality toward any particular group member to the exclusion or detriment of any other member(s). It is likely that group counselors will favor some members over others, yet all group members deserve to be treated equally.

(c) Group counselors ensure equitable use of group time for each member by inviting silent members to become involved, acknowledging nonverbal attempts to communicate, and discouraging rambling and monopolizing of time by members.

(d) If a large group is planned, counselors consider enlisting another qualified professional to serve as a co-leader for the group sessions.

9. *Dual Relationships:* Group counselors avoid dual relationships with group members that might impair their objectivity and professional judgment, as well as those which are likely to compromise a group member's ability to participate fully in the group.

(a) Group counselors do not misuse their professional role and power as group leader to advance personal or social contacts with members throughout the duration of the group.

(b) Group counselors do not use their professional relationship with group members to further their own interest either during the group or after the termination of the group.

(c) Sexual intimacies between group counselors and members are unethical.

(d) Group counselors do not barter (exchange) professional services with group members for services.

(e) Group counselors do not admit their own family members, relatives, employees, or personal friends as members to their groups.

(f) Group counselors discuss with group members the potential detrimental effects of group members engaging in intimate inter-member relationships outside of the group.

(g) Students who participate in a group as a partial course requirement for a group course are not evaluated for an academic grade based upon their degree of participation as a member in a group. Instructors of group counseling courses take steps to minimize the possible negative impact on students when they participate in a group course by separating course grades from participation in the group and by allowing students to decide what issues to explore and when to stop.

(h) It is inappropriate to solicit members from a class (or institutional affiliation) for one's private counseling or therapeutic groups.

10. *Use of Techniques:* Group counselors do not attempt any technique unless trained in its use or under supervision by a counselor familiar with the intervention.

(a) Group counselors are able to articulate a theoretical orientation that guides their practice, and they are able to provide a rationale for their interventions.

(b) Depending upon the type of an intervention, group counselors have training commensurate with the potential impact of a technique.

(c) Group counselors are aware of the necessity to modify their techniques to fit the unique needs of various cultural and ethnic groups.

212

(d) Group counselors assist members in translating in-group learnings to daily life.

11. *Goal Development:* Group counselors make every effort to assist members in developing their personal goals.

(a) Group counselors use their skills to assist members in making their goals specific so that others present in the group will understand the nature of the goals.
(b) Throughout the course of a group, group counselors assist members in assessing the degree to which personal goals are being met, and assist in revising any goals when it is appropriate.
(c) Group counselors help members clarify the degree to which the goals can be met within the context of a particular group.

12. *Consultation:* Group counselors develop and explain policies about between-session consultation to group members.

(a) Group counselors take care to make certain that members do not use between-session consultations to avoid dealing with issues pertaining to the group that would be dealt with best in the group.
(b) Group counselors urge members to bring the issues discussed during between-session consultations into the group if they pertain to the group.
(c) Group counselors seek out consultation and/or supervision regarding ethical concerns or when encountering difficulties which interfere with their effective functioning as group leaders.
(d) Group counselors seek appropriate professional assistance for their own personal problems or conflicts that are likely to impair their professional judgment and work performance.
(e) Group counselors discuss their group cases only for professional consultation and educational purposes.
(f) Group counselors inform members about policies regarding whether consultations will be held confidential.

13. *Termination from the Group:* Depending upon the purpose of participation in the group, counselors promote termination of members from the group in the most efficient period of time.

(a) Group counselors maintain a constant awareness of the progress made by each group member and periodically invite the group members to explore and reevaluate their experiences in the group. It is the responsibility of group counselors to help promote the independence of members from the group in a timely manner.

14. *Evaluation and Follow-up:* Group counselors make every attempt to engage in ongoing assessment and to design follow-up procedures for their groups.

(a) Group counselors recognize the importance of ongoing assessment of a group, and they assist members in evaluating their own progress.
(b) Group counselors conduct evaluation of the total group experience at the final meeting (or before termination), as well as ongoing evaluation.
(c) Group counselors monitor their own behavior and become aware of what they are modeling in the group.
(d) Follow-up procedures might take the form of personal contact, telephone contact, or written contact.
(e) Follow-up meetings might be with individuals, or groups, or both to determine the degree to which: (i) members have reached their goals, (ii) the group had a positive or negative effect on the participants, (iii) members could profit from some type of referral, and (iv) as information for possible modification of future groups. If there is no follow-up meeting, provisions are made available for individual follow-up meetings to any member who needs or requests such a contact.

15. *Referrals:* If the needs of a particular member cannot be met within the type of group being offered, the group counselor suggests other appropriate professional referrals.

(a) Group counselors are knowledgeable of local community resources for assisting group members regarding professional referrals.
(b) Group counselors help members seek further professional assistance, if needed.

16. *Professional Development:* Group counselors recognize that professional growth is a continuous, ongoing, developmental process throughout their career.

(a) Group counselors maintain and upgrade their knowledge and skill competencies through educational activities, clinical experiences, and participation in professional development activities.
(b) Group counselors keep abreast of research findings and new developments as applied to groups.

Safeguarding Ethical Practice and Procedures for Reporting Unethical Behavior

The preceding remarks have been advanced as guidelines which are generally representative of ethical and professional group practice.

They have not been proposed as rigidly defined prescriptions. However, practitioners who are thought to be grossly unresponsive to the ethical concerns addressed in this document may be subject to a review of their practices by the AACD Ethics Committee and ASGW peers.

- For consultation and/or questions regarding these ASGW Ethical Guidelines or group ethical dilemmas, you may contact the Chairperson of the ASGW Ethics Committee. The name, address, and telephone number of the current ASGW Ethics Committee Chairperson may be acquired by telephoning the AACD office in Alexandria, Virginia at (703) 823-9800.

- If a group counselor's behavior is suspected as being unethical, the following procedures are to be followed:

  (a) Collect more information and investigate further to confirm the unethical practice as determined by the ASGW Ethical Guidelines.

  (b) Confront the individual with the apparent violation of ethical guidelines for the purposes of protecting the safety of any clients and to help the group counselor correct any inappropriate behaviors. If satisfactory resolution is not reached through this contact then:

  (c) A complaint should be made in writing, including the specific facts and dates of the alleged violation and all relevant supporting data. The complaint should be included in an envelope marked "CONFIDENTIAL" to ensure confidentiality for both the accuser(s) and the alleged violator(s) and forwarded to all of the following sources:

    1. The name and address of the Chairperson of the state Counselor Licensure Board for the respective state, if in existence.

    2. The Ethics Committee
       c/o The President
       American Association for Counseling and Development
       5999 Stevenson Avenue
       Alexandria, Virginia 22304

    3. The name and address of all private credentialing agencies that the alleged violator maintains credentials or holds professional membership. Some of these include the following:

       National Board for Certified Counselors, Inc.
       5999 Stevenson Avenue
       Alexandria, Virginia 22304

National Council for Credentialing of Career Counselors
c/o NBCC
5999 Stevenson Avenue
Alexandria, Virginia 22304

National Academy for Certified Clinical Mental Health Counselors
5999 Stevenson Avenue
Alexandria, Virginia 22304

Commission on Rehabilitation Counselor Certification
162 North State Street, Suite 317
Chicago, Illinois 60601

American Association for Marriage and Family Therapy
1717 K Street, N.W., Suite 407
Washington, D.C. 20006

American Psychological Association
1200 Seventeenth Street, N.W.
Washington, D.C. 20036

American Group Psychotherapy Association, Inc.
25 East 21st Street, 6th Floor
New York, New York 10010

NATIONAL CAREER DEVELOPMENT ASSOCIATION ETHICAL STANDARDS, 1987

These Ethical Standards were developed by the National Board for Certified Counselors (NBCC), an independent, voluntary, not-for-profit organization incorporated in 1982. Titled "Code of Ethics" by NBCC and last amended in February 1987, the Ethical Standards were adopted by the National Career Development Association (NCDA) Board of Directions at its April 1987 meeting in New Orleans, LA. Only minor changes in wording (e.g., the addition of specific references to NCDA members) were made.

Preamble

NCDA is an educational, scientific, and professional organization dedicated to the enhancement of the worth, dignity, potential, and uniqueness of each individual and, thus, to the service of society. This code of ethics enables the NCDA to clarify the nature of ethical responsibilities for present and future professional career counselors.

Section A: General

1. NCDA members influence the development of the profession by continuous efforts to improve professional practices, services, and research. Professional growth is continuous through the career counselor's career and is exemplified by the development

of a philosophy that explains why and how a career counselor functions in the helping relationship. Career counselors must gather data on their effectiveness and be guided by their findings.

2. NCDA members have a responsibility to the clients they are serving and to the institutions within which the services are being performed. Career counselors also strive to assist the respective agency, organization, or institution in providing the highest caliber of professional services. The acceptance of employment in an institution implies that the career counselor is in agreement with the general policies and principles of the institution. Therefore, the professional activities of the career counselor are in accord with the objectives of the institution. If, despite concerted efforts, the career counselor cannot reach agreement with the employer as to acceptable standards of conduct that allow for changes in institutional policy that are conducive to the positive growth and development of clients, then terminating the affiliation should be seriously considered.

3. Ethical behavior among professional associates (e.g., career counselors) must be expected at all times. When accessible information raises doubt as to the ethical behavior of professional colleagues, the NCDA member must take action to attempt to rectify this condition. Such action uses the respective institution's channels first and then uses procedures established by the American Association for Counseling and Development, of which NCDA is a division.

4. NCDA members neither claim nor imply professional qualifications which exceed those possessed, and are responsible for correcting any misrepresentations of these qualifications by others.

5. NCDA members must refuse a private fee or other remuneration for consultation or counseling with persons who are entitled to their services through the career counselor's employing institution or agency. The policies of some agencies may make explicit provisions for staff members to engage in private practice with agency clients. However, should agency clients desire private counseling or consulting services, they must be apprised of other options available to them. Career counselors must not divert to their private practices, legitimate clients in their primary agencies or of the institutions with which they are affiliated.

6. In establishing fees for professional counseling services, NCDA members must consider the financial status of clients and the respective locality. In the event that the established fee status is inappropriate for a client, assistance must be provided in finding comparable services of acceptable cost.

7. NCDA members seek only those positions in the delivery of professional services for which they are professional qualified.

8. NCDA members recognize their limitations and provide services or only use techniques for which they are qualified by training and/or experience. Career counselors recognize the need, and seek continuing education, to assure competent services.

9. NCDA members are aware of the intimacy in the counseling relationship, maintain respect for the client, and avoid engaging in activities that seek to meet their personal needs at the expense of the client.

10. NCDA members do not condone or engage in sexual harassment which is defined as deliberate or repeated comments, gestures, or physical contacts of a sexual nature.

11. NCDA members avoid bringing their personal or professional issues into the counseling relationship. Through an awareness of the impact of sterotyping and discrimination (i.e., biases based on age, disability, ethnicity, gender, race, religion, or sexual preference), career counselors guard the individual rights and personal dignity of the client in the counseling relationship.

12. NCDA members are accountable at all times for their behavior. They must be aware that all actions and behaviors of a counselor reflect on professional integrity and, when inappropriate, can damage the public trust in the counseling profession. To protect public confidence in the counseling profession, career counselors avoid public behavior that is clearly in violation of accepted moral and legal standards.

13. NCDA members have a social responsibility because their recommendations and professional actions may alter the lives of others. Career counselors remain fully cognizant of their impact and are alert to personal, social, organizational, financial, or political situations or pressures which might lead to misuse of their influence.

14. Products or services provided by NCDA members by means of classroom instruction, public lectures, demonstrations, written articles, radio or television programs, or other types of media must meet the criteria cited in Sections A through F of these Ethical Standards.

Section B: Counseling Relationship

1. The primary obligation of NCDA members is to respect the integrity and promote the welfare of the client, regardless of whether the client is assisted individually or in a group relationship. In a group setting, the career counselor is also responsible for taking reasonable precautions to protect individuals from physical and/or psychological trauma resulting from interaction within the group.

2. The counseling relationship and information resulting from it remains confidential, consistent with the legal obligations of the NCDA member. In a group counseling setting, the career counselor sets a norm of confidentiality regarding all group participants' disclosures.

3. NCDA members know and take into account the traditions and practices of other professional groups with whom they work, and they cooperate fully with such groups. If a person is receiving similar services from another professional, career counselors do not offer their own services directly to such a person. If a career counselor is contacted by a person who is already receiving similar services from another professional, the career counselor carefully considers that professional relationship and proceeds with caution and sensitivity to the therapeutic issues as well as the client's welfare. Career counselors discuss these issues with clients so as to minimize the risk of confusion and conflict.

4. When a client's condition indicates that there is a clear and imminent danger to the client or others, the NCDA member must take reasonable personal action or inform responsible authorities. Consultation with other professionals must be used where possible. The assumption of responsibility for the client's behavior must be taken only after careful deliberation, and the client must be involved in the resumption of responsibility as quickly as possible.

5. Records of the counseling relationship, including interview notes, test data, correspondence, audio or visual tape recordings, electronic data storage, and other documents are to be considered professional information for use in counseling. They should not be considered a part of the records of the institution or agency in which the NCDA member is employed unless specified by state statute or regulation. Revelation to others of counseling material must occur only upon the expressed consent of the client; career counselors must make provisions for maintaining confidentiality in the storage and disposal of records. Career counselors providing information to the public or to subordinates, peers, or supervisors have a responsibility to ensure that the content is general; unidentified client information should be accurate and unbiased, and should consist of objective, factual data.

6. NCDA members must ensure that data maintained in electronic storage are secure. The data must be limited to information that is appropriate and necessary for the services being provided and accessible only to appropriate staff members involved in the provision of services by using the best computer security methods available. Career counselors must also ensure that electronically stored data are destroyed when the information is no longer of value in providing services.

7. Data derived from a counseling relationship for use in counselor training or research shall be confined to content that can be disguised to ensure full protection of the identity of the subject/client and shall be obtained with informed consent.

8. NCDA members must inform clients before or at the time the counseling relationship commences, of the purposes, goals, techniques, rules and procedures, and limitations that may affect the relationship.

9. All methods of treatment by NCDA members must be clearly indicated to prospective recipients and safety precautions must be taken in their use.

10. NCDA members who have an administrative, supervisory and/or evaluative relationship with individuals seeking counseling services must not serve as the counselor and should refer the individuals to other professionals. Exceptions are made only in instances where an individual's situation warrants counseling intervention and another alternative is unavailable. Dual relationship with clients that might impair the career counselor's objectivity and professional judgment must be avoided and/or the counseling relationship terminated through referral to another competent professional.

11. When NCDA members determine an inability to be of professional assistance to a potential or existing client, they must, respectively, not initiate the counseling relationship or immediately terminate the relationship. In either event, the career counselor must suggest appropriate alternatives. Career counselors must be knowledgeable about referral resources so that a satisfactory referral can be initiated. In the event that the client declines a suggested referral, the career counselor is not obligated to continue the relationship.

12. NCDA members may choose to consult with any other professionally competent person about a client and must notify clients of this right. Career counselors must avoid placing a consultant in a conflict-of-interest situation that would preclude the consultant's being a proper party to the career counselor's efforts to help the client.

13. NCDA members who counsel clients from cultures different from their own must gain knowledge, personal awareness, and sensitivity pertinent to the client populations served and must incorporate culturally relevant techniques into their practice.

14. When NCDA members are engaged in intensive, short-term therapy, they must ensure that professional counseling assistance is available to the client(s) during and following the counseling.

216

15. NCDA members must screen prospective group counseling participants, especially when the emphasis is on self-understanding and growth through self-disclosure. Career counselors must maintain an awareness of each group participant's welfare throughout the group process.

16. When electronic data and systems are used as a component of counseling services, NCDA members must ensure that the computer application, and any information it contains, is appropriate for the respective needs of clients and is nondiscriminatory. Career counselors must ensure that they themselves have acquired a facilitation level of knowledge with any system they use including hands-on application, search experience, and understanding of the uses of all aspects of the computer-based system. In selecting and/or maintaining computer-based systems that contain career information, career counselors must ensure that the systems provide current, accurate, and locally relevant information. Career counselors must also ensure that clients are intellectually, emotionally, and physically compatible to using the computer application and understand its purpose and operation. Client use of a computer application must be evaluated to correct possible problems and assess subsequent needs.

17. NCDA members who develop self-help, stand-alone computer software for use by the general public, must first ensure that it is initially designed to function in a stand-alone manner, as opposed to modifying software that was originally designed to require support from a counselor. Secondly, the software must include program statements that provide the user with intended outcomes, suggestions for using the software, descriptions of inappropriately used applications, and descriptions of when and how counseling services might be beneficial. Finally the manual must include the qualifications of the developer, the development process, validation data, and operating procedures.

Section C: Measurement and Evaluation

1. NCDA members must provide specific orientation or information to an examinee prior to and following the administration of assessment instruments or techniques so that the results may be placed in proper perspective with other relevant factors. The purpose of testing and the explicit use of the results must be made known to an examinee prior to testing.

2. In selecting assessment instruments or techniques for use in a given situation or with a particular client, NCDA members must evaluate carefully the instrument's specific theoretical bases and characteristics, validity, reliability, and appropriateness. Career counselors are professionally responsible for using unvalidated information with special care.

3. When making statements to the public about assessment instruments or techniques, NCDA members must provide accurate information and avoid false claims or misconceptions concerning the meaning of psychometric terms. Special efforts are often required to avoid unwarranted connotations of terms such as IQ and grade-equivalent scores.

4. Because many types of assessment techniques exist, NCDA members must recognize the limits of their competence and perform only those functions for which they have received appropriate training.

5. NCDA members must note when tests are not administered under standard conditions or when unusual behavior or irregularities occur during a testing session and the results must be designated as invalid or of questionable validity. Unsupervised or inadequately supervised assessments, such as mail-in tests, are considered unethical. However, the use of standardized instruments that are designed to be self-administered and self-scored, such as interest inventories, is appropriate.

6. Because prior coaching or dissemination of test materials can invalidate test results, NCDA members are professionally obligated to maintain test security. In addition, conditions that produce most favorable test results must be made known to an examinee (e.g., penalty for guessing).

7. NCDA members must consider psychometric limitations when selecting and using an instrument, and must be cognizant of the limitations when interpreting the results. When tests are used to classify clients, career counselors must ensure that periodic review and/or re-testing are conducted to prevent client stereotyping.

8. An examinee's welfare, explicit prior understanding, and agreement are the factors used when determining who receives the test results. NCDA members must see that appropriate interpretation accompanies any release of individual or group test data (e.g., limitations of instrument and norms).

9. NCDA members must ensure that computer-generated test administration and scoring programs function properly thereby providing clients with accurate test results.

10. NCDA members who are responsible for making decisions based on assessment results, must have appropriate training and skills in educational and psychological measurement—including validation criteria, test research, and guidelines for test development and use.

11. NCDA members must be cautious when interpreting the results of instruments that possess insufficient technical data, and must

explicitly state to examinees the specific purposes for the use of such instruments.

12. NCDA members must proceed with caution when attempting to evaluate and interpret performances of minority group members or other persons who are not represented in the norm group on which the instrument was standardized.

13. NCDA members who develop computer-based test interpretations to support the assessment process, must ensure that the validity of the interpretations is established prior to the commercial distribution of the computer application.

14. NCDA members recognize that test results may become obsolete, and avoid the misuse of obsolete data.

15. NCDA members must avoid the appropriation, reproduction, or modification for published tests or parts thereof without acknowledgment and permission from the publisher.

Section D: Research and Publication

1. NCDA members will adhere to relevant guidelines on research with human subjects. These include:
   a. *Code of Federal Regulations*, Title 45, Subtitle A, Part 46, as currently issued.
   b. American Psychological Association. (1982). *Ethical principles in the conduct of research with human participants*. Washington, DC: Author.
   c. American Psychological Association. (1981). Research with human participants. *American Psychologist, 36*, 633–638.
   d. Family Educational Rights and Privacy Act. (Buckley Amendment to P.L. 93-380 of the Laws of 1974).
   e. Current federal regulations and various state privacy acts.

2. In planning research activities involving human subjects, NCDA members must be aware of and responsive to all pertinent ethical principles and ensure that the research problem, design, and execution are in full compliance with the principles.

3. The ultimate responsibility for ethical research lies with the principal researcher, though others involved in the research activities are ethically obligated and responsible for their own actions.

4. NCDA members who conduct research with human subjects are responsible for the subjects' welfare throughout the experiment and must take all reasonable precautions to avoid causing injurious psychological, physical, or social effects on their subjects.

5. NCDA members, who conduct research must abide by the following basic elements of informed consent:

a. a fair explanation of the procedures to be followed, including an identification of those which are experimental
b. a description of the attendant discomforts and risks
c. a description of the benefits to be expected
d. a disclosure of appropriate alternative procedures that would be advantageous for subjects
e. an offer to answer any inquiries concerning the procedures
f. an instruction that subjects are free to withdraw their consent and to discontinue participation in the project or activity at any time

6. When reporting research results, explicit mention must be made of all the variables and conditions known to the NCDA member that may have affected the outcome of the study or the interpretation of the data.

7. NCDA members who conduct and report research investigations must do so in a manner that minimizes the possibility that the results will be misleading.

8. NCDA members are obligated to make available sufficient original research data to qualified others who may wish to replicate the study.

9. NCDA members who supply data, aid in the research of another person, report research results, or make original data available, must take due care to disguise the identity of respective subjects in the absence of specific authorization from the subject to do otherwise.

10. When conducting and reporting research, NCDA members must be familiar with, and give recognition to, previous work on the topic, must observe all copyright laws, and must follow the principles of giving full credit to those to whom credit is due.

11. NCDA members must give due credit through joint authorship, acknowledgment, footnote statements, or other appropriate means to those who have contributed significantly to the research and/or publication, in accordance with such contributions.

12. NCDA members should communicate to others the results of any research judged to be of professional value. Results that reflect unfavorably on institutions, programs, services, or vested interests must not be withheld.

13. NCDA members who agree to cooperate with another individual in research and/or publication must incur an obligation to cooperate as promised in terms of punctuality of performance and with full regard to the completeness and accuracy of the information required.

14. NCDA members must not submit the same manuscript, or one essentially similar in

content, for simultaneous publication consideration by two or more journals. In addition, manuscripts that are published in whole or substantial part in another journal or published work should not be submitted for publication without acknowledgment and permission from the previous publication.

Section E: Consulting

Consultation refers to a voluntary relationship between a professional helper and help-needing individual, group, or social unit in which the consultant is providing help to the client(s) in defining and solving a work-related problem or potential work-related problem with a client or client system.

1. NCDA members, acting as consultants, must have a high degree of self-awareness of their own values, knowledge, skills, limitations, and needs in entering a helping relationship that involves human and/or organizational change. The focus of the consulting relationship must be on the issues to be resolved and not on the person(s) presenting the problem.

2. In the consulting relationship, the NCDA member and client must understand and agree upon the problem definition, subsequent goals, and predicted consequences of interventions selected.

3. NCDA members must be reasonably certain that they, or the organization represented, have the necessary competencies and resources for giving the kind of help that is needed or that may develop later, and that appropriate referral resources are available to the consultant.

4. NCDA members in a consulting relationship must encourage and cultivate client adaptability and growth toward self-direction. NCDA members must maintain this role consistently and not become a decision maker for clients or create a future dependency on the consultant.

5. NCDA members conscientiously adhere to the NCDA Ethical Standards when announcing consultant availability for services.

Section F: Private Practice

1. NCDA members should assist the profession by facilitating the availability of counseling services in private as well as public settings.

2. In advertising services as private practitioners, NCDA members must advertise in a manner that accurately informs the public of the professional services, expertise, and counseling techniques available.

3. NCDA members who assume an executive leadership role in a private practice organization do not permit their names to be used in professional notices during periods of time when they are not actively engaged in the private practice of counseling.

4. NCDA members may list their highest relevant degree, type, and level of certification and/or license, address, telephone number, office hours, type and/or description of services, and other relevant information. Listed information must not contain false, inaccurate misleading, partial, out-of-context, or otherwise deceptive material or statements.

5. NCDA members who are involved in a partnership or corporation with other professionals must, in compliance with the regulations of the locality, clearly specify the separate specialties of each member of the partnership or corporation.

6. NCDA members have an obligation to withdraw from a private-practice counseling relationship if it violates the NCDA Ethical Standards, if the mental or physical condition of the NCDA member renders it difficult to carry out an effective professional relationship, or if the counseling relationship is no longer productive for the client.

SECTION F: PROCEDURES FOR PROCESSING ETHICAL COMPLAINTS

As a division of the American Association for Counseling and Development (AACD), the National Career Development Association (NCDA) adheres to the guidelines and procedures for processing ethical complaints and the disciplinary sanctions adopted by AACD. A complaint against an NCDA member may be filed by any individual or group of individuals ("complainant"), whether or not the complainant is a member of NCDA. (Action will not be taken on anonymous complaints.) For specifics on how to file ethical complaints and a description of the guidelines and procedures for processing complaints, contact:

AACD Ethics Committee
c/o Executive Director
American Association for Counseling and
Development
5999 Stevenson Avenue
Alexandria, VA 22304

APPENDIX B

NATIONAL BOARD FOR CERTIFIED COUNSELORS CODE OF ETHICS

Amended, 1989

Preamble

The National Board for Certified Counselors (NBCC) is an educational, scientific, and professional organization dedicated to the enhancement of the worth, dignity, potential, and uniqueness of each individual and, thus, to the service of society. This code of ethics enables the NBCC to clarify the nature of ethical responsibilities for present and future certified counselors.

Section A: General

1. Certified counselors influence the development of the profession by continuous efforts to improve professional practices, services, and research. Professional growth is continuous throughout the certified counselor's career and is exemplified by the development of a philosophy that explains why and how a certified counselor functions in the helping relationship. Certified counselors must gather data on their effectiveness and be guided by their findings.

2. Certified counselors have a responsibility to the clients they are serving and to the institutions within which the services are being performed. Certified counselors also strive to assist the respective agency, organization, or institution in providing the highest caliber of professional services. The acceptance of employment in an institution implies that the certified counselor is in agreement with the general policies and principles of the institution. Therefore, the professional activities of the certified counselor are in accord with the objectives of the institution. If, despite concerted efforts, the certified counselor cannot reach agreement with the employer as to acceptable standards of conduct that allow for changes in institutional policy that are conducive to the positive growth and development of clients, then terminating the affiliation should be seriously considered.

3. Ethical behavior among professional associates (i.e., both certified and non-certified counselors) must be expected at all times. When accessible information raises doubt as to the ethical behavior of professional colleagues, whether certified counselors or not, the certified counselor must take action to attempt to rectify this condition. Such action uses the respective institution's channels first and then uses procedures established by the NBCC.

4. Certified counselors neither claim nor imply professional qualifications which exceed those possessed, and are responsible for correcting any misrepresentations of these qualifications by others.

5. Certified counselors must refuse a private fee or other remuneration for consultation or counseling with persons who are entitled to these services through the certified counselor's employing institution or agency. The policies of some agencies may make explicit provisions for staff members to engage in private practice with agency clients. However, should agency clients desire private counseling or consulting services, they must be apprised of other options available to them. Certified counselors must not divert to their private practices, legitimate clients in their primary agencies or of the institutes with which they are affiliated.

6. In establishing fees for professional counseling services, certified counselors must consider the financial status of clients and the respective locality. In the event that the established fee status is inappropriate for a client, assistance must be provided in finding comparable services of acceptable cost.

7. Certified counselors seek only those positions in the delivery of professional services for which they are professionally qualified.

8. Certified counselors recognize their limitations and provide services or only use techniques for which they are qualified by training and/or experience. Certified counselors recognize the need, and seek continuing education, to assure competent services.

9. Certified counselors are aware of the intimacy in the counseling relationship, maintain respect for the client, and avoid engaging in activities that seek to meet their personal needs at the expense of the client.

10. Certified counselors do not condone or engage in sexual harassment which is defined

as deliberate or repeated comments, gestures, or physical contact of a sexual nature.

11. Certified counselors avoid bringing their personal or professional issues into the counseling relationship. Through an awareness of the impact of stereotyping and discrimination (i.e., biases based on age, disability, ethnicity, gender, race, religion, or sexual preference), certified counselors guard the individual rights and personal dignity of the client in the counseling relationship.

12. Certified counselors are accountable at all times for their behavior. They must be aware that all actions and behaviors of the counselor reflect on professional integrity and, when inappropriate, can damage the public trust in the counseling profession. To protect public confidence in the counseling profession, certified counselors avoid public behavior that is clearly in violation of accepted moral and legal standards.

13. Certified counselors have a social responsibility because their recommendations and professional actions may alter the lives of others. Certified counselors remain fully cognizant of their impact and are alert to personal, social, organizational, financial, or political situations or pressures which might lead to misuse of their influence.

14. Products or services provided by certified counselors by means of classroom instruction, public lectures, demonstrations, written articles, radio or television programs or other types of media must meet the criteria cited in Sections A through F of these Standards.

Section B: Counseling Relationship

1. The primary obligation of certified counselors is to respect the integrity and promote the welfare of a client, regardless of whether the client is assisted individually or in a group relationship. In a group setting, the certified counselor is also responsible for taking reasonable precautions to protect individuals from physical and/or psychological trauma resulting from interaction within the group.

2. The counseling relationship and information resulting from it remains confidential, consistent with the legal obligations of the certified counselor. In a group counseling setting, the certified counselor sets a norm of confidentiality regarding all group participants' disclosures.

3. Certified counselors know and take into account the traditions and practices of other professional groups with whom they work and cooperate fully with such groups. If a person is receiving similar services from another professional, certified counselors do not offer their own services directly to such a person. If a certified counselor is contacted by a person who is already receiving similar services from another professional, the certified counselor carefully considers that professional relationship as well as the client's welfare and proceeds with caution and sensitivity to the therapeutic issues. Certified counselors discuss these issues with clients so as to minimize the risk of confusion and conflict.

4. When a client's condition indicates that there is a clear and imminent danger to the client or others, the certified counselor must take reasonable personal action or inform responsible authorities. Consultation with other professionals must be used where possible. The assumption of responsibility for the client's behavior must be taken only after careful deliberation, and the client must be involved in the resumption of responsibility as quickly as possible.

5. Records of the counseling relationship, including interview notes, test data, correspondence, audio or visual tape recordings, electronic data storage, and other documents are to be considered professional information for use in counseling. They should not be considered a part of the records of the institution or agency in which the counselor is employed unless specified by state statute or regulation. Revelation to others of counseling material must occur only upon the expressed consent of the client; certified counselors must make provisions for maintaining confidentiality in the storage and disposal of records. Certified counselors providing information to the public or to subordinates, peers, or supervisors have a responsibility to ensure that the content is general; unidentified client information should be accurate and unbiased, and should consist of objective, factual data.

6. Certified counselors must ensure that data maintained in electronic storage are secure. By using the best computer security methods available, the data must be limited to information that is appropriate and necessary for the services being provided and accessible only to appropriate staff members involved in the provision of services. Certified counselors must also ensure that the electronically stored data are destroyed when the information is no longer of value in providing services.

7. Any data derived from a client relationship, and used in training or research, shall be so disguised that the client's identity is fully protected. Any data which cannot be so disguised may be used only as expressly authorized by the client's informed and uncoerced consent.

8. Certified counselors must inform clients before or at the time the counseling relationship commences, of the purposes, goals, techniques, rules and procedures, and limitations that may affect the relationship.

9. All methods of treatment by certified counselors must be clearly indicated to prospective recipients and safety precautions must be taken in their use.

10. Certified counselors who have an administrative, supervisory and/or evaluative relationship with individuals seeking counseling services must not serve as the counselor and should refer the individuals to other professionals. Exceptions are made only in instances where an individual's situation warrants counseling intervention and another alternative is unavailable. Dual relationships with clients that might impair the certified counselor's objectivity and professional judgement must be avoided and/or the counseling relationship terminated through referral to another competent professional.

11. When certified counselors determine an inability to be of professional assistance to a potential or existing client, they must, respectively, not initiate the counseling relationship or immediately terminate the relationship. In either event, the certified counselor must suggest appropriate alternatives. Certified counselors must be knowledgeable about referral resources so that a satisfactory referral can be initiated. In the event that the client declines a suggested referral, the certified counselor is not obligated to continue the relationship.

12. Certified counselors may choose to consult with any other professionally competent person about a client and must notify clients of this right. Certified counselors must avoid placing a consultant in a conflict-of-interest situation that would preclude the consultant's being a proper party to the certified counselor's efforts to help the client.

13. Certified counselors who counsel clients from cultures different from their own must gain knowledge, personal awareness, and sensitivity pertinent to the client populations served and must incorporate culturally relevant techniques into their practice.

14. When certified counselors are engaged in intensive, short-term therapy, they must ensure that professional counseling assistance is available to the client(s) during and following the counseling.

15. Certified counselors must screen prospective group counseling participants, especially when the emphasis is on self-understanding and growth through self-disclosure.·Certified counselors must maintain an awareness of each group participant's welfare throughout the group process.

16. When electronic data and systems are used as a component of counseling services, certified counselors must ensure that the computer application, and any information it contains, is appropriate for the respective needs of clients and is non-discriminatory. Certified counselors must ensure that they themselves have acquired a facilitation level of knowledge with any system they use including hands-on application, search experience, and understanding of the uses of all aspects of the computer-based system. In selecting and/or maintaining computer-based systems that contain career information, counselors must ensure that the system provides current, accurate, and locally relevant information. Certified counselors must also ensure that clients are intellectually, emotionally, and physically compatible to using the computer application and understand its purpose and operation. Client use of a computer application must be evaluated to correct possible problems and assess subsequent needs.

17. Certified counselors who develop self-help/stand-alone computer software for use by the general public, must first ensure that it is initially designed to function in a stand-alone manner, as opposed to modifying software that was originally designed to require support from a counselor. Secondly, the software must include program statements that provide the user with intended outcomes, suggestions for using the software, descriptions of inappropriately used applications, and descriptions of when and how counseling services might be beneficial. Finally, the manual must include the qualifications of the developer, the development process, validation date, and operating procedures.

Section C: Measurement and Evaluation

1. Certified counselors must provide specific orientation or information to an examinee prior to and following the administration of assessment instruments or techniques so that the results may be placed in proper perspective with other relevant factors. The purpose of testing and the explicit use of the results must be made known to an examinee prior to testing.

2. In selecting assessment instruments for techniques for use in a given situation or with a particular client, certified counselors must evaluate carefully the instrument's specific theoretical bases and characteristics, validity, reliability and appropriateness. Certified counselors are professionally responsible for using invalidated information carefully.

3. When making statements to the public about assessment instruments or techniques, certified counselors must provide accurate information and avoid false claims or misconceptions concerning the meaning of psychometric terms. Special efforts are often required to avoid unwarranted connotations of terms such as IQ and grade-equivalent scores.

4. Because many types of assessment techniques exist, certified counselors must recog-

nize the limits of their competence and perform only those functions for which they have recieved appropriate training.

5. Certified counselors must note when tests are not administered under standard conditions or when unusual behavior or irregularities occur during a testing session, and the results must be designated as invalid or of questionable validity. Unsupervised or inadequately supervised assessments, such as mail-in tests, are considered unethical. However, the use of standardized instruments that are designed to be self-administered and self-scored, such as interest inventories, is appropriate.

6. Because prior coaching or dissemination of test materials can invalidate test results, certified counselors are professionally obligated to maintain test security. In addition, conditions that produce most favorable test results must be made known to an examinee (e.g., penalty for guessing).

7. Certified counselors must consider psychometric limitations when selecting and using an instrument, and must be cognizant of the limitations when interpreting the results. When tests are used to classify clients, certified counselors must ensure that periodic review and/or retesting are made to prevent client stereotyping.

8. An examinee's welfare, explicit prior understanding, and agreement are the factors used when determining who receives the test results. Certified counselors must see that appropriate interpretation accompanies any release of individual or group test data (e.g., limitations of instrument and norms).

9. Certified counselors must ensure that computer-generated test administration and scoring programs function properly thereby providing clients with accurate test results.

10. Certified counselors, who are responsible for making decisions based on assessment results, must have appropriate training and skills based on educational and psychological measurement, validation criteria, test research, and guidelines for test development and use.

11. Certified counselors must be cautious when interpreting the results of instruments that possess insufficient technical data, and must explicitly state to examinees the specific purposes for the use of such instruments.

12. Certified counselors must proceed with caution when attempting to evaluate and interpret performances of minority group members or other persons who are not represented in the norm group on which the instrument was standardized.

13. Certified counselors who develop computer-based test interpretations to support the assessment process, must ensure that the validity of the interpretations is established prior to the commercial distribution of the computer application.

14. Certified counselors recognize that test results may become obsolete, and avoid the misuse of obsolete data.

15. Certified counselors must avoid the appropriation, reproduction, or modification of published tests or parts thereof without acknowledgement and permission from the publisher except as permitted by the 'fair educational use' provisions of the U.S. copyright law.

Section D: Research and Publication

1. Certified counselors will adhere to relevant guidelines on research with human subjects. These include the:
   a. Ethical Principles in the Conduct of Research with Human Participants, Washington, D.C.: American Psychological Association Inc., 1982
   b. Code of Federal Regulations, Title 45, Subtitle A, Part 46, as currently issued
   c. Ethical Principles of Psychologists, American Psychological Association, Principle #9: Research with Human Participants
   d. Buckley Amendment
   e. current federal regulations and various state rights privacy acts

2. In planning research activities involving human subjects, certified counselors must be aware of and responsive to all pertinent ethical principles and ensure that the research problem, design, and execution are in full compliance with the principles.

3. The ultimate responsibility for ethical research lies with the principal researcher, though others involved in the research activities are ethically obligated and responsible for their own actions.

4. Certified counselors who conduct research with human subjects, are responsible for the subjects' welfare throughout the experiment and must take all reasonable precautions to avoid causing injurious psychological, physical, and social effects on their subjects.

5. Certified counselors, who conduct research, must abide by the following basic elements of informed consent:
   a. a fair explanation of the procedures to be followed, including an identification of those which are experimental
   b. a description of the attendant discomforts and risks
   c. a description of the benefits to be expected
   d. a disclosure of appropriate alternative procedures that would be advantageous for subjects
   e. an offer to answer any inquiries concerning the procedures

f. an instruction that subjects are free to withdraw their consent and to discontinue participation in the project or activity at any time

6. When reporting research results, explicit mention must be made of all the variables and conditions known to the investigator that may have affected the outcome of the study or the interpretation of the data.

7. Certified counselors who conduct and report research investigations must do so in a manner that minimizes the possibility that the results will be misleading.

8. Certified counselors are obligated to make available sufficient original research data to qualify others who may wish to replicate the study.

9. Certified counselors who supply data, aid in the research of another person, report research results, or make original data available, must take due care to disguise the identity of respective subjects in the absence of specific authorization from the subjects to do otherwise.

10. When conducting and reporting research, certified counselors must be familiar with, and give recognition to, previous work on the topic, must observe all copyright laws, and must follow the principles of giving full credit to those to whom credit is due.

11. Certified counselors must give due credit through joint authorship, acknowledgement, footnote statements, or other appropriate means to those who have contributed significantly to the research and/or publication, in accordance with such contributions.

12. Certified counselors should communicate to other counselors the results of any research judged to be of professional value. Results that reflect unfavorably on institutions, programs, services, or vested interests must not be withheld.

13. Certified counselors who agree to cooperate with another individual in research and/or publication must incur an obligation to cooperate as promised in terms of punctuality of performance and with full regard to the completeness and accuracy of the information required.

14. Certified counselors must not submit the same manuscript, or one essentially similar in content, for simultaneous publication consideration by two or more journals. In addition, manuscripts that are published in whole or substantial part in another journal or published work should not be submitted for publication without acknowledgement and permission from the previous publication.

Section E: Consulting

Consultation refers to a voluntary relationship between a professional helper and helpneeding individual, group, or social unit in which the consultant is providing help to the client(s) in defining and solving a work-related problem or potential work-related problem with a client or client system.

1. Certified counselors, acting as consultants, must have a high degree of self awareness of their own values, knowledge, skills, limitations, and needs in entering a helping relationship that involves human and/or organizational change. The focus of the consulting relationship must be on the issues to be resolved and not on the person(s) presenting the problem.

2. In the consulting relationship, the certified counselor and client must understand and agree upon the problem definition, subsequent goals, and predicted consequences of interventions selected.

3. Certified counselors must be reasonably certain that they, or the organization represented, have the necessary competencies and resources for giving the kind of help that is needed or that may develop later, and that appropriate referral resources are available to the consultant.

4. Certified counselors in a consulting relationship must encourage and cultivate client adaptability and growth toward self-direction. Certified counselors must maintain this role consistently and not become a decision maker for clients or create a future dependency on the consultant.

5. Certified counselors conscientiously adhere to the NBCC Code of Ethics when announcing consultant availability for services.

Section F: Private Practice

1. Certified counselors should assist the profession by facilitating the availability of counseling services in private as well as public settings.

2. In advertising services as a private practitioner, certified counselors must advertise in a manner that accurately informs the public of the professional services, expertise, and techniques of counseling available.

3. Certified counselors who assume an executive leadership role in a private practice organization do not permit their names to be used in professional notices during periods of time when they are not actively engaged in the private practice of counseling.

4. Certified counselors may list their highest relevant degree, type and level of certification and/or license, address, telephone number, office hours, type and/or description of services, and other relevant information. Listed information must not contain false, inaccurate, misleading, partial, out-of-context, or otherwise deceptive material or statements.

5. Certified counselors who are involved in a partnership/corporation with other certified counselors and/or other professionals, must clearly specify the separate specialties of each member of the partnership or corporation, in compliance with the regulations of the locality.

6. Certified counselors have an obligation to withdraw from a private practice counseling relationship if it violates the Code of Ethics, the mental or physical condition of the certified counselor renders it difficult to carry out an effective professional relationship, or the counseling relationship is no longer productive for the client.

Appendix: Certification Examination

1. Applicants for the National Counselor Examination must have fulfilled all current eligibility requirements, and are responsible for the accuracy and validity of all information and/or materials provided by themselves or by others for fulfillment of eligibility criteria.

2. Participation in the National Counselor Examination by any person under the auspices of eligibility ascribed to another person (i.e., applicant) is prohibited. Applicants are responsible for ensuring that no other person participates in the National Counselor Examination through use of the eligibility specifically assigned to the applicant.

3. Participants in the National Counselor Examination must refrain from the use of behaviors and/or materials which would afford them unfair advantage for performance on the Examination. These behaviors and/or materials include, but are not limited to, any form of copying of responses from another participant's answer sheet, use of unauthorized notes or other informational materials, or communication with other participants during the Examination.

4. Participants in the National Counselor Examination must, at the end of the regularly scheduled Examination period, return all Examination materials to the test administrator.

5. After completing the National Counselor Examination, participants must not disclose, in either verbal or written form, items which appeared on the Examination form.

Approved on July 1, 1982
Amended on February 21, 1987 and
January 6, 1989

Acknowledgement

Reference documents, statements, and sources for the development of the NBCC Code of Ethics were as follows:

The Ethical Standards of the American Association for Counseling and Development, Responsible Uses for Standardized Testing (AMECD), codes of ethics for the American Psychological Association, National Academy of Certified Clinical Mental Health Counselors, and the National Career Development Association, Handbook of Standards for Computer-Based Career Information Systems (ACSCI) and Guidelines for the Use of Computer-Based Career Information and Guidance Systems (ACSCI).

APPENDIX C

AACD POLICIES AND PROCEDURES FOR PROCESSING COMPLAINTS OF ETHICAL VIOLATIONS

(Approved by AACD Governing Council, March 17–19, 1988)

The American Association for Counseling and Development, hereinafter referred to as the "Association" or the "AACD", as an educational scientific, and charitable organization, is dedicated to enhancing the worth, dignity, potential, and uniqueness of each individual and rendering service to society.

The Association, in furthering its objectives, administers Ethical Standards that have been developed and approved by the AACD Govering Council.

The purpose of this document is to facilitate the work of the AACD Ethics Committee by specifying procedures for processing cases of alleged violations of the AACD Code of Ethics, codifying options for sanctioning members, and stating appeal procedures. The intent of the Association is to monitor the professional conduct of its members to ensure sound ethical counseling practices.

The Ethics Committee

The Ethics Committee is a standing committee of the Association. The Committee consists of six (6) appointed members, including the Chairperson. The editor of the *Ethical Standards Casebook* serves as an *ex officio* member of this Committee without vote. Two members are appointed annually for a three (3) year term by the President-Elect; appointments are subject to confirmation by the AACD Governing Council. Any vacancy occurring on the Committee will be filled by the President in the same manner, and the person appointed shall serve the unexpired term of the member whose place he or she took. Committee members may be reappointed to not more than one (1) additional consecutive term.

The Chairperson of the Committee is appointed annually by the incumbent President-Elect, subject to confirmation by the AACD Governing Council. A Chairperson may be reappointed to one additional term during any three-year period.

Role and Function of the Ethics Committee

The role of the Ethics Committee of the Association is to assist in the arbitration and conciliation of conflicts among members of the Association, except where appropriate client concerns may be expressed. The Committee also is responsible for:

1. Educating the membership as to the Association's Ethical Standards.

2. Periodically review and recommend changes in the Ethical Standards of the Association as well as the Policies and Procedures for Processing Complaints of Ethical Violations,

3. Receiving and processing complaints of alleged violations of the Ethical Standards of the Association, and

4. Receiving and processing questions.

In processing complaints about alleged ethical misconduct, the Committee will compile an objective, factual account of the dispute in question and make the best possible recommendation for the resolution of the case. The Committee, in taking any action, shall do so only for cause, shall only take that degree of disciplinary action that is reasonable, shall utilize these procedures with objectivity and fairness, and in general shall act only in furthering of interests and objectives of the Association and its membership.

The AACD Ethics Committee itself will not initiate any ethical violation charges against an AACD member.

Of the six (6) voting members of the Committee, a vote of four (4) is necessary to conduct business, and a unanimous vote is necessary to expel a member from the Association.

Members of the Committee

The members of the Ethics Committee must be conscious that their position is extremely important and sensitive and that their decisions involve the rights of many individuals, the reputation of the counseling and human development community, and the careers of the members. The Committee members have an obligation to act in an unbiased manner, to work expeditiously, to safeguard the confidentiality of the Committee's activities, and to follow procedures that protect the rights of all individuals involved.

The Chairperson

In addition to the above guidelines for members of the Committee, the Chairperson has the responsibilities of:

1. receiving (via AACD Headquarters) complaints that have been certified for membership status of the accused,

2. notifying the complainant and the accused of receipt of the case,

3. notifying the members of the Ethics Committee of the case within ten (10) days after it is received,

4. presiding over the meetings of the Committee,

5. preparing and sending (by certified mail) communications on the recommendations and decisions of the Committee, and

6. arranging for legal advice with assistance and financial approval of the AACD Executive Director.

Procedures for Submitting Complaints

All correspondence, records, and activities of the AACD Ethics Committee will remain confidential.

The AACD Ethics Committee will not act on anonymous complaints, nor will it act on complaints currently under civil or criminal litigation.

The AACD Ethics Committee will act only on those cases where the accused is a current member of AACD or was a member of AACD at the time of the alleged violation. State Division and State Branch Ethics Committees will act only on those cases where the accused is a member of the State Division or State Branch and not a member of AACD.

The procedures for submission of complaints to the Ethics Committee are as follows:

1. If feasible, the complainant should discuss with utmost confidentiality the nature of the complaint with a colleague to see if he/she views the situation as an ethical violation.

2. Whenever feasible, the complainant is to approach the accused directly to discuss and resolve the complaint.

3. In cases where a resolution is not forthcoming at the personal level, the complainant shall prepare a formal written statement of the complaint, stating the details of the alleged violation and shall submit it to the AACD Ethics Committee. Action or consideration by the AACD Ethics Committee may not be initiated until this requirement is satisfied.

4. Written statements must include a statement indicating the section or sections of the Ethical Standards that are allegedly being violated as well as the date(s) of the alleged violation. The written statement must also contain the accused member's full name and complete address.

5. All complaints that are directed to the AACD Ethics Committee should be mailed to:
The Ethics Committee
C/o The Executive Director
American Association for Counseling and
  Development
5999 Stevenson Avenue
Alexandria, Virginia 22304
The envelope must be marked "CONFIDENTIAL". This procedure is necessary to ensure the confidentiality of the person submitting the complaint and the person accused in the complaint.

Processing Complaints

1. The AACD Executive Director, or in his/her absence, the Assistant Executive Director for Association and Professional Relations (staff), shall: (a) check on the membership status of the accused in the case, (b) confer with legal counsel and secure a legal opinion, and (c) send the case to the Chairperson of the AACD Ethics Committee within ten (10) working days after it is received in AACD Headquarters.

Staff verification of membership of the accused and the AACD legal opinion on the legitimacy of the complaint shall be included among the documents sent to the Committee.

2. Within ten (10) days of receipt of a written statement of the alleged violation of ethical practices, the Chairperson of the AACD Ethics Committee shall do the following:

(a) acknowledge receipt of the complaint,
(b) review the complaint and recommendations from the AACD legal counsel,
(c) direct a letter to the complainant acknowledging receipt of the complaint, informing the complainant that the case will be investigated by the Committee, and outlining the procedures to be followed in the investigation,
(d) direct a letter to the accused member informing the member of accusations lodged against him/her, asking for a response and requesting that relevant information be submitted to the Chairperson within thirty (30) days, and
(e) direct a letter to the members of the AACD Ethics Committee notifying them of the case and presenting them with an action plan for investigation.

3. The AACD Ethics Committee will review the case and make recommendations for disposition and/or resolution of the case within two hundred (200) days following its receipt.

4. The AACD Ethics Committee Chairperson may ask the President of AACD to appoint an investigating committee at the local or state level to gather and submit relevant information concerning the case to the Committee.

Options Available to the Ethics Committee

After reviewing the information submitted by the accused, the Ethics Committee shall have the power to:

1. dismiss the charges, find that no violation has occurred, and dismiss the complaint, or

2. find that the practice(s) in which the member engages is (are) the subject of the complaint and is (are) unethical, notify the accused of this determination, and request the member to voluntarily cease and desist in the practice(s) without impositions of further sanctions, or

3. find that the practice(s) in which the member engages, that is (are) the subject of the complaint, is (are) unethical, notify the accused of this determination, and impose sanctions.

Hearings

At the discretion of the Ethics Committee, a hearing may be conducted when the results of the Ethics Committee's preliminary determination indicate that additional information is needed. The Chairperson shall schedule a formal hearing on the case and notify both the complainant and the accused of their right to attend.

The hearing will be held before a panel made up of the Ethics Committee and, if the accused member chooses, a representative of the accused member's primary Division. This hearing representative will be identified by the Division President and will have voting privileges.

Recommended Hearing Procedures

1. *Purpose of Hearings*
   The purpose for which hearings shall be conducted by the Ethics Committee are: (a) to determine whether a breach of the Ethical Standards of AACD has occurred, and (b) if so, to determine what disciplinary action should be taken by the AACD. No disciplinary action will be taken by AACD until after the accused member has been given reasonable notice of the hearing and the specific charges raised against him/her and has had the opportunity to be heard and to present evidence in his/her behalf.
   The Committee will be guided in its deliberations by principles of basic fairness and professionalism. The hearings will be formally conducted and presided over by the Chair of the Committee, but the Committee recognizes it is not a court of law and will keep its deliberations as confidential as possible, except as provided herein.

2. *Notice*
   At least forty-five (45) days before the hearing, the accused member should be advised in writing of the time and place of the hearing and of the charges involved. Notice shall be given either personally or by certified or registered mail and shall be signed by the Committee Chair. The notice should be addressed to the accused member at his/her address as it appears in the membership records of the AACD.
   The notice should include a brief statement of the offense(s) charged and should be supported by the evidence. The accused is under no duty to respond to the notice, but the Committee will not be obligated to delay or postpone its hearing unless the accused so requests, with good cause, in advance. Failure of the accused to appear at the hearing should not be relied upon by the Committee as sufficient ground for taking disciplinary action.

3. *Conduct of the Hearing*
   A. *Accommodations*
      The Committee shall provide a private room to conduct the hearings, and no observers shall be permitted. The location of the hearing shall be determined at the discretion of the Committee, taking into consideration the convenience of the Committee and the parties involved.
   B. *Presiding Officer*
      The Chair of the Ethics Committee shall preside over the hearing and deliberations of the Committee. In the event the Chair or any other member of the Committee has a personal interest in the case, he/she shall withdraw from the hearing and deliberations and shall not participate therein. The Committee shall select from among its members a presiding officer for any case where the Chair has excused him/herself.
   C. *Record*
      A record of the hearing shall be made and preserved, together with any documents presented as evidence, at the AACD Headquarters for a period of three (3) years following the hearing and decision. The record may consist of a summary of testimony

received, or a verbatim transcript, at the discretion of the Committee.

D. *Right to Counsel*

The parties shall be entitled to have counsel present to advise them throughout the hearing. Legal counsel for AACD shall also be present at the hearing to advise the Committee and shall have the privilege of the floor.

Legal Counsel may be brought to hearings as advisors for the complainant or the accused, but they may not participate beyond advising.

E. *Witness*

Either party shall have the right to call witnesses to substantiate his/her version of the case. The Committee shall also have the right to call witnesses it believes may provide further insight into the matter before the Committee.

Witnesses shall not be present during the hearings except when they are called upon to testify. The presiding officer shall allow questions to be asked of any witness by the opposition or members of the Committee and shall ensure that questions and testimony are relevant to the issues in the case. Should the hearing be disturbed by disparaging or irrelevant testimony or by the flare-up of tempers, the presiding officer shall call a brief recess until order can be restored.

Witnesses shall be excused upon completion of their testimony. All expenses associated with witnesses or counsel on behalf of the parties shall be borne by the respective parties.

F. *Presentation of Evidence*

(1) A member of the Committee shall be called upon first to present the charge(s) made against the accused and to briefly describe the evidence supporting the charge(s).

(2) The complainant or a member of the Committee shall then be called upon to present the case against the accused. Witnesses who can substantiate the case shall be called upon to testify and answer questions of the accused and the Committee.

(3) If he/she has exercised the right to be present at the hearing, the accused shall be called upon last to present any evidence he/she may have to refute the charges against him/her. This includes the presentation of witnesses as in Subsection (2) above. The accused member has the right to refuse to make a statement in his/

her behalf. The accused will not be found guilty simply because he/she refuses to testify. Once the accused chooses to testify, however, he/she may be cross-examined by the members of the Committee or the complainant.

(4) The Committee will endeavor to conclude the hearing within a period of approximately three (3) hours. The parties will be requested to be considerate of this time frame in planning their testimony. Testimony that is merely cumulative or repetitious may, at the discretion of the presiding officer, be excluded.

(5) The accused has the right to be present at all times during the hearing and to challenge all of the evidence presented against him/her.

G. *Relevancy of Evidence*

The Ethics Committee is not a court of law and is not required to observe the rules of evidence that apply in the trial of lawsuits. Consequently, evidence that would be inadmissable in a court of law may be admissable in the hearing before the Committee, if it is relevant to the case. That is, if the evidence offered tends to explain, clarify, or refute any of the important facts of the case, it should generally be considered. The Committee will not receive evidence or testimony for the purpose of supporting any charge that was not set forth in the notice of the hearing or that is not relevant to the issues of the case.

4. *Deliberation of the Committee*

A. After the hearing with the parties is completed, the Committee shall meet in a closed session to review the evidence presented and reach a conclusion. The Committee shall be the sole trier of fact and shall weigh the evidence presented and judge the credibility of the witnesses. The act of a majority of the members of the Committee shall be the decision of the Committee.

B. *Burden of Proof*

The burden of proving a violation of the Ethical Standards is on the complainant and/or the Committee. It is not up to the accused to prove his/her innocence of any wrong-doing. Although the charge(s) need not be proved "beyond a reasonable doubt," the Committee will not find the accused guilty in the absence of substantial, objective, and believable evidence to sustain the charge(s).

C. Decision and Appropriate Discipline
  (1) *Guilt or Innocence*
      The Committee will first resolve the issue of the guilt or innocence of the accused. Applying the burden of proof in paragraph B above, the Committee will vote by secret ballot, unless the members of the Committee consent to an oral vote. Only those members of the Committee who were present throughout the entire hearing shall be eligible to vote. The vote of a majority of the members of the Committee shall be the act of the Committee. In the event a majority of the members of the Committee do not find the accused guilty, the charges shall be dismissed and the parties notified.
  (2) *Appropriate Discipline*
      If the Committee finds the accused has violated the Ethical Standards, it must then determine what disciplinary action is appropriate. The Committee may take any of the following actions:
      (a) issue a reprimand with recommendations for corrective action, subject to review by the Committee, or
      (b) withdraw eligibility for membership in AACD for a specified period of time, or
      (c) place the member on probation for a specified period of time, subject to review by the Committee, or
      (d) expel the member from AACD permanently.
      The Committee may consider extenuating circumstances before deciding on the penalty to be imposed.
      At the conclusion of the hearing and deliberation of the Committee, the Chair shall promptly notify the accused and complainant of the Committee's decision in writing. All of the written evidence, the record of the hearing, and a summary of the decision of the Committee shall be forwarded to the President of AACD.
  (3) *Consequences of Discipline*
      A. In the event a member is expelled from AACD member-

ship, he/she shall lose all rights and privileges of membership in AACD and its divisions permanently. The expelled member shall not be entitled to a refund of dues already paid.

B. A suspended member forfeits the rights and privileges of membership only for the period of his/her suspension.

C. A reprimand carries with it no loss of membership rights or privileges.

D. After any right to appeal has been exhausted, the Committee will notify the appropriate State Licensing Board(s) of the disciplined member's status with AACD. Notice will also be given to the National Board for Certified Counselors, the AACD divisions of which the disciplined party is a member, the members of AACD, and the complainant. Such notice shall only state the discipline imposed and the sections of the AACD Ethical Standards that were violated. Further elaboration shall not be disclosed.

E. Should a member resign from the Association after a complaint has been brought against him/her and before the Ethics Committee has completed its deliberations, that member is considered to have been expelled from the Association for failure to respond in a timely and complete manner to the Ethics Committee.

Appeal Procedures

Appeals will be heard only in such cases wherein the appellant presents evidence that the sanction imposed by the Committee has been arbitrary or capricious or that the procedures outlined in the "Policy Document" have not been followed.

The complainant and accused shall be advised of the appeal procedure by the Chairperson of the AACD Ethics Committee. The following procedures shall govern appeals:

1. A three (3) member review committee composed of the Executive Director of the AACD, the President of the AACD Division

with which the accused member is most closely identified, and the immediate Past President of the AACD. The AACD attorney shall serve as legal advisor.

2. The appeal with supporting documentation must be made in writing within sixty days by certified mail to the AACD Executive Director and indicate the basis upon which it is made. If the member requires a time extension, he/she must request it in writing by certified mail within thirty days of the receipt of the decision by the AACD Ethics Committee. The extension will consist of ninety days beginning from that request.

3. The review committee shall review all materials considered by the AACD Ethics Committee.

4. Within thirty (30) days of this review, the members on the review committee shall submit to the President of the AACD a written statement giving their opinion regarding the decision of the Ethics Committee. Each member shall concur with or dissent from the decision of the Ethics Committee.

5. Within fifteen (15) days of receiving this opinion, the President of AACD will reach a decision based on the considered opinions of the review committee from the following alternatives:

(a) support the decision of the Ethics Committee, or
(b) reverse the decision of the Ethics Committee.

6. The parties to the appeal shall be advised of the action in writing.

Legal counsel for the AACD has the privilege of the floor and shall advise the review committee.

Records

Records of the AACD Ethics Committee and the review committee shall remain at the AACD Headquarters.

Procedures for Submitting and Interpreting Questions of Ethical Conduct

The procedures for submitting questions to the Ethics Committee are as follows:

1. Whenever possible, the questioner is first advised to consult other colleagues seeking interpretation of questions.

2. If a national level resolution is deemed appropriate, the questioner shall prepare a written statement, detailing the conduct in question. Statements should include the section or sections of the Ethical Standards to be interpreted relative to the conduct in question. All questions that are directed to the Ethics Committee should be mailed to: Ethics Committee, C/o AACD Executive Director.

3. The AACD Ethics Committee Chairpersons or his/her designee shall:

(a) confer with legal counsel, and
(b) direct a letter to the questioner acknowledging receipt of the question, informing the member that the questions will be interpreted by the Committee, and outlining the procedures to be involved in the interpretation.

4. The Ethics Committee will review and interpret the question and, if requested by the questioner, make recommendations for conduct.

Non-Member Accusations

The AACD Ethics Committee recognizes the rights of non-AACD members to file grievances concerning a member. Ordinarily this non-member will be a client of an AACD member who believes that the AACD member has acted unethically.

In such cases, the complainant shall contact the Chairperson of the AACD Ethics Committee outlining, in writing, those behaviors he/she feels were unethical in nature. The Chairperson will delineate the complaint process to the complainant.

APPENDIX D

AACD LEGAL ACTION PROGRAM

(Approved by AACD Governing Council, April 1987)

(The Legal Defense Program was established by the APGA Board of Directors, December 8–10, 1977 and revised by the Board of Directors, July 12–15, 1979. It was further revised by the AACD Governing Council April 1987)

I. Statement of Purpose

The AACD Legal Defense Program for AACD members was established by the APGA Board of Directors at its meeting, December 8–10, 1977, to assist members in their legal efforts to redress discrimination or unfair practices in employment related matters. In 1987, the AACD Governing Council revised the program and renamed it the Legal Action Program. The kind of legal disputes for which members (heretofore defined for the purposes of this program as AACD members in good standing with membership in at least one division, state or national divisions or state branches) may request financial assistance are cases in which facts are at issue that are deemed by the Review Panel to discriminate clearly against counselors in general or against the counseling profession. Cases will not be funded if a counselor's performance, judgement or competence is at issue, unless the Review Panel determines that the allegations, even if proven accurate, do not constitute unprofessional, unethical, or illegal conduct. For funding under this program to be authorized, an actual case must be pending. In civil suits, a bill of complaint and responsive pleadings must have been filed. In a criminal suit, charges must have been filed. In appellate cases, the appeal must have been filed.

The purpose of this program is to provide assistance to eligible AACD members to enable them to resolve legal disputes in matters relating to their primary responsibilities or interests in the area of counseling and human development [see AACD Bylaws, Article II, Section 2(a)].

An AACD member eligible for this program must be a member in good standing for at least one year prior to the onset of the legal dispute. State and national divisions and state branches are automatically eligible provided their charter has been current for one year.

II. Obtaining the Revenue for the Legal Action Program

A. The Governing Council establishes the budget and authorizes membership solicitation of additional voluntary contributions for the fund.

B. Policies and guidelines to govern the program's operation shall be the sole responsibility of the AACD Governing Council, based upon monitoring reports from the Counselor Advocacy Committee.

C. The Executive Director shall report the activities and the fiscal condition of the Program to the Governing Council at each meeting of the Council.

III. Review Panel and Guidelines

A. The President, Past President, Executive Director of AACD, President of the applicant's primary and most relevant division (subject to the desire of the applicant) and the Chair of the AACD Committee on Counselor Advocacy shall serve as a review panel for all applications for assistance from the Legal Action Program. AACD Counsel will serve as a consultant to the Review Panel. The Judgement of the Review Panel shall be made in accordance with the guidelines established by the AACD Governing Council.

1. Applicants seeking support from these funds will be notified of the decision of the Review Panel within sixty (60) working days of receipt of the application and all supporting documents.

2. Rejected applications may be appealed to the AACD Governing Council at its next meeting.

B. The guidelines for members obtaining financial support from this program include:

1. Two hundred and fifty dollars ($250) of legal fees and expenses must be paid by the AACD member.

2. After the $250 of legal expenses are paid by the member, a minimum of $250.00 shall be provided by any of the following:
a. state branch
b. state division
c. national division
d. professional or private source

3. After ascertaining that the expenditures made by the member and other sources total

at least $500.00, a sum not to exceed $1,000.00 may be provided to the approved member from the AACD Legal Action Fund.

4. Should the receipted expenditures exceed the initial $1,000.00, costs above that $1,000.00 may be reimbursed up to an additional $4,000.00 sum per member per act or occurrence. If more than one member is involved in the same occurrence under litigation, only $5,000.00 payment will be authorized, except as determined by the AACD Governing Council.

5. Expenditures will be limited to the authorized sums in the legal action fund.

6. State or national divisions, and state branches may apply for up to $5,000.00 provided they have evidenced expenditure of or committed funds of a matching amount of money designated for such legal action.

7. If a funded case is appealed to a higher court, an additional $5,000.00 may be authorized.

C. Excluded from eligibility would be cases such as:

1. Non-professionally related criminal suits or charges.

2. Licensure outside of the counseling profession.

3. Professional liability suits.

4. Other cases determined by the Review Panel to be inappropriate for commitment of AACD Legal Action Funds.

IV. Application Procedures for Members

A. The AACD member requests from AACD Headquarters an "Application for Assistance from the AACD Legal Action Fund" claim. The completed claim forms are sent to the Executive Director. The member shall complete these forms during the legal proceedings. All forms, documentation and records shall be treated as confidential documents.

B. Upon receipt of the completed forms and supporting documents signed by the applicant, representing attorney, and official representative of the group contributing the additional $250.00 to guarantee expenditures of at least $500.00, the Executive Director will review all of the information in relation to the established policies and procedures and, then, submit this information to the Review Panel for determination of eligibility.

C. Once the eligibility for assistance is determined, the member will be notified and a check for the authorized amount, not to exceed the appropriate guidelines, will be authorized and mailed payable to the attorney.

D. If the Review Panel determines the member is ineligible for assistance, the member may appeal this decision to the AACD Governing Council. The Governing Council shall notify the member of the results of its deliberations, including the reasons for its actions.

E. Falsification of any document or the submission of any fraudulent statements or materials shall render the application null and void. If such falsification or fraudulence is discovered before or after payment is made, AACD reserves the right to take whatever action is necessary that is appropriate legally and ethically, to recover allocated funds or expenditures related to processing such an application.

AMERICAN ASSOCIATION FOR COUNSELING AND DEVELOPMENT

5999 Stevenson Avenue
Alexandria, VA 22304

APPLICATION FOR ASSISTANCE FROM THE AACD LEGAL ACTION FUND

Date of Application _____

AACD Membership Number _____

Name _____

Business Address _____

_____

Home Address _____

Business Phone _____ Home Phone _____

Brief Statement of Dispute:

In order for this application to be completed and reviewed, a copy of all pleadings filed in the case must be attached.

Which is your primary Division? _____

Do you wish to have Division President on Review Panel? _____ Yes _____ No

I hereby certify that I have contributed a minimum of $250.00 of my own personal funds to this case. I also hereby certify that all of the information in this application is true and correct to the best of my knowledge.

_____   _____
Date   Signature of Applicant

I hereby certify that I or my organization have contributed a minimum of $250.00 to the above-stated legal action. My signature indicates I have not provided any false or misleading information.

_____   _____
Signature   Organization

AMERICAN ASSOCIATION FOR COUNSELING AND DEVELOPMENT

5999 Stevenson Avenue
Alexandria, VA 22304

FINANCIAL AFFIDAVIT FOR AACD LEGAL ACTION FUND

Name of AACD Member _____

Name of Attorney _____

Attorney's Address _____

_____

Member's Address _____

_____

Statement of Legal Costs:

Received by Attorney $_____

Remaining Fees $_____

This information we hereby present is true and correct.

_____   Date _____
   AACD Member's Signature

_____   Date _____
   Member's Attorney's Signature

AMERICAN ASSOCIATION FOR COUNSELING AND DEVELOPMENT

5999 Stevenson Avenue
Alexandria, VA 22304

APPLICATION FOR ADDITIONAL ASSISTANCE FROM AACD LEGAL ACTION FUND

Date of Application _____

AACD Membership Number _____

Name _____

Business Address _____

_____

Home Address _____

Business Phone _____ Home Phone _____

Applications for additional assistance from AACD Legal Action Fund will not be considered unless one of the following conditions has been met:

1. An initial request for funds has been approved up to $1,000.00.
2. All possible assistance has been granted and the case is now in appeal.

Member Expenditure on Case to Date $_____

Sum of All Legal Action Funds Awarded to Date $_____

Statement of Total Sum of Attorney's Fees $_____

Status of Case? _____ initial proceedings _____ appellate proceedings

Amount(s) Granted from Other Sources $_____

The information we hereby present is true and correct.

_____   Date _____
AACD Member's Signature

_____   Date _____
Member's Attorney's Signature

The AACD Ethics Committee maintains and periodically updates an extensive Ethics Bibliography. To obtain a copy, write to:

ETHICS BIBLIOGRAPHY

American Association for Counseling and Development
5999 Stevenson Avenue
Alexandria, VA 22304